FUNDAMENTALISM
in
American Religion
1880 - 1950

A forty-five-volume facsimile series
reproducing often extremely rare material
documenting the development of one of the
major religious movements of our time

■ *Edited by*
Joel A. Carpenter
Billy Graham Center, Wheaton College
■ *Advisory Editors*
Donald W. Dayton,
Northern Baptist Theological Seminary
George M. Marsden,
Duke University
Mark A. Noll,
Wheaton College
Grant Wacker,
University of North Carolina

A GARLAND SERIES

■ The Fundamentals
A Testimony to Truth

VOLUME 4

Edited by
George M. Marsden

Garland Publishing, Inc.
New York & London 1988

For a list of the titles in this series, see the final pages of this volume.

This facsimile has been made from a copy in the Billy Graham Center of Wheaton College.

Library of Congress Cataloging in Publication Data

The Fundamentals

   (Fundamentalism in American religion, 1880-1950)
    1. Fundamentalism. 2. Theology, Doctrinal.
   I. Marsden, George M., 1939-   . II. Series.
   BT82.2.F86 1988   230'.044   88-21407
   ISBN 0-8240-5015-0 (alk. paper)

Design by Valerie Mergentime
Printed on acid-free, 250-year-life paper.
Manufactured in the United States of America

The Fundamentals

A Testimony to the Truth

"To the Law and to the Testimony"
Isaiah 8:20

Volume X

Compliments of
Two Christian Laymen

TESTIMONY PUBLISHING COMPANY
(Not Inc.)
808 La Salle Ave., Chicago, Ill., U. S. A.

FOREWORD

The tenth volume of "THE FUNDAMENTALS" goes free to all English-speaking Protestant religious workers who requested it by signing the card which we inclosed in the ninth volume and mailing it to our business office, "Testimony Publishing Company, 808 La Salle Avenue, Chicago, Illinois." It will be sent free to other Christian workers who request it. (See Publishers' Notice, page 128.)

We send it out with special thanksgiving to God, because He has so wonderfully blessed the previous volumes. Since the ninth volume reached our readers, hundreds of letters have come to us from them, telling us of their gratitude and appreciation, thanking the generous Two Christian Laymen, and reporting specific cases of blessing received. Thus we know that by the gracious influence of the Holy Spirit "THE FUNDAMENTALS" have been used to the conversion of sinners, to the strengthening of wavering believers, and to the full surrender and consecration to His service of earnest Christian men and women. To God be all the praise. May He bless the tenth volume as He did its predecessors, and use it to His glory and to the advancement of His cause.

Our Circle of Prayer has grown again since we sent out the ninth volume. We do not publish special literature for the thousands who have joined it, but we simply ask them to pray in faith, (1) for the Two Christian Laymen, whose consecration and liberality make possible the publication and free distribution of "THE FUNDAMENTALS" and who are more than three score years and ten, that the Lord keep them and prosper all the work at home and abroad which they support; (2) for all who are connected with the great work of "THE FUNDAMENTALS," including the writer of these lines who has been seriously ill since the beginning of November and is writing these lines while being under treatment in a sanatorium.

Grace be with all them that love our Lord Jesus Christ in sincerity. Amen.

(Signed) The Executive Secretary "THE FUNDAMENTALS."

Address all editorial correspondence to "Box 8, Monrovia, California, U. S. A."

(See Publishers' Notice, Page 128.)

CONTENTS

THE FUNDAMENTALS

VOLUME X

CHAPTER I

WHY SAVE THE LORD'S DAY?

BY REV. DANIEL HOFFMAN MARTIN, D. D.,
GLENS FALLS, NEW YORK

The only command in the Decalogue which begins with the word "Remember" is the fourth: "Remember the Sabbath day to keep it holy," as if the Divine writer realized there would be more danger of forgetting this than any of the others, and of yielding to the subtle temptations of caprice and convenience as an excuse for violating it. "Remember" stands like a solitary sentinel in front of this solemn command, yet it has been chafed under, from the ancient Jew who was stoned for gathering sticks on the Sabbath, down to the Sunday saloon-keeper who, in commercializing his fellow-man's weakness, breaks three laws, that of the Sabbath, the State, and brotherly love.

Jesus declared the Sabbath was made for man, that is, for *mankind*. It is to be kept holy, that is *wholesomely*, so that our threefold nature, body, mind and soul, may benefit. No law more wise and merciful ever came from the loving heart of God; a law as all-embracing in its design as sunlight, meeting the needs of king and peasant, master and servant, parent and child. Whence came the wisdom condensed in this fourth commandment? Not from the Greeks, called the wisest of nations, for these words were written a thousand years before Socrates was born. Not from the Romans, masters of jurisprudence, for these words antedate the founding of Rome, by seven hundred and fifty years. They come from our Heavenly Father and they embody the great septenary law which runs through nature; therefore it is of equal application to every nation on earth. The Sabbath is the savings bank of human existence. It conserves man's physical, mental, spiritual and eternal welfare.

WHY THE FIRST DAY INSTEAD OF THE SEVENTH?

If you ask why the Jewish Saturday once observed as Lord's Day was changed to the First Day, the answer is that Jesus proclaimed Himself Lord also of the Sabbath day, therefore greater than the statute law of Moses. Jesus is the incarnate Legislator of the world. As Lord of the Sabbath, Jesus had the right to interpret and ennoble the day, so that it might be the greatest institution for the culture of the three-fold man. The Scribes and Pharisees had misconceived the genius of the Sabbath law. They missed its underlying principle, encumbered it with intricate and inflexible rules, assuming themselves to be the judges of every act. "The letter killeth, the spirit giveth life." Jesus rescued the Sabbath from its burial under a mass of ceremonialism, and revealed its true spirit and meaning. "Jesus did for the Sabbath what a skipper does for his ship, when she comes laboring into port, unable to make headway, because her hulk is covered with barnacles. He puts her into drydock, and scrapes off the barnacles. He does not scuttle the ship. So our Lord does not repeal nor annul the Sabbath law when He strips it of the intolerable burdens which the ceremonialists had heaped upon it." In order to emphasize His new idea of the old Sabbath the disciples chose a new day as Lord's Day.

The disciples also desired to commemorate the greatest of all events since the world's creation, namely, the resurrection of our Lord, for it was on the first day of the week that

Jesus made His first five appearances. It was also on the first day of the week that the Holy Spirit was given, therefore Pentecost was commemorated on that day. (Acts 2.) It was on this day also that the great tidings of salvation were first preached to the multitudes. (Acts 2.) The first day became the day in which all the early Christians assembled for worship, and for communion. (Acts 20:7 and 1 Cor. 11:23.) It was the day also in which the prophecy of Revelation was granted to St. John on Patmos. (Rev. 1:10.) All the church fathers kept the Lord's Day instead of the Jewish Sabbath, and thus the Christian Sabbath became the weekly holy day of the Christian dispensation, and is the only Sabbath day mentioned as a sacred rest day after the resurrection.

HAVE WE OUTGROWN THE SABBATH DAY?

Is this king of days, created by our Father, sanctified by our Saviour, preserved by the Church, worth saving? Some would have us think we have outgrown it, that it belongs to another time, governed by different conditions. A moment's thought will show that it is impossible to outgrow a law of nature, such as this septenary law is proved to be. And here are a few of the reasons:

THE BODY NEEDS IT

First, man has a body. Experience proves that the normal level of bodily energy cannot be maintained without the regular observance of a stated day of rest. We are like seven-day clocks that run down and have to be rewound. We are like musical instruments that play well for a time and get out of tune. We are storage batteries that leak their vital currents, and must be recharged. There was never an age when humanity needed this weekly rest-day more than now. Think of the fierce competition of modern business, and the relentless law of the survival of the strongest! Think of the

feverish hurry and hustle of our American people! Ian
Maclaren wrote thus about us: "I am now in New York,
where everybody seems to be in a hurry. I asked a police-
man what the excitement was all about. He thought I was
joking. No one walks to business who can ride in a street
car; none rides in a street car who can ride in a steam car,
and he regrets there is no pneumatic tube by which he might
be shot to his office or shop. When there, he does not write
letters if he can telegraph, or telegraph if he can telephone,
and regrets there is no occupation for his feet while waiting
at the phone." There is magnetism in our oxygen which
stimulates our blood and explains our American push and
rush.

The difficulty, with our splendid American activity and
achievement, is to arrest the momentum. Men rush so hard
through the week that the Day of Rest finds them in the rush-
ing mood. It is hard to stop. They want to do something
or go somewhere, or keep up the pace by some dissipating use
of the Lord's Day. Hence the Sunday excursions which generally make an incursion into the week's wages, and leave the
working man more tired on that night than any other of the
week. And there are Sunday amusements and dinner parties
and receptions. But the human organism is not a machine of
iron to run without rest, but a delicate bundle of nerves and
tissues. But even iron machinery does better work and lasts
longer when it has periodic rests, as the superintendent of the
Pennsylvania railroad said recently about their locomotives.

THE MIND NEEDS IT

Second, man has a mind. It is a fact of common record
that no set of men can keep working the same mental tread-
mill day after day without blunting the keen edge of their
intellectual faculties. Note the employees who are held at
their monotonous grind seven days out of seven, month after
month, and you will observe that the average intelligence and

moral standards are low. They read scarcely anything and take practically no interest in current events. A boy asked his father to take him "next Sunday to see the animals at the Bronx Zoo." The father has to work seven days a week, and he replied, "You needn't go to the Bronx to see animals; look at me, I am not much different from the horses I drive in front of my milk wagon." Do you wonder Jesus said the Sabbath was made for man? For man, that he might be something different from an animal. As soon as God had created man He ordained the Sabbath, because He knew the needs of man.

We can ill afford to make light of God's merciful provision of this weekly arrest of physical and mental toil. Science supports the Divine law by showing in the analysis of the blood, that during our application to work through the week we recover in one night's rest only five-sixths of the ounce of oxygen consumed out of our system by the day's labor. Each morning finds one-sixth of an ounce lacking, so that a man is run down at the end of the week to the extent of that whole ounce of vitality. The Lord's Day is a physiological necessity for the restoration of that one ounce. When a man presumes to be wiser than this law of nature and of God, he usually pays the penalty by breaking down with that peculiar malady "Americanitis," a compound of insomnia and nervous debility. Then the physician most likely prescribes a sea voyage, for that will be an enforced rest for the depleted system. But a proper observance of the Lord's day would have supplied that very need, because the Lord's Day is a sea voyage between the two continents of monotony and drudgery. There would be little need of prolonged trips abroad, or sojourns in a sanatarium, if the Sabbath could have its claims respected. Fifty-two Sabbaths a year mean nearly two months vacation to every worker. When a man wipes the Sabbath out of his calendar he breaks a law of nature, and nature always squares accounts with broken law. Of many another could this doggerel be truthfully spoken concerning a man:

> 'Who spent his health to get his wealth,
> And then with might and main
> He turned around and spent his wealth
> To get his health again."

THE SOUL NEEDS IT

Third, man has a soul. A great jurist recently said: "In this strenuous age, our republic, instead of making light of one Sabbath, ought to have *two* each week, not only to repair its jaded nerves, but to tone up its moral sense." We have not fulfilled all the command when we have rested the body and diverted the mind. The soul has its rights, and not to recognize them is to leave our nature a truncated cone, the highest, finest part left undeveloped. We read of Jesus that "He went *as His custom was* into the synagogue on the Sabbath day." That His soul might keep its tryst with God, have larger breathing space, clearer light, and glimpses of the center of the spiritual universe, in which our spirits join and have their being. If Jesus needed that privilege, much more do we ordinary men. The shell fishes on the sea-shore live without water while the tide is out, but they depend upon the tide's return. If any of them are tossed by the waves beyond the reach of the tides, they die. Our souls are refreshed and nourished by communion with our Father in prayer, and through the means of grace provided by Divine worship on the Lord's Day. It is then we lay hold of our best yearnings, and stiffen them into fighting fibre for victorious warfare with the world, the flesh and the devil.

The artist Turner kept on his easel a handful of precious stones of beautiful colors. For a half hour each morning he would silently sit and gaze at those glorious tints. He said he did this to keep his color-sense acute. If the artist's eye needed that influence to keep its color sense toned up, surely the human soul needs the tonic influence of spiritual worship. What is the cloud that looms over every man's path every day? Not sorrow, not poverty, not sickness, not business reverses. The cloud that looms over every path is TEMPTATION. Some time ago a man who had not been in church for many years, secured a pew in his old church, and is now one of its regular attendants. Someone asked him the reason. He said, "I have a growing family of sons and daughters. I have been watching my boys with some anxiety. I am alarmed at what I read in the daily papers about the ways of the world, the ease with which men under temptation go down like reeds in the wind, the frequency with which husbands and wives break up their homes. I am convinced there is only one place to bring up a family of children, and that is the church." Who will question that father's judgment? He does not want his sons to grow up without moral anchorage, he does not want his daughters to marry those who will play fast and loose with honor, and he knows that the church with its worship is the place where ideals are burnished up, where the dust is cleansed from the soul's wings, where false standards are corrected.

If a busy brain worker could see a photograph of his mind as it appears on Saturday night, with its six layers of toil and grime, representing the six days contact with the world, he would see himself much in need of a spiritual bath on the Lord's Day. The average breadwinner is a human football, tossed hither and yon from the goal of Monday to the goal of Saturday, and literally dumped into the Sabbath morning bruised from the battle. He is apt to feel soured and out of sorts; and nothing so soothes the wounds as contact with the people of God in the Lord's house.

A COMPLETE MAN

So the Sabbath was made for man, that he might be in every sense MAN! Something more than a beast of burden, something more than a cash-register, something more than a pendulum swinging between his home and his business. In an ordinary lifetime of seventy years there are ten years of Sundays. Therefore the manner in which a man keeps those three thousand six hundred and forty Sabbaths will make its impress on the man's life for all eternity.

When a man says and thinks that he has a right to do as he pleases on the Lord's Day, with no reference to the sacredness of the day, or its claims upon his soul, we may conclude that man has not accepted his Heavenly Father's estimate of the worth of a man. He assesses himself at a lower value. God created man in His own image, in the image of God created He him. But the man says, "I will rub out the Divine lineaments. God started me on an immortal journey but I am satisfied to let it end in the graveyard." There isn't much use trying to reason with a man who puts the body first and last, who regards his face as a mere opening for the alimentary canal, and who allows the lower nature to preside at the funeral of the higher.

Man, do you think the Almighty God made a mistake when He started you on an eternal journey? Is your soul a joke? Has God not said: "If thou turn away thy foot from the Sabbath, from doing thy pleasure on My holy day and call the Sabbath a delight, holy of the Lord and honorable and shall honor Him in not doing thy own ways, nor finding thy own pleasure, nor speaking thy own words, then shalt thou delight thyself in the Lord, and I will cause thee to ride upon the high places of the earth, for the mouth of the Lord hath spoken it." (Isa. 58:13, 14.)

THE LAW OF LIBERTY

There are those who say, "If the Sabbath was made for man, why may he not do as he pleases with it?" Because it was made for man's liberty, not for man's license, and the highest liberty is always found in conformity to law. So long as my doings affect no one else's liberty, I may do as I choose, but the moment I cross some one else's rights, I am not free to do as I choose. I am limited by the higher law of brotherly love. If you think you are at liberty to travel on the Lord's Day or attend a ball-game or concert on that day, you are not conforming to the law of brotherly love in that you force your fellow man to work for you on the day that you enjoy your freedom. But you reply, "Those people who toil on the Lord's Day receive extra pay." Extra pay! My friend, there is not gold enough in the bosom of the eternal hills to compensate a single toiler for his loss of the day of rest. EVERY MAN HAS A RIGHT TO HIS MAN-HOOD, AND NO MONEY COMPENSATION CAN RE-PLACE THE LOSS OF MANHOOD. "But the train of cars that I board on the Sabbath would run anyway, and I might as well go on it." My friend, how does that cancel your share of the moral responsibility for having forced your brother man to violate the law of the Sabbath?

"Well, I am so busy during the week that I have no other day for recreation. From Monday to Saturday I grind like Samson at the mill." Yes, but you are no busier than the Sabbath-keeping toilers who manage to get their recreation at other times. If you honestly believe that you have no other day than the Lord's Day for your pleasure seeking, I ask you in all solemnity, have you any other day for the culture of your spiritual life? When are you going to attend to your immortal soul? Now is the accepted time, what are you doing with it? Some one has said, "The Lord's Day is like a rented house; it belongs to the proprietor, it is occupied by the tenant, but the tenant has no right to say, 'I will do what I please with this house, damage it, desecrate it, turn it into an evil resort.' No, the house is his to use and not abuse. The Sabbath is ours in the same way; he who diverts it from its proper purpose is dishonest. Will a man rob God? If a tramp tells me a pitiful tale and I have seven silver dollars and give six of them, what would you think of the ingrate if you were told he came at night and robbed me of the seventh? I wonder what God thinks of the man to whom He gives six days for his own free use and finds the man appropriating to himself that which is specially stamped as *God's.*"

What is the use of a Lord's Day if it is to be swamped between the secular tide of one worldly week gone, and of another coming, and to have nothing about it that distinguishes it from all the other days, except in some fanciful alteration in the style of its wordliness or carnality? Look at the people who have spent the entire Sabbath in pleasure-seeking. Not one gleam of spiritual light in their faces, not one crumb of spiritual food in their souls, going to bed at night a day's march nearer home. Home? Yes, if home is the grave and eternal death . Otherwise a day's march farther from home, if home is God, and if heaven is an experience into which men graduate from this earthly season of moral training and spiritual acquisition.

BLUE LAWS BETTER THAN RED ANARCHY

We are not pleading for a Puritan Sunday of bigotry or intolerance. We are not pleading for blue laws. But as between bigotry and a mush of concession give us bigotry every time. And even the bluest of blue laws would be preferable to red anarchy. We appeal for a safe and sane Sabbath, not in the interests of the Church or religion, but in the interests of all the people, believers and unbelievers, because the Sabbath was made for mankind. When I stood the other day in the little log cabin where Abraham Lincoln first saw the light, I thought of his regard for the Sabbath, and there came to my mind these words of his: "As we keep, or break, the Sabbath day, we nobly save, or meanly lose, the last best hope by which man rises."

It is true there are many noble people who never get a Sabbath to themselves. They are busy in works of necessity and mercy. Jesus Himself sets the example of this, and leaves to our enlightened consciences to judge what is necessary, and what is not, to do on His day. The fundamental principle is to be "in the spirit on the Lord's Day," to be in tune with our Lord's mind, to be in harmony with our Lord's will. So if you ask what rules do you suggest for the proper observance of the Lord's Day I answer, THERE IS NO RULE BUT THE GOLDEN RULE THAT CAN GOVERN OUR RE- LATION TO THE LORD'S DAY. Therefore, before I give a Sunday house party, or travel for my own pleasure, or talk a lot of twaddle at the telephone on the Lord's Day I will say, "I would *not* like to be obliged myself to work on Sunday; therefore it is wrong for me to oblige others to work. I will not buy a Sunday paper, knowing that I am forcing a hundred and fifty thousand compositors and press- men to work seven days out of seven, and robbing a great army of men and boys of their right to a day of rest and wor- ship. True, that newsboy is poor, and needs the money, but I refuse to take advantage of that boy's poverty by contrib- uting to his moral detriment. It is bad that he is poor, it is worse that I should make him a law-breaker." All over this country a hundred thousand boys are training for manhood with no reverence for the Sabbath, and no respect for au- thority, in order to supply a Sunday newspaper for people who would be infinitely better off to have one whole day in which the dust and rubbish of six secular days could not enter. When the attempt to introduce a Sunday newspaper was made in London, the "Evening Post" commented: "The best view which can be taken of our own Sunday newspapers must be that they are a nuisance. They are twice cursed; they curse him that prints them and him that reads them. They add new terrors to Sunday. On purely humanitarian grounds, without allowing theological reasons to have any weight whatever, we could wish them all away. If there is any more pathetic sight than a man deliberately sitting down to wade through a sextuple Sunday newspaper, we do not know what it is."

That is the new indictment of the Sunday press from a secular viewpoint. We may easily see the harm it does from a spiritual viewpoint. A mind that has waded through the Sunday sheet is no more prepared for spiritual thoughts than is a man's clothing for appearance at church after rambling over fields of burdocks and nettles. The very purpose of the Sabbath was to give God's children one whole day free from the suggestions and contaminations of a wicked world.

IN THE NAME OF HUMANITY

O men, does it not touch a tender place in your hearts when you hear of the multitudes of wage earners who are pleading for a Sabbath restday? Railroad men, miners, actors, craftsmen of all sorts, signing petitions for a recognition of their right to a weekly day of rest, making their appeal on the grounds of common humanity. Here is one from a member of the bartenders' union. He said: "I cannot of course appeal to you from the standpoint of religion, but we have some interests in common with other men. I am myself the father of three children, but I scarcely know them. I am up in the morning before they are awake, and I return at night after they are in bed. This I do seven days a week, year in and year out." That from the bartenders' union. And similar appeals are made from thousands of other toilers; because every man has a right to his manhood, and the Sabbath was made for man.

THE PLAIN DUTY OF A CHRISTIAN

For Christian men and women there can be only one course of action. There may be perplexing situations at times, where even a Christian will be puzzled to decide just what to do; but with a mind brought, as the Apostle says, "into captivity to the obedience of Christ" the ground is level and the air cleared for meeting them. When we fully recognize the Lord's lordship of this Day of days, we will never go far astray. Every question as to the proper observance of it will be dealt with in its Divine relations to our Divine Master. It is more than half the answer to any question to be in tune with the principles involved in the solution of the question. "I was in the spirit on the Lord's Day," said the Apostle. To keep that pregnant phrase in mind will settle the details of every program of conduct on that day.

God help us all to resist the drift of Sabbath secularization. Doubtless it will cost us something to be loyal to principle in this day of many jelly fish Christians, who have opinions without convictions, and prejudices without principles. A refreshing shadow of a great rock in a weary land is the man of convictions and principles who can resist the drifting sands of a loose interpretation of the Divine commands. The demand today is for rock Christians. We are living in a time when the people who settle questions of right and wrong for themselves seem to be in a minority. In matters of morals and dress most of us go in droves. A few people act as brain for the many, a few people act as conscience for the many. But we who have the light of God's Word need not be mastered by the mob. One is our Master, even Christ. A great many people are doing certain things on the Lord's Day, not because they have settled the question, as between themselves and their Lord, but because they have settled it as between themselves and their own preferences, or as between themselves and their associates.

Let us be rock Christians, who will keep the Lord's Day holy because it holds us in touch with eternal and Divine things, and because it celebrates our relation to our Divine Master; and because the Lord's Day is the guerdon of our national prosperity, the hope of our civilization; and because the mouth of Jehovah hath spoken: "Them that honor Me I will honor."

CHAPTER II

THE INTERNAL EVIDENCE
OF THE FOURTH GOSPEL

BY CANON G. OSBORNE TROOP, M. A.,
MONTREAL, CANADA

The whole Bible is stamped with the Divine "Hall-Mark"; but the Gospel according to St. John is *primus inter pares.* Through it, as through a transparency, we gaze entranced into the very holy of holies, where shines in unearthly glory "the great vision of the face of Christ". Yet man's perversity has made it the "storm center" of New Testament criticism, doubtless for the very reason that it bears such unwavering testimony both to the deity of our Lord and Saviour, Jesus Christ, and to His perfect humanity. The Christ of the Fourth Gospel is no unhistoric, idealized vision of the later, dreaming church, but is, as it practically claims to be, the picture drawn by "the disciple whom Jesus loved", an eye-witness of the blood and water that flowed from His pierced side. These may appear to be mere unsupported statements, and as such will at once be dismissed by a scientific reader. Nevertheless the appeal of this article is to the instinct of the "one flock" of the "one Shepherd". "They know His voice" . . . "a stranger will they not follow."

1. There is one passage in this Gospel that flashes like lightning—it dazzles our eyes by its very glory. To the broken-hearted Martha the Lord Jesus says with startling suddenness, "*I am* the resurrection and the life; he that believeth on Me, though he die, yet shall he live; and whosoever liveth and believeth in Me, shall never die."

It is humbly but confidently submitted that these words are utterly beyond the reach of human invention. It could never have entered the heart of man to say, "*I am* the resurrection and the life." "There is a resurrection and a life," would have been a great and notable saying, but *this Speaker* identifies *Himself* with the resurrection and with life eternal. The words can only be born from above, and He who utters them is worthy of the utmost adoration of the surrendered soul.

In an earlier chapter John records a certain question addressed to and answered by our Lord in a manner which has no counterpart in the world's literature. "What shall we do," the eager people cry; "What shall we do that we might work the works of God?" "This is the work of God", our Lord replies, "that ye believe on Him whom He hath sent" (John 6:28, 29). I venture to say that such an answer to such a question has no parallel. This is the work of God that ye accept ME. I am the Root of the tree which bears the only fruit pleasing to God. Our Lord states the converse of this in chapter 16, when He says that the Holy Spirit will "convict the world of sin . . . because they believe not on ME." The root of all evil is unbelief in Christ. The condemning sin of the world lies in the rejection of the Redeemer. Here we have the root of righteousness and the root of sin in the acceptance or rejection of His wondrous personality. This is unique, and proclaims the Speaker to be "separate from sinners" though "the Lord hath laid on Him the iniquity of us all." Truly,

> "He is His own best evidence,
> His witness is within."

2. Pass on to the fourteenth chapter, so loved of all Christians. Listen to that Voice, which is as the voice of many waters, as it sounds in the ears of the troubled disciples: "Let not your heart be troubled; ye believe in God, believe *also* in *ME*. In My Father's house are many mansions: *if it were not so, I would have told you.* I go to prepare a place

for you. And if I go and prepare a place for you, I will
come again, and receive you unto Myself; that where I am,
there ye may be also."

Who is he who dares to say: "Ye believe in *God*, believe
also in Me"? He ventures thus to speak because He is the
Father's Son. Man's son is man: can God's Son be anything
less than God? Elsewhere in this Gospel He says: "I and
the Father are one". The fourteenth chapter reveals the
Lord Jesus as completely at home in the heavenly company.
He speaks of His Father and of the Holy Spirit as Himself
being one of the utterly holy Family. He knows all about His
Father's house with its many mansions. He was familiar
with it before the world was. Mark well, too, the exquisite
touch of transparent truthfulness: "If it were not so, I
would have told you." An *ear*-witness alone could have
caught and preserved that touching parenthesis, and who
more likely than the disciple whom Jesus loved?

As we leave this famous chapter let us not forget to
note the wondrous words in verse 23: "If a man love Me,
he will keep My words; and My Father will love him, and
WE will come unto him and make our abode with him."

This saying can only be characterized as blasphemous, if
it be not the true utterance of one equal with God. On the
other hand, does any reasonable man seriously think that
such words originated in the mind of a forger? "Every one
that is of the truth heareth My voice", and surely that voice
is here.

3. When we come to chapter 17 we pass indeed into the
very inner chamber of the King of kings. It records the
high-priestly prayer of our Lord, when He "lifted up His eyes
to heaven and said, Father, the hour is come, glorify Thy
Son that Thy Son may also glorify Thee." Let any man
propose to himself the awful task of forging such a prayer,
and putting it into the mouth of an imaginary Christ. The
brain reels at the very thought of it. It is, however, per-

fectly natural that St. John should record it. It must have fallen upon the ears of himself and his fellow-disciples amidst an awe-stricken silence in which they could hear the very throbbing of their listening hearts. For their very hearts were listening through their ears as the Son poured out His soul unto the Father. It is a rare privilege, and one from which most men would sensitively shrink, to listen even to a fellow-man alone with God. Yet the Lord Jesus in the midst of His disciples laid bare His very soul before His Father, as really as if He had been alone with Him. He prayed with the cross and its awful death full in view, but in the prayer there is no slightest hint of failure or regret, and there is no trace of confession of sin or need of forgiveness. These are all indelible marks of genuineness. It would have been impossible for a sinful man to conceive such a prayer. But all is consistent with the character of Him who "spake as never man spake", and could challenge the world to convict Him of sin.

With such thoughts in mind let us now look more closely into the words of the prayer itself.

"Father, the hour is come; glorify Thy Son, that Thy Son also may glorify Thee: As Thou hast given Him power over all flesh, that He should give eternal life to as many as Thou hast given Him. And this is life eternal, that they might know Thee, the only true God, and *Jesus Christ whom Thou hast sent."*

Here we have again the calm placing of Himself on a level with the Father in connection with eternal life. And it is not out of place to recall the consistency of this utterance with that often-called "Johannine" saying recorded in St. Matthew and St. Luke: "All things are delivered unto Me of My Father: and no man knoweth the Son, but the Father; neither knoweth any man the Father, save the Son, and he to whomsoever the Son willeth to reveal Him."

We read also in St. John 14:6: "No man cometh unto

the Father but by Me". And as we reverently proceed further in the prayer we find Him saying: "And now, O Father, glorify Thou Me with Thine own self, with the glory which I had with Thee *before the world was.*"

These words are natural to the Father's Son as we know and worship Him, but they are beyond the reach of an uninspired man, and who can imagine a forger inspired of the Holy Ghost? Such words would, however, be graven upon the very heart of an ear-witness such as the disciple whom Jesus loved.

We have in this prayer also the fuller revelation of the "one flock" and "one Shepherd" pictured in chapter ten: "Neither pray I for these alone, but for them also which shall believe on Me through their word; that they all may be one; *as Thou, Father, art in Me, and I in Thee, that they also may be one in us:* That *the world* may believe that Thou hast sent Me. And the glory which Thou gavest Me I have given them; that they may be one, even as we are one: I in them, and Thou in Me, that they may be perfected into one; and that the world may know that Thou hast sent Me, and *hast loved them, as Thou hast loved Me.*"

In these holy words there breathes a cry for such a unity as never entered into the heart of mortal man to dream of. It is no cold and formal ecclesiastical unity, such as that suggested by the curious and unhappy mistranslation of "one fold" for "one flock" in St. John 10:16. It is the living unity of the living flock with the living Shepherd of the living God. It is actually the same as the unity subsisting between the Father and the Son. And according to St. Paul in Rom. 8:19; the creation is waiting for its revelation. The one Shepherd has from the beginning had His one flock in answer to His prayer, but the world has not yet seen it, and is therefore still unconvinced that our Jesus is indeed the Sent of God. The world has seen the Catholic Church and the Roman Catholic Church, but the Holy Catholic Church no eye as yet has seen but God's. For the Holy Catholic Church and the Shepherd's one flock are one and the same, and the world will not see either "till He come." The *Holy Catholic Church* is an object of faith and not of sight, and so is the one flock. In spite of all attempts at elimination and organization wheat and tares together grow, and sheep and wolves-in-sheep's-clothing are found together in the earthly pasture grounds. But when the Good Shepherd returns He will bring His beautiful flock with Him, and eventually the world will see and believe. "O the depth of the riches both of the wisdom and knowledge of God! How unsearchable are His judgments, and His ways past finding out!"

The mystery of this spiritual unity lies hidden in the high-priestly prayer, but we may feel sure that no forger could ever discover it, for many of those who profess and call themselves Christians are blind to it even yet.

4. The "Christ before Pilate" of St. John is also stamped with every mark of sincerity and truth. What mere human imagination could evolve the noble words: "My kingdom is not of this world; if My kingdom were of this world, then would My servants fight, that I should not be delivered to the Jews: but now is My kingdom not from hence . . . To this end was I born, and for this cause came I into the world, that I should bear witness unto the truth. Every one that is of the truth heareth My voice"?

The whole wondrous story of the betrayal, the denial, the trial, the condemnation and crucifixion of the Lord Jesus, as given through St. John, breathes with the living sympathy of an eye-witness. The account, moreover, is as wonderful in the delicacy of its reserve as in the simplicity of its recital. It is entirely free from sensationalism and every form of exaggeration. It is calm and judicial in the highest degree. If it is written by the inspired disciple whom Jesus loved, all is natural and easily "understood of the people"; while on

any other supposition, it is fraught with difficulties that cannot be explained away. "I am not credulous enough to be
an unbeliever," is a wise saying in this as in many similar
connections.

5. The Gospel opens and closes with surpassing grandeur.
With Divine dignity it links itself with the opening words of
Genesis: *"In the beginning* was the Word, and the Word
was with God, and the Word was *God.* . . . And the
Word became flesh, and dwelt among us, and we beheld His
glory, the glory as of the Only Begotten of the Father, full
of grace and truth." What a lifelike contrast with this sublime
description is found in the introduction of John the Baptist:
"There came *a man* sent from God whose name was John".
In the incarnation Christ did not become *a* man but *man*.
Moreover in this St. Paul and St. John are in entire agreement.

"There is one God", says St. Paul to Timothy; "one
Mediator also between God and man—*Himself Man*—Christ
Jesus." The reality of the Divine Redeemer's human nature
is beautifully manifested in the touching interview between
the weary Saviour and the guilty Samaritan woman at the
well; as also in His perfect human friendship with Mary and
Martha and their brother Lazarus, culminating in the price-
less words, "Jesus wept".

And so by the bitter way of the Cross the grandeur of
the incarnation passes into the glory of the resurrection. The
last two chapters are alive with thrilling incident. If any one
wishes to form a true conception of what those brief chapters
contain, let him read "Jesus and the Resurrection," by the
saintly Bishop of Durham (Dr. Handley Moule) and his cup
of holy joy will fill to overflowing. At the empty tomb we
breathe the air of the unseen kingdom, and presently we gaze
enraptured on the face of the Crucified but risen and ever-
living King. Mary Magdalene, standing in her broken-hearted
despair, is all unconscious of the wondrous fact that holy

angels are right in front of her and standing behind her is her living Lord and Master. Slowly but surely the glad story spreads from lip to lip and heart to heart, until even the honest but stubborn Thomas is brought to his knees, crying in a burst of remorseful, adoring joy, "My Lord and my God!"

Then comes the lovely story of the fruitless all-night toil of the seven fishermen, the appearance at dawn of the Stranger on the beach, the miraculous draught of fishes, the glad cry of recognition, "It is the Lord!" the never-to-be-forgotten breakfast with the risen Saviour, and His searching interview with Peter, passing into the mystery of St. John's old age.

In all these swiftly-drawn outlines we feel ourselves instinctively in the presence of the truth. We are crowned with the Saviour's beatitude: "Blessed are they that have not seen, and yet have believed," and we are ready to yield a glad assent to the statement which closes chapter twenty: "Many other signs truly did Jesus in the presence of His disciples, which are not written in this book; but these are written that ye might believe that Jesus is the Christ, the Son of God; and that believing ye might have life in His Name."

THE NATURE OF REGENERATION

BY THOMAS BOSTON (1676-1732)

I. For the better understanding of the nature of regeneration, take this along with you, in the first place, that as there are false conceptions in nature, so there are also in grace: by these many are deluded, mistaking some partial changes made upon them for this great and thorough change. To remove such mistakes, let these few things be considered:

1. Many call the Church their mother, whom God will not own to be His children. "My mother's children," that is, false brethren, "were angry with me" (Cant. 1:6). All that are baptized, are not born again. Simon was baptized, yet still "in the gall of bitterness, and in the bond of iniquity" (Acts 8:13-23). Where Christianity is the religion of the country, many are called by the name of Christ, who have no more of Him than the name: and no wonder, for the devil had his goats among Christ's sheep, in those places where but few professed the Christian religion. "They went out from us, but they were not of us" (1 John 2:19).

2. Good education is not regeneration. Education may chain up men's lusts, but cannot change their hearts. A wolf is still a ravenous beast, though it be in chains. Joash was very devout during the life of his good tutor Jehoiada; but afterwards he quickly showed what spirit he was of, by his sudden apostasy (2 Chron. 24:2-18). Good example is of mighty influence to change the outward man; but that change often goes off when a man changes his company; of which the world affords many sad instances.

3. A turning from open profanity to civility and sobriety falls short of this saving change. Some are, for a while, very

loose, especially in their younger years; but at length they reform, and leave their profane courses. Here is a change, yet only such as may be found in men utterly void of the grace of God, and whose righteousness is so far from exceeding, that it does not come up to the righteousness of the scribes and Pharisees.

4. One may engage in all the outward duties of religion, and yet not be born again. Though lead be cast into various shapes, it remains still but a base metal. Men may escape the pollutions of the world, and yet be but dogs and swine (2 Pet. 2:20-22). All the external acts of religion are within the compass of natural abilities. Yea, hypocrites may have the counterfeit of all the graces of the Spirit: for we read of "true holiness" (Eph. 4:23); and "faith unfeigned" (1 Tim. 1:15); which shows us that there is a counterfeit holiness, and a feigned faith.

5. Men may advance to a great deal of strictness in their own way of religion, and yet be strangers to the new birth. "After the most straitest sect of our religion I lived a Pharisee" (Acts 26:5). Nature has its own unsanctified strictness in religion. The Pharisees had so much of it that they looked on Christ as little better than a mere libertine. A man whose conscience has been awakened, and who lives under the felt influence of the covenant of works, what will he not do that is within the compass of natural abilities? It is a truth, though it came out of a hellish mouth, that "skin for skin, all that a man hath will he give for his life" (Job 2:4).

6. A person may have sharp soul-exercises and pangs, and yet die in the birth. Many "have been in pain," that have but, as it were, "brought forth wind." There may be sore pangs and throes of conscience, which turn to nothing at last. Pharaoh and Simon Magus had such convictions as made them desire the prayers of others for them. Judas repented himself; and under terrors of conscience, gave back his ill-gotten pieces of silver. All is not gold that glitters. Trees may blos-

som fairly in the spring, on which no fruit is to be found in the harvest: and some have sharp soul exercises, which are nothing but foretastes of hell.

The new birth, however in appearance hopefully begun, may be marred two ways: *First,* Some, like Zarah (Gen. 38:28, 29), are brought to the birth, but go back again. They have sharp convictions for a while; but these go off, and they become as careless about their salvation, and as profane as ever and usually worse than ever; "their last state is worse than their first" (Matt. 12:45). They get awakening grace, but not converting grace and that goes off by degrees, as the light of the declining day, till it issue in midnight darkness.

Secondly, Some, like Ishmael, come forth too soon; they are born before the time of the promise. (Gen. 16:2; compare Gal. 4:22, etc.) They take up with a mere law-work, and stay not till the time of the promise of the Gospel. They snatch at consolation, not waiting till it be given them; and foolishly draw their comfort from the law that wounded them. They apply the healing plaster to themselves, before their wound is sufficiently searched. The law, that rigorous husband, severely beats them, and throws in curses and vengeance upon their souls; then they fall to reforming, praying, mourning, promising, and vowing, till this ghost be laid; which done, they fall asleep again in the arms of the law: but they are never shaken out of themselves and their own righteousness, nor brought forward to Jesus Christ.

Lastly, There may be a wonderful moving of the affections, in souls that are not at all touched with regenerating grace. Where there is no grace, there may, notwithstanding, be a flood of tears, as in Esau, "who found no place of repentance, though he sought it carefully with tears" (Heb. 12:17). There may be great flashes of joy; as in the hearers of the Word, represented in the parable by the stony ground, who "anon with joy receive it" (Matt. 13:20). There may also be great desires after good things, and great delight in them too; as in those hypocrites described in Isa. 58:2: "Yet they seek Me daily, and delight to know My ways: they take delight in approaching to God." See how high they may sometimes stand, who yet fall away (Heb. 6:4-6). They may be "enlightened, taste of the heavenly gift," be "partakers of the Holy Ghost, taste the good Word of God, and the powers of the world to come." Common operations of the Divine Spirit, like a land flood, make a strange turning of things upside down: but when they are over, all runs again in the ordinary channel. All these things may be, where the sanctifying Spirit of Christ never rests upon the soul, but the stony heart still remains; and in that case these affections cannot but wither, because they have no root.

But regeneration is a real thorough change, whereby the man is made a new creature. (2 Cor. 5:17.) The Lord God makes the creature a new creature, as the goldsmith melts down the vessel of dishonor, and makes it a vessel of honor. Man is, in respect of his spiritual state, altogether disjointed by the fall; every faculty of the soul is, as it were, dislocated: in regeneration the Lord loosens every joint, and sets it right again. Now this change made in regeneration, is:

1. *A change of qualities or dispositions*: it is not a change of the substance, but of the qualities of the soul. Vicious qualities are removed,and the contrary dispositions are brought in, in their room. "The old man is put off" (Eph. 4:22); "the new man put on" (ver. 24). Man lost none of the rational faculties of his soul by sin: he had an understanding still, but it was darkened; he had still a will, but it was contrary to the will of God. So in regeneration, there is not a new substance created, but new qualities are infused; light instead of darkness, righteousness instead of unrighteousness.

2. *It is a supernatural change;* he that is born again, is born of the Spirit. (John 3:5.) Great changes may be made by the power of nature, especially when assissted by external revelation. Nature may be so elevated by the common in-

fluences of the Spirit, that a person may thereby be turned into another man, as Saul was, (1 Sam. 10:6,) who yet never becomes a new man. But in regeneration, nature itself is changed, and we become partakers of the Divine nature; and this must needs be a supernatural change. How can we, that are dead in trespasses and sins, renew ourselves, more than a dead man can raise himself out of his grave? Who but the sanctifying Spirit of Christ can form Christ in a soul, changing it into the same image? Who but the Spirit of sanctification can give the new heart? Well may we say, when we see a man thus changed: "This is the finger of God."

3. *It is a change into the likeness of God.* "We, beholding, as in a glass, the glory of the Lord, are changed into the same image" (2 Cor. 3:18). Everything that generates, generates its like; the child bears the image of the parent; and they that are born of God, bear God's image. Man aspiring to be as God, made himself like the devil. In his natural state he resembles the devil, as a child doth his father. "Ye are of your father the devil" (John 8:44). But when this happy change comes, that image of Satan is defaced, and the image of God is restored. Christ Himself, who is the brightness of His Father's glory, is the pattern after which the new creature is made. "For whom He did foreknow, He also did predestinate, to be conformed to the image of His Son" (Rom. 8:29). Hence He is said to be formed in the regenerate. (Gal. 4:19.)

4. *It is a universal change;* "all things become new," (2 Cor. 5:17). Original sin infects the whole man; and regenerating grace, which is the salve, goes as far as the sore. This fruit of the Spirit is in all goodness; goodness of the mind, goodness of the will, goodness of the affections, goodness of the whole man. He gets not only a new head, to know religion, or a new tongue to talk of it; but a new heart, to love and embrace it in the whole of his conversation.

CHAPTER IV

REGENERATION — CONVERSION — REFORMATION

BY REV. GEORGE W. LASHER, D. D., LL. D.,
Author of "Theology for Plain People"
CINCINNATI, OHIO

In his "Twice-Born Men," Mr. Harold Begbie gives us a series of instances wherein men of the lowest grade, or the most perverse nature, became suddenly changed in thought, purpose, will and life. Without intentionally ignoring the word "regeneration," or the fact of regeneration, he emphasises the act of conversion in which he includes regeneration which, in our conception, is the origin of conversion and a true reformation as a permanent fact. A weakness in much of the teaching of modern times is in that conversion and reformation are thrust to the front, while regeneration is either ignored, or minimized to nothingness.

Jesus Christ did not say much about regeneration, using the equivalent word in the Greek (*paliggenesis*) only once, and then (Matt. 19:28) having reference to created things, a new order in the physical universe, rather than to a new condition of the individual soul. But He taught the great truth in other words, the needful fact by which He made it evident that a regeneration is what the human soul needs and must have to fit it for the kingdom of God.

In the other Gospels, Jesus is represented as teaching things which involve a new birth, without which it is impossible to meet Divine requirements; but in John's Gospel it is distinctly set forth in the very first chapter, and the idea is carried through to the end. When (in John 1:12, 13) it is said that those who received the Word of God received also "power," or right, to become God's children, it is expressly declared that this power, or right, is not inherent in human nature, is not found in the natural birth, but involves a new birth—"who are born not of blood, nor of the will of the flesh, nor of the will of man, but of God." It is this new or second birth which produces children of God. The declaration of John (3:3) puts to confusion the very common claim that God is the Father of universal humanity, and makes it absurd to talk of "the Fatherhood of God," "the Heavenly Father," "the Divine Fatherhood," and other such phrases with which we are surfeited in these modern days. Nothing is farther from truth, and nothing is more dangerous and seductive than the claim that the children of Adam are, by nature, God's children. It is the basis of much false reasoning with regard to the future state and the continuity of future punishment. It is said, in words, that, though a father may chastise his son, "for his profit," yet the relation of fatherhood and sonship forbids the thought that the father can thrust his son into the burning and keep him there forever. No matter what the offense, it can be expiated by suffering, the father heart will certainly relent and the prodigal will turn again and will be received with joy and gladness by the yearning father.

Of course, the fallacy of the argument is in the assumption that all men are, by nature, the children of God, a thing expressly denied by the Lord Jesus (John 8:42) who declared to certain ones that they were of their father the devil. The conversation with Nicodemus gives us the condition upon which once-born men may see the kingdom of God, namely, by being twice-born, once of the flesh, and a second time of the Spirit. "Except a man be born again [*anothen*, from above] he cannot see the kingdom of God." There must be a birth from heaven before there can be a heavenly inheritance. Nicodemus, though a teacher of Israel, did not understand it. He had read in vain the word through Jeremiah (33:31) relative to the "new covenant" which involves a new heart. He had failed to discern between the natural man and the spiritual man. He had no conception of a changed condition as the basis of genuine reformation. But Nicodemus was not alone in his misconception. After all these centuries, many students of the New Testament, accepting the Gospel of John as canonical and genuine, stumble over the same great truth and "pervert the right ways of the Lord." Taking the fifth verse of John 3, they accept the doctrine of regeneration, but couple it with an external act without which, in their view, the regeneration is not and cannot be completed. In their rituals they distinctly declare that water baptism is essential to and is productive of the regeneration which Jesus declares must be from heaven. They stumble over, or pervert the words used, and make "born of water" to be baptism, of which nothing is said in the verse or in the chapter, and which the whole tenor of Scripture denies.

The lexicographers, the grammarians and evangelical theologians are all pronounced against the interpretation put upon the words of Jesus when He said: "Except a man [any one] be born of water *kai* spirit, he cannot enter into the kingdom of God." The lexicographers tell us that the conjunction *k a i* (Greek) may have an epexegetical meaning and may be (as it frequently is) used to amplify what has gone before; that it may have the sense of "even," or "namely." And thus they justify the reading: "Except a man be born of water, even [or namely] spirit, he cannot enter into the kingdom of God." The grammarians tell us the same thing, and innumerable instances of such usage can be cited from both classic and New Testament Greek. The theologians are explicit in their denial that regeneration can be effected by baptism. They hold to a purely spiritual experience, either before baptism, or after it, and deny that the spiritual birth is effected by the water, no matter how applied. And yet some who take this position in discussions of the "new birth" fall away to the ritualistic idea when they come to treat of baptism, its significance and place in the Christian system. (It would be easy to justify all these statements by reference to authors and books, but space forbids the quotations here. So patent are they that we can hardly doubt the acceptance of the assertion by the intelligent reader, without citations in proof.)

PAUL AS AN INTERPRETER OF JESUS

The best interpreter of Jesus who ever undertook to represent Him was the man who was made a "chosen vessel," to bear the Gospel of the kingdom to the pagan nations of his own time, and to transmit his interpretations to us of the twentieth century. He could say: "The Gospel which was preached of me is not after man, neither was I taught it, but by revelation of Jesus Christ." And Paul speaks of this work wrought in the human soul as a "new creation"—something that was not there before. "If any man be in Christ, he is a new creature" (creation). "Neither circumcision availeth anything, nor uncircumcision, but a new creature" (creation). Never once, in all his discussions of the way of salvation, does Paul intimate that the new creation is effected by a ritual observance. It is always and everywhere regarded and treated as a spiritual experience wrought by the Spirit of God, the subject of it knowing only, as the healed man said of himself, "Whereas I was blind now I see."

THE TESTIMONY OF EXPERIENCE

The prayers of the Bible, especially those of the New Testament, do not indicate that the suppliant asks for a regeneration—a new heart. He may have been taught the need of it, and may be brought face to face with the great and decisive fact; but his thought is not so much of a new heart as it is of his sins and his condemnation. What he wants is deliverance from the fact and the consequences of sin. He finds himself a condemned sinner, under the frown of a God of justice, and he despairs. But he is told of Jesus and the forgiving grace of God, and he asks that the gracious provision be applied to his own soul. "Mercy, and not sacrifice," is the argument, the mercy secured by the work of Him whom God hath appointed to be the propitiation for our sins. But when the supplicating and believing sinner awakes to a consciousness that his prayer has been heard, he finds that he is a new creature. The work has been wrought without his consciousness of it at the moment. All he knows is that something has taken place within him—a great "change." He is a new creature. He dares to hope and to believe that he is a son of God; and he cries in the ecstacy of a new life: "Abba, Father" (Dear Father)! "The Spirit Himself beareth witness with our spirit that we are the children of God," and subsequently we learn that we are heirs of a rich Father— "heirs of God and joint-heirs with Jesus Christ," with whom we are to both suffer and reign.

CONVERSION (which really means only "change"), we have said, is included in the idea of regeneration; but the words do not mean the same thing. Regeneration implies conversion; but there may be conversion without regeneration. The danger is that the distinction may not be observed and that, because there is a visible conversion, it may be supposed that there must be a prevenient regeneration. Conversion may be a mere mental process; the understanding convinced, but the heart unchanged. It may be effected as education and refinement are effected. The schools are constantly doing it. It is what they are for. Regeneration involves a change of mind; but conversion may be effected while the moral condition remains unchanged. Regeneration can occur but once in the experience of the same soul; but conversion can occur many times. Regeneration implies a new life, eternal life, Divine life, the life of God in the soul of man, a Divine sonship, the continuous indwelling of the Holy Spirit. Conversion may be like that of King Saul, when he took a place among the prophets of Jehovah, or like that of Simon the sorcerer, who said: "Pray ye the Lord for me, that none of these things which ye have spoken come upon me."

Conversion may be the result of a conviction that, after all, a change of life may be profitable for the life that is to come, as well as for the life that now is; that in the future world a man gets what he earns in this life. It does not imply a heart in love with God and the things of God. Men of the world are converted many times. They change their minds, and often change their mode of living, for the better; not because they have been regenerated and brought into sacred relations with God in Christ, being renewed by the power of the Holy Spirit.

One of the most imminent dangers of the religious life of today is the putting of conversion in the place of regeneration, and counting converted men as Christian men, counting "converts" in revival meetings as regenerated and saved, because they have mentally, and, for the moment, changed. Men are converted, politically, from one party to another; from one set of principles to another. Christians, after regeneration, may change their religious views and pass from one denomination to another. Few Christians pass through many years without a need of conversion. They grow cold of heart, blind to the things of God, and wander from the straight path to which they once committed themselves; and they need conversion. Most revivals of religion begin with the conversion of saints. Rarely are souls, in considerable numbers, regenerated while regenerated men and women are unconscious of their high calling and are in need of conversion, in order to their hearty engagement in efforts for those around them. First, a converted church, then regenerated and converted souls.

REFORMATION implies conversion, but it does not imply regeneration. Regeneration insures reformation, but reformation does not imply regeneration. Reformers have been abroad in all ages, and are known to paganism as well as to

Christianity. The Buddha was a reformer. Confucius was a reformer. Zoroaster was a reformer. Mahomet was a reformer. Kings and priests have been reformers, while knowing nothing of the life of God in the human soul. A Christian man is a reformed man, though his reformation may be far from complete and may need a great many reforming impulses. The most glaring and fatal mistake in the religious world today is the effort to reform men and reform society by making the reformation a substitute for regeneration.

The social life of today is full of devices and expedients for bettering the physical condition of individuals, families and communities, while yet the soul-life is untouched. Human devices are taking the place of the Divine ideal, and those who cannot reach the inner life are contenting themselves, if they can reach and better the outer life, the mere incident of being. We have civic organizations without number, each of which has for its highest object the betterment not simply of worldly conditions, but of the character of the brotherhood. An argument for the existence of many of these organizations is that they may make better men by reason of the confidence and fraternity secured by the contact effected, by the oaths and vows taken, and by the cultivation of the social life. A willingness to learn and to receive instruction is a condition of initiation into the order.

That reformatory agencies are good and accomplish good is not denied. Each has its good points and helps to elevate the tone of society in the aggregate. But a fatal mistake is in the notion that the elevation of society, the eliminating of its miseries, is conducive to a religious life and promotive of Christianity. Perhaps the greatest hindrances to the conquest sought by Christianity today, in civilized and nominally Christian countries, are the various agencies intended to reform society. They are improving the exterior, veneering and polishing the outside, while the inside is no better than before because the heart remains wicked and sinful. "Now do ye Pharisees make clean the outside of the cup and the platter, but your inward part is full of ravening and wickedness."

The Pharisees were the best people of their day; and yet they were the greatest failures. Against no others did Jesus hurl so fierce denunciations. Why? Because they put reformation in the place of repentance and faith; because they were employing human means for accomplishing what only the Holy Spirit could accomplish. And so, today, every device for the betterment of society which does not strike at the root of the disease and apply the remedy to the seat of life, the human soul, is Pharisaical and is doing a Pharisee's work. It is polishing the outside, while indifferent to the inside. The road to hell from a church door is as short as is that from a hangman's noose, or an electric chair. More church members than murderers have gone to the hell of the unbeliever. "The good is always the enemy of the best"; and so reformation is always an enemy of the cross of Christ.

*Mr. Begbie's "twice-born men" were reformed, and they made proof of it in their subsequent lives because they were regenerated, twice born; but there were beside them, a great multitude of "reformed" men, who were no less heirs of hell than before their "reformation." He tells us of only a few of the great multitude of those reformed—a few of thousands.

Fundamental to the Christian system is a conviction of sin which compels a cry for mercy, responded to by the Holy Spirit, who regenerates the soul, converts it, reforms it and fits it for the blessedness of heaven.

*By reference to Mr. Begbie's book, the writer means no criticism, for he is in full accord with the facts and purposes of the book. He uses it only as a striking illustration of the point he wishes to make.

CHAPTER V

OUR LORD'S TEACHINGS ABOUT MONEY

BY ARTHUR T. PIERSON

Our Lord's teachings as to money gifts, if obeyed, would forever banish all limitations on church work and all concern about supplies. These teachings are radical and revolutionary. So far are they from practical acceptance that, although perfectly explicit, they seem more like a dead language that has passed out of use than like a living tongue that millions know and speak. Yet, when these principles and precepts of our Lord on giving are collated and compared, they are found to contain the materials of a complete ethical system on the subject of money, its true nature, value, relation and use. Should these sublime and unique teachings be translated into *living*, the effect not only upon benevolent work, but upon our whole spiritual character, would be incalculable. Brevity compels us to be content with a simple outline of this body of teaching, scattered through the four Gospel narratives, but gathered up and methodically presented by Paul in that exhaustive discussion of Christian giving in 2 Cor. 8 and 9.

I. THE PRINCIPLE OF STEWARDSHIP

The basis of Christ's teaching about money is the fundamental conception of *stewardship*. (Luke 12:42; 16:1-8.) Not only money, but every gift of God, is received in trust for His use. Man is not an owner, but a trustee, managing another's goods and estates, God being the one original and inalienable Owner of all. The two things required of stewards are that they be "faithful and wise," that they study to employ God's gifts with fidelity and sagacity—fidelity so that God's entrustments be not perverted to self-indulgence; sagacity, so that they be converted into as large gains as possible.

This is a perfectly plain and simple basal principle, yet it is not the accepted foundation of our money-making and using. The vast majority, even of disciples, practically leave God out of their thoughts when they engage in finance. Men consider themselves owners; they "make money" by their industry, economy, shrewdness, application; it is theirs to do as they will with it. There is little or no sense of stewardship or of its implied obligation. If they give, it is an act, not of duty, but of generosity; it ranks, not under law, but under grace. Hence there is no inconsistency felt in hoarding or spending vast sums for worldly ends and appropriating an insignificant fraction to benevolent purposes. Such methods and notions would be utterly turned upside down could men but think of themselves as stewards, accountable to the one Master for having wasted His goods. The great day of account will bring an awful reckoning, not only to wasters, but to hoarders; for even the unfaithful servants brought back to their lord the talent and the pound at last, but without profit, and the condemnation was for not having used so as to increase the entrusted goods.

II. THE PRINCIPLE OF INVESTMENT

In our Lord's teachings we find this kindred principle of investment: "Thou oughtest to have put my money to the exchangers" (Matt. 25:27). Money-changing and investing is an old business. The "exchangers," as Luke renders, are the *bankers*, the ancient Trapezitae, who received money on deposit and paid interest for its use, like modern savings institutions. The argument of our Lord refutes the unfaithful servant on his own plea, which his course showed to be not an excuse, but a pretext. It was true that he dared not risk trading on his own account; why not, without such risk, get a moderate interest for his Master by lending to professional traders? It was not fear but sloth that lay behind his unfaithfulness and unprofitableness.

Thus indirectly is taught the valuable lesson that timid souls, unfitted for bold and independent service in behalf of the kingdom, may link their incapacity to the capacity and sagacity of others who will make their gifts and possessions of use to the Master and His Church.

James Watt, in 1773, formed a partnership with Matthew Boulton, of Soho, for the manufacture of steam engines— Watt, to furnish brains, and Boulton, hard cash. This illustrates our Lord's teaching. The steward has money, or it may be other gifts, that can be made of use, but he lacks faith and foresight, practical energy and wisdom. The Lord's "exchangers" can show him how to get gain for the Master. The Church boards are God's bankers. They are composed of practical men, who study how and where to put money for the best results and largest returns, and when they are what they ought to be, they multiply money many-fold in glorious results. The Church partly exists that the strength of one member may help the weakness of another, and that by co-operation of all, the power of the least and weakest may be increased.

III. THE SUBORDINATION OF MONEY

Another most important principle is *the subordination of money,* as emphatically taught and illustrated in the rich young ruler. (Matt. 19:16-26.) This narrative, rightly regarded, presents no enigma. With all his attractive traits, this man was a slave. Money was not his servant, but his master; and because God alone is to be supreme, our Lord had no alternative. He must demolish this man's idol, and when He dealt a blow at his money, the idolatry became apparent, and the slave of greed went away sorrowful, clinging to his idol. It was not the man's having great possessions that was wrong, but that his possessions *had* the man; they possessed him and controlled him. He was so far the slave of money that he could not and would not accept freedom by the breaking of its fetters. His "trust" was in riches—how could it be in God? Behind all disguises of respectability and refinement, God sees many a man to be an abject slave, a victim held in bonds by love of money; but covetousness is idolatry, and no idolater can enter the kingdom of God. How few rich men keep the mastery and hold money as their servant, in absolute subordination to their own manhood, and the masterhood of the Lord!

IV. THE LAW OF RECOMPENSE

We ascend a step higher, and consider our Lord's teaching as to the *law of recompense*. "Give, and it shall be given unto you" (Luke 6:38). We are taught that getting is in order to giving, and consequently that giving is the real road to getting. God is an economist. He entrusts larger gifts to those who use the smaller well. Perhaps one reason of our poverty is that we are so far slaves of parsimony. The future may reveal that God has been withholding from us because we have been withholding from Him.

It can scarcely be said by any careful student of the New Testament that our Lord encourages His disciples to look or ask for earthly wealth. Yet it is equally certain that hundreds of devout souls who have chosen voluntary poverty for His sake have been entrusted with immense sums for His work. George Müller conducted for over sixty years enterprises requiring at least some hundred and twenty-five thousand dollars a year. Note also the experiences of William Quarrier and Hudson Taylor, and D. L. Moody and Dr. Barnardo. Such servants of God, holding all as God's, spending little or nothing for self, were permitted to receive and use millions for God, and in some cases, like Müller's, without any appeal to men, looking solely to God. This great saint of Bristol found, in a life that nearly rounded out a century, that it was safe to give to God's purposes the last penny at any moment, with the perfect assurance that more would come in before another need should arise. And there was never one failure for seventy years!

V. SUPERIOR BLESSEDNESS

Kindred to this law of recompense is the law of *superior blessedness.* "It is more blessed to give than to receive" (Acts 20:35). Paul quotes this as a saying of our Lord, but it is not to be found in either of the Gospel narratives. Whether he meant only to indicate what is substantially our Lord's teaching, or was preserving some precious words of our Great Teacher, otherwise unrecorded, is not important. It is enough that this saying has the authority of Christ. Whatever the blessedness of receiving, that of giving belongs to a higher plane. Whatever I get, and whatever good it brings to me, I only am benefited; but what I give brings good to others—to the many, not the one. But, by a singular decree of God, what I thus surrender for myself for the sake of others comes back even to me in larger blessing. It is like the moisture which the spring gives out in streams and evaporation, returning in showers to supply the very channels which filled the spring itself.

VI. COMPUTATION BY COMPARISON

We rise a step higher in considering God's *law of computation.* How does He reckon gifts? Our Lord teaches us that it is *by comparison.* No one narrative is more telling on this theme than that of the poor widow* who dropped into the treasury her two mites. The Lord Jesus, standing near, watched the offerings cast into the treasury. There were rich givers that gave large amounts. There was one poor woman, a widow, who threw in two mites, and He declared her offering to be more than any of all the rest, because, while they

*Mark 12:41-44; Luke 21:1-4.

gave out of a superfluity she gave out of a deficiency—they of their abundance, she of her poverty.

She who cast her two mites into the sacred treasury, by so doing became rich in good works and in the praise of God. Had she kept them she had been still only the same poor widow. Are not two sparrows sold for a farthing? And the two mites "make a farthing." He who, as the Superintending Providence of nature, watches the fall of a sparrow, so that "one of them is not forgotten before God," also, as the Overseer of the treasury, invisibly sits and watches the gifts that are dropped into the chest, and even the widow's mite is not forgotten.

He tells us here how He estimates money gifts—not by what we *give*, but by what we *keep*—not by the amount of our contributions, but by their *cost* in self-denial. This widow's whole offering counted financially for but a farthing (κοδράντης, a quadrant, equal to four mills, or two fifths of a cent, as three-fourths of an English farthing). What could be much more insignificant? But the two mites constituted *her whole means of subsistence.* The others reserved what they needed or wanted for themselves, and then gave out of their superabundance (περισσεύοντος). The contrast is emphatic; she "out of her *deficiency*," they "out of their *supersufficiency*."

Not all *giving*—so-called—has rich reward. In many cases the keeping hides the giving, in the sight of God. Self-indulgent hoarding and spending spread a banquet; the crumbs fall from the table, to be gathered up and labeled "charity." But when the one possession that is dearest, the last trusted resource, is surrendered to God, then comes the vision of the treasure laid up in heaven.

VII. UNSELFISHNESS IN GIVING

We ascend still higher to the law of unselfishness in giving. "Do good and lend, *hoping for nothing again*" (Luke 6:35).

Much giving is not giving at all, but only lending or exchanging. He who gives to another of whom he expects to receive as much again, is trading. He is seeking gain, and is selfish. What he is after is not another's profit, but his own advantage. To invite to one's table those who will invite him again, is simply as if a kindness were done to a business acquaintance as a basis for boldness in asking a similar favor when needed. This is reciprocity, and may be even mean and calculating.

True giving has another's good solely in view, and hence bestows upon those who cannot and will not repay, who are too destitute to pay back, and too degraded, perhaps, to appreciate what is done for them. That is like God's giving to the evil and unthankful. That is the giving prompted by love.

To ask, therefore, "Will it pay?" betrays the selfish spirit. He is the noblest, truest giver who thinks only of the blessing he can bring to another's body and soul. He casts his bread-seed beside all waters. He hears the cry of want and woe, and is concerned only to supply the want and assuage the woe. This sort of giving shows God-likeness, and by it we grow into the perfection of benevolence.

VIII. SANCTIFIED GIVING

Our Lord announces also a law of sanctification. "The altar sanctifieth the gift"—*association gives dignity to an offering* (Matt. 23:19). If the cause to which we contribute is exalted it ennobles and exalts the offering to its own plane. No two objects can or ought to appeal to us with equal force unless they are equal in moral worth and dignity, and a discerning giver will respond most to what is worthiest. God's altar was to the Jew the central focus of all gifts; it was associated with His worship, and the whole calendar of fasts and feasts moved round it. The gift laid upon it acquired a new dignity by so being deposited upon it. Some objects which appeal for gifts we are at liberty to set aside because they are not sacred. We may give or not as we judge best, for they depend on man's enterprises and schemes, which we may not altogether approve. But some causes have Divine sanction, and that hallows them; giving becomes an act of worship when it has to do with the altar.

IX. TRANSMUTATION

Another law of true giving is that of *transmutation*. "Make to yourselves friends of the mammon of unrighteousness; that, when ye fail, they may receive you into everlasting habitations" (Luke 16:9). This, though considered by many an obscure parable, contains one of the greatest hints on money gifts that our Lord ever dropped.

Mammon here stands as the equivalent for *money*, practically worshipped. It reminds us of the golden calf that was made out of the ear-rings and jewels of the crowd. Now our Lord refers to a second transmutation. The golden calf may in turn be melted down and *coined into Bibles,* churches, books, tracts, and even *souls of men.* Thus what was material and temporal becomes immaterial and spiritual, and eternal. Here is a man who has a hundred dollars. He may spend it all on a banquet, or an evening party, in which case the next day there is nothing to show for it. It has secured a temporary gratification of appetite—that is all. On the other hand, he invests in Bibles at ten cents each, and it buys a thousand copies of the Word of God. These he judiciously sows as seed of the Kingdom, and that seed springs up a harvest, not of Bibles, but of souls. Out of the unrighteous mammon he has made immortal friends, who, when he fails, receive him into everlasting habitations. May this not be what is meant by the *true riches*—the treasure laid up in heaven in imperishable good?

What revelations await us in that day of transmutation! Then, whatever has been given up to God as an offering of the heart, "in righteousness," will be seen as transfigured. Not only the magi's gold, frankincense and myrrh, and the alabaster box of ointment of spikenard, very precious, and the houses and lands of such as Barnabas, but fishermen's boats and nets, the abandoned "seat of custom," the widow's mites, and the cup of cold water—yes, when we had nothing else to give, the word of counsel, the tear of pity, the prayer of intercession. Then shall be seen both the limitless possibilities and the "transcendent riches" of consecrated poverty.

Never will the work of missions, or any other form of service to God and man, receive the help it ought until there is a new conscience and a new consecration in the matter of money. The influence of the world and the worldly spirit is deadening to unselfish giving. It exalts self-indulgence, whether in gross or refined form. It leads to covetous hoarding or wasteful spending. It blinds us to the fact of obligation, and devises flimsy pretexts for diverting the Lord's money to carnal ends. The few who learn to give on Scriptural principles learn also to *love* to give. These gifts become abundant and systematic and self-denying. The stream of beneficence flows perpetually—there is no period of drought.

Once it was necessary to proclaim to the people of God that what they had brought "was more than enough," and to "restrain them from bringing" (Ex. 36:6). So far as known, this is the one and only historic instance of such excess of generosity. But should not that always be the case? Is it not a shame and disgrace that there ever should be a lack of "meat in God's house"? When His work appeals for aid, should there ever be a reluctance to respond or a doling out of a mere pittance? Surely His unspeakable gift should make all giving to Him a spontaneous offering of love that, like Mary's, should bring its precious flask of spikenard and lavish its treasures on His feet, and fill the house with the odor of self-sacrifice!

CHAPTER VI

SATAN AND HIS KINGDOM*

BY MRS. JESSIE PENN-LEWIS,
LEICESTER, ENGLAND

I. SATAN'S ORIGIN AND HOME

The Scriptures give but veiled glimpses of his origin and home, for their purpose is more expressly to reveal God in His character; and Christ as the Redeemer of men; with the history of the redeemed from the fall of Adam, their salvation through the Cross, and their eternal destiny, when Christ shall have "abolished all rule and all authority and power" (1 Cor. 15:24), contrary to the reign of God, and God Himself shall be All in all.

Our Lord says of Satan, "he was a murderer from the beginning" (John 8:44) and John says of him that he "sinneth from the beginning" (1 John 3:8).

II. SATAN'S POSITION AND CHARACTER

In regard to the position and character of Satan we know that he is the very embodiment of a lie, for "There is no truth in him . . . he is a liar, and the father of it," said the Lord. The various names by which he is described in the Scriptures reveal his power. Fallen though he be, he is called by the Lord Jesus no less than three times the "prince of this world" (John 12:31; 14:30; 16:11), thus plainly recognizing his rule over the earth. That he is a personage of rank and power we learn from Jude: "Michael, the archangel, when contending with the devil, he disputed about the

*Condensed from "The Warfare with Satan and the Way of Victory."
Published by Marshall Brothers, 10 Paternoster Row, London, E. C., England.

body of Moses, *durst not* bring against him a railing judgment, but said, *The Lord* rebuke thee" (Jude 9). He is also called the "god of this age" (2 Cor. 4:4, margin), for men obey and worship him, even unconsciously, when they do not obey and worship the Creator.

The fallen archangel is moreover described as the "prince of the power of the air" (Eph. 2:2), meaning wicked spiritual powers dwelling in the aerial heavens, for it seems the "Satanic confederation has its seat in the atmospheric heaven —in the spaces above and around our world" (Seiss). That the "prince of the power of the air" has power (when permission is granted) to wield the forces of the air we see in the history of Job; for at his bidding lightning fell from heaven to consume the flocks of the faithful servant of God, and he caused a wind to blow Job's house down and kill his children. In relation to his attacks upon the children of men the prince of this world is called the "tempter" (1 Thess. 3:5), because it is his fiendish delight to tempt others from loyal obedience to God. And he is named "the devil" (1 Tim. 3:6, 7)—a word *never used in the plural*, and always, and only, of Satan himself. "The Hebrew name Satan occurs in the New Testament thirty-five times interchangeably with the Greek Diabolos, which is also used thirty-five times. The word Diabolos signifies "separator and slanderer" (Blackstone), or "malignant accuser." Satan is the great separator, and he separates by slandering. He separated the race of man from God in Eden, and ever since he has been separating men from each other, with hatred, malice, envy and jealousy. He is especially named the "accuser of the brethren" (Rev. 12:10), and we find him also described as "the great dragon," the "old serpent," and the "deceiver of the whole inhabited earth."

That the adversary still has the world under his rule, is unmistakably shown in his attack upon the Lord Jesus in the wilderness. The Lord was led, under the constraint of the

Holy Spirit, into the wilderness to be "tempted of the devil," and after other temptations, the devil showed Him "all the kingdoms of the inhabited earth. And the devil said unto Him, *To Thee will I give all this authority,* and the glory of them: for it hath been delivered unto me; and to whomsoever I will I give it. If Thou therefore wilt worship before me, it shall all be Thine" (Luke 4:5, 6, 7, *margin*).

What a daring condition to put to the Son of God. The fallen archangel is craving for worship still.

The extent of His claim to *"all the kingdoms of the inhabited earth"* the Son of God did not deny, and later the Lord plainly speaks of Satan's *kingdom.* "If Satan also is divided against himself, how shall his kingdom stand"? (Luke 11:18.) And He adds, "The strong man fully armed guardeth his own court," until "a Stronger than he" comes upon him, and sets his captive free. How fitting therefore the petition, "Deliver us from the *evil one*" (Matt. 6:13)! John also emphasizes the universality of Satan's rule, for he writes, "The whole world lieth in the evil one" (1 John 4:19)—it is sunk in the darkness which is his sphere, and is under the rule of the *"world-rulers of this darkness"* (Eph. 6:12). The Scripture makes no distinction between high and low, or between cultured and ignorant, when it states that the "whole world"—heathen and Christendom—lies "in" the realm of the evil one.

In heathen lands, the deceiver is daring in his tyranny, holding men and women in gross and open sin. In civilized countries, the god of this age needs must veil his working. In these last days, however, he is beginning to more openly manifest himself as the prince of the world. He is familiarizing people with his name. Books to be popular must be about him, and in fashion's realm serpents have been the favorite ornaments of dress, while palmistry, clairvoyance, planchette, and other means of intercourse with the spirits of evil, abound on every hand.

The adversary has also his organized governments, which the Apostle Paul describes as "principalities . . . powers . . . sovereigns of this present darkness" (Eph. 6:12, C. H.). We read of "Satan's throne" (Rev. 2:13); of "his ministers" (2 Cor. 11:15); of his "principalities" and his "powers"; and of his hosts of "spirits of evil" (Eph. 6:12, C. H.) in the heavens. Daniel's account of his interview with the messenger from God supports the view that these principalities and powers of Satan are given charge of specified countries; for the Satanic "prince of Persia" withstood the heavenly messenger, who said that on his return he would again have to meet with the same Prince, together with the "Prince of Greece" (Dan. 10:13, 20). Satan therefore reigns over an aerial kingdom of hierarchies and spiritual powers, and a kingdom on earth in the world of men, and he governs by means of an organized government.

But let us not forget that all these hosts are compelled to acknowledge the Sovereign Lord of the Universe! *Unbelievers in God are alone to be found on earth,* for the powers of evil "believe and shudder" (James 2:19), knowing that they are reserved unto judgment.

III. SATAN'S SYSTEM OF RELIGION

In his organized government the adversary has also a *religion* for those whom he can delude and deceive, showing his perfect mimicry of the worship of the true God.

WORSHIP OF IDOLS

In 1 Corinthians one aspect of Satan's religion is revealed as we are shown what *idol-worship* actually means. They who would walk in fellowship with God must "flee from idolatry," lest they would hold *"communion with demons."* They dare not partake of the "table of the Lord," and of the "table of demons." (1 Cor. 10:19-22, C. H.). The matter was vital to the Corinthians, as it now is to native Christians in heathen lands, for oftentimes the meat offered for sale had first been offered to idols, and some of the Corinthian Christians had accepted invitations to feasts celebrated in the temple of heathen gods—feasts which were acts of idolatrous worship. Thus we see how the fallen archangel not only deceives, and holds in darkness the human race, but he adds to their destruction, by seeking to meet the desire for an object of worship which lies dormant in every breast.

OUTWARD PROFESSION OF GODLINESS

But apart from direct Satanic worship, Satan has other ways of meeting the need for some religion. Paul writes to the Romans, "Thou that abhorrest idols, dost *thou* commit sacrilege?" (Rom. 2:22, *margin*) as he shows that no outward rite or ceremonial fulfillment of the law is acceptable to God. Satan knows this, and therefore persuades men that outward obedience to some creed is enough, thus deluding multitudes into a false peace by causing them to rest upon an outward ceremony or form of words.

In the Lord's message to the church at Smyrna, He spoke of those who *"say* they are Jews, and are not, but are the synagogue of Satan" (Rev. 2:9). It appears by this that the adversary has not only a religion which gives him worship through material images, but that his "synagogue" or congregation is made up of professors of religion who are without the inward truth. John writes, "If we *say* that we have fellowship with Him, and walk in darkness [i. e. in sin], we lie, and do not the truth" (1 John 1:6, A. V.); and the most severe words that ever passed the lips of Christ were His scathing exposures of the Pharisees. "They *say* and do not" He said, and "outwardly appear righteous unto men," when inwardly full of hypocrisy. He told them they were of their "father the devil," and called them "serpents," and the "offspring of vipers" (Matt. 23:15). And yet the Pharisees claimed *God as their Father*, and were the straitest sect in

Israel in the outward fulfilling of the law! The Lord's strong words make it appear that Satan's invisible "church" is filled with those who make religion a cloak while they are really his subjects.

SATAN'S DOCTRINES

The Apostle Paul wrote to Timothy that the Holy Spirit had expressly told him that in the latter days the adversary would seek to draw many away from the faith by the teaching of spirits inculcating "doctrines of demons" (1 Tim. 4: 1, *m.*). So that Satan has "doctrines" as well as system of worship—a "cup," a "table," and a "synagogue!" Paul said that the teaching would be given through men who would *profess to be what they were not,* and whose consciences would be seared as with a hot iron.

These "teachings of demons," through false teachers acting under their control, had already begun in the first century, and seducing spirits were evidently at work in the church at Thyatira drawing servants of God from their Lord through the "deep things of Satan" (Rev. 2:24). One calling herself a prophetess was leading souls astray, teaching them to "eat things sacrificed to idols." The Lord's complaint was that the church suffered these things to be in its midst—things upon which He pronounced the most awful warning of certain judgment. Satan's religion has always one clearly defined mark in the *omission of the Gospel of Calvary.* And by this test all "gospels" that are not the Gospel may be recognized! The atoning death of the Son of God; His propitiation for sin; His blotting out of sin; His deliverance from the power of sin by the severing power of the Cross; His call of the blood-redeemed soul to the Cross in humiliation of self, and sacrifice for others—in brief, *all that Calvary means,* is emphatically repudiated, or else always carefully omitted, in the doctrines of the seducing spirits which are evolved in hell! Let everyone thus test the tenets of Theosophy, of Christian (?) Science, and all other teachings now being poured into the world by spirits of evil, who do not hesitate to appropriate for their purposes the very language describing the effects, and blessings of the Gospel.

It cannot always be said that there is no *mention* of the Cross (and in his later workings, even of the *Blood* of Christ), in Satan's religious teaching, but it is *the Cross as only an outward symbol* without the inward power, for he knows that it is only the real acceptance of the death of Christ—or Cross of Christ—which saves from sin and delivers the soul from the power of Satan.

IV. SATAN'S SUBJECTS

"The whole world lieth in the evil one," declares the Apostle John, but it is of the supremest importance to the prince of this world that those who dwell in his realm should not know it. To keep men ignorant of their position *he blinds their minds!* "The god of this world hath blinded the minds [*m.*, thoughts] of the unbelieving, that the light of the Gospel . . . should not dawn upon them" (2 Cor. 4:4).

The adversary dreads the light of God, for light reveals things as they are, both in the natural and in the spiritual world. "Ye shall know the truth, and the truth shall make you free" (John 8:32). The truth about the love of God to men, of men as sinners needing a Saviour, and of God's gift of a perfect Saviour when really apprehended by the soul, must set free, and so the adversary hides the truth from his captives. They are kept "darkened in their understanding" and are thus "alienated from the life of God because of the ignorance that is in them" (Eph. 4:18).

That the truth must reach the *understanding* to be effectual in delivering the soul is evident from the Lord's words that the good ground which received the seed was in the one "that heareth the Word, and *understandeth it*" (Matt. 13:23; see also Col. 1:9; 1 John 5:20). The adversary therefore labors to keep the understanding darkened, blinding the mind with (1) wrong thoughts about God, (2) prejudices of all kinds, (3) philosophy of earth, (4) false reasonings concerning spiritual things, or else he occupies the thoughts with earthly things, earthly idols, or the cares and pleasures of this life. The Spirit of God alone can defeat the evil one, and destroy the veil which darkens men's minds.

The adversary seeks to snatch away the Word of truth. "When anyone heareth the Word . . . and understandeth it not, then cometh the evil one, and snatcheth away" (Matt. 13:19). The adversary, or his minions, attends every preaching of the Word of truth, and when it does not enter the understanding it is easily snatched away. Once the smallest seed of the Word of truth enters the *understanding* it is sure to bring forth fruit in its season, unless it is choked by other things entering in.

The adversary keeps his subjects in a false peace. "The strong man fully armed guardeth his own court," and "his goods are in peace" (Luke 11:21). Here the adversary is pictured as in full control of the darkened sinner, keeping him in peace, and the sinner is guarded carefully by the terrible one who is "fully armed" to meet every attempt to deliver the captive from his bonds. The poor soul resents his peace being disturbed, and cries, "Let me alone," but the time comes when the "Stronger than he"—the Man of Calvary—lays hold of the captive soul, and he is delivered "out of the power of darkness, and translated . . . into the kingdom of the Son" (Col. 1:13).

The adversary counterfeits the true work of God. "While men slept, his enemy came, and sowed tares also among the wheat" (Matt. 13:25, 38, 39). The "tares are the sons of the evil one . . . the enemy that sowed them is the devil." *The attention of the world must be drawn to the counterfeits, and the true living seed of God hidden,* for the tares look like the wheat until the time of fruit! And God looks on! "Let both grow together till the harvest," He cries, for the tares cannot be uprooted without danger to the growing wheat. And the adversary also works on! The Lord's wheat, and the adversary's tares; the true and the counterfeit; are always found side by side throughout the inhabited earth.

We must face the fact that the Scriptures declare these things to be true concerning all men, be they high or low, rich or poor, cultured or ignorant. There is no trace given of neutral ground. The Scripture "hath shut up all things under sin" (Gal. 3:22) that "every mouth may be stopped, and all the world may become guilty before God" (Rom. 3:19, A. V.). "He that doeth sin is of the devil" (1 John 3:8). The Divine life which comes from God, and is implanted in the child of God, does not sin, for the good tree bears good fruit. The fallen life must also bring forth its own fruit of sin. Sin in greater or lesser degree it is true, but *sin* as God calls sin. *We are children of the one by whose life we live.* Children of God if His life is imparted to us, or "children of the devil" if we live under his control.

The arch-fiend has studied the fallen race of Adam for many thousand years, and knows how to allure his subjects. Among the sons of men there are some with more spirit-capacity than others, and these are the ones especially open to his snares, and most likely to become his tools to work out his will. These souls would not be allured by the "flesh," nor would vain philosophy and reasonings charm them. Beguiled, as the serpent beguiled Eve, by the fascination of the knowledge of good and evil, he draws them on into unlawful dealings with the spirit-world, until some are given "a spirit of divination" (Acts 16:16) like the damsel at Philippi, or like Simon the sorcerer, and are led into "magical arts" as in the days of Paul. Such are the workings of the adversary today in spiritism, palmistry, crystal-gazing, and such like things. In the twentieth century professed Christian people are once more practising the "abominations" which caused the Lord to cast out the nations of Canaan before His people Israel. Abominations which Jehovah solemnly forbade Israel to touch. (Read Deut. 18:9-12.)

But all is in fulfillment of the Apostle Paul's forecast of the latter days. The grievous times are upon us. Men are "lovers of self, lovers of money, . . . lovers of pleasure rather than lovers of God; holding a form of godliness" while denying the power thereof (2 Tim. 3:1-6).

V. SATAN CONQUERED AT CALVARY

Satan was conquered at Calvary. The disobedience of the first Adam was met by the obedience of the second—the Lord from heaven. The punishment of death was carried out upon the sinless One who took upon Him the sins of the world, and died as the Representative Man. The fallen race of Adam which God said must be "blotted out" (Gen. 6:7, *m.;* Gen. 7:23, *m.*), because, "every imagination of the thoughts of the heart was only evil continually," was nailed to the Cross in the person of the second Adam, and by the Cross the Lord from heaven triumphed over the prince of darkness. *"Through death"*—the very result of sin; *"through death"*— the very weapon by which the evil one held his subjects in bondage; *through death*—the Prince of Life destroyed "him that had the power of death, that is, the devil" (Heb. 2:14). Satan has fallen from heaven. He was "cast out," his power destroyed, his kingdom shaken, at the place called Calvary.

But though the adversary was conquered at Calvary and cast down from his throne of power, he is left at large while the proclamation of the victory is sent throughout his dominions, for the purpose of giving the choice of masters to every human being. How bitterly the adversary resists the work of the Holy Spirit in men as their eyes are opened to the truth! But far more keenly does he resist the full enlightenment of the believer which makes him so possessed by the Holy Spirit that he becomes an equipped and aggressive warrior in the army of the Lord.

VI. SATAN'S DEVICES AGAINST THE FULL DELIVERANCE OF HIS CAPTIVES

Note some of the ways in which the adversary resists the full deliverance of the soul after the light of the Gospel has dawned upon him:

He seeks to keep back the soul from full surrender to God. "Ananias, why hath *Satan* filled thy heart to deceive the Holy Ghost, and to keep back part . . . ?" (Acts 5:3, *m.*) It was when all were placing their possessions entirely at the disposal of the Lord! Ananias laid part of his possessions at the Apostle's feet, pretending that it was "all"! Peter, filled with the Spirit discerned the truth, and his stern words at once unveil the source of the sin! *Satan* had "filled his heart" to make him "keep back part." Keep back part for self, is the tempter's whisper, for something kept for self gives place to the devil, and keeps the Redeemer from His Throne in the heart.

He resists the removal of the filthy garments spotted by the flesh. "Satan standing at his right hand to be his adversary" (Zech. 3:1). Joshua is seen standing before the Lord clothed in filthy garments with Satan as his adversary. Even so does the devil resist every child of God as he stands before the Lord seeking to be clothed with change of raiment. Clothed in the garments spotted by the flesh, the redeemed one stands in dumb helplessness before the Lord. The simple words, "The Lord rebuke thee, O Satan," are spoken and the foe is silenced. The soul seeking deliverance is here shown the way of victory over the adversary! Just as we are, we must stand before the Lord in our deep need, and count upon Him to rebuke the evil one.

He uses others to tempt us from the way of the Cross. "Be it far from Thee, Lord . . . But He turned and said unto Peter, Get thee behind Me, Satan" (Matt. 16:22, 23). When the soul has yielded all in full surrender, and in dumb helplessness ceases from his own efforts to save himself, he knows by the Holy Spirit that he must take the Cross, and deny himself, if Christ is to see of the travail of His soul, and be satisfied. But "Be it far from thee," cries the adversary, through the lips of even servants of God, who have dimmer visions of the things of God, and know not the eternal loss to the soul who listens to their plea. But "Get thee behind me, Satan," the redeemed one must cry as he looks behind the human voice, and sees the adversary of God.

He inflames the life of nature into division and strife. "If ye have bitter jealousy and faction in your heart . . . . [it] is earthly, natural [or animal], *devilish*" (Jas. 3:14, 15, *m.*).

James points out that all "jealousy" and "faction" has its source in the life which he calls animal, and "devilish"! Satan is shown here to be the real power working through the fallen life of nature. Possibly when the believer has taken the Cross for himself, circumstances arise when "loyalty demands that he should stand up for a friend!" The spirit of faction comes in, or jealousy for others, and the adversary triumphs. The Apostle says that the wisdom which is from above is "without partiality." All *faction*, all *jealousy* for the "own," in friends, or denomination, is instigated by the evil one *to keep the believer in the sphere* lying under his rule.

The wiles of the devil concerning "revelations." "I know a man in Christ . . . caught up into paradise" (2 Cor. 12:2, 4). "I will love him, and will manifest Myself unto him" (John 14:21), is a promise made by the Lord on the eve of His passion. There is a moment when the promise is fulfilled, and Christ reveals Himself to the obedient heart, and the believer knows the Risen Lord. To some He is manifested in light above the brightness of the sun, as to Paul in a wondrous heavenly vision, and others are but conscious of His Presence in a peace and joy unspeakable. In any case the glorified Christ now becomes a living reality to the soul. What are the wiles of the adversary now but an attempt to personate the Lord! The believer must know that the evil one can fashion himself as an angel of light, and work with all "power and signs and lying wonders" (2 Thess. 2:9) to lead astray the very elect.

We need to walk carefully with God at this stage of the spiritual life, not coveting wonderful experiences, but rather an ever-deepening conformity to the death of Jesus (Phil. 3:10), so that the life of Jesus may be manifested (2 Cor. 4:10, 11) to all around. "Visions and revelations" are not given to the soul for its own enjoyment, but for some definite purpose, as with the Apostle Paul when he was stoned in Lystra; called to Macedonia; or needed clearer guidance to remain in Athens.

The wiles concerning the voice of God. "The sheep follow Him, for they know His voice . . . they know not the voice of strangers" (John 10:4, 5). The Lord does speak to His children, and makes them to know His voice from the voice of strangers. They know it as a *babe knows its mother's voice,* but like the babe they may not be able to say how or why. When the believer is brought by the Spirit into the Spirit-sphere, and Christ is manifested to him, one of the first results is a knowledge of the voice of the Lord, in a way the soul has never realized before. The adversary knows that the believer has but little knowledge of his foe, so the wiles are soon planned to counterfeit the voice of the Lord, so as to confuse or to mislead the soul, either to *destroy his faith in the guidance of the Spirit,* or else to lead him in obedience to the voice of the devil, and in strong delusion to believe a lie.

The believer who would overcome must now know how to distinguish the voice of the Lord from the voice of the foe. This may be done by its effect, and by its object. The voice of the Lord brings a deep calm over the spirit, whereas the voice of the devil often causes confusion, restlessness, agitation and uncertainty. The voice of the Lord is invariably in accord with the teaching of the Word of God, although the adversary also can quote Scripture, but it is usually texts with the portions omitted which safeguard, or interpret the whole, or else he uses isolated words wrenched from the context which explains them! The wiles of the adversary are the most subtle, and likely to succeed, in the early days of the life in the Spirit-sphere, for as the believer matures in the knowledge of God, the *"mind* of Christ" becomes the mind of the one closely in fellowship with God. It is well that the believer should understand this, lest he give advantage to the enemy by falling into discouragement, or depression, when the transition from childhood to manhood takes place, and God is teaching him how to use his spiritual senses, discerning good and evil. (Heb. 5:14.)

The wiles concerning guidance. "As many as are led by the Spirit of God, these are sons of God" (Rom. 8:14). There is scarcely any subject connected with the spiritual life more difficult to explain, and more misunderstood than the subject of guidance! The words, "I was 'led' to do this or that," are so often used when there is no evidence of any leading at all. There are many wiles of the adversary around the subject. One tactic of the evil one is to make souls confused and distracted over what is the will of God; others he deludes into throwing aside all use of their judgment and knowledge, to act upon some isolated text, or some "thought" that came to them in prayer; others are beguiled into an attitude of judgment upon the walk of others, or else into a position not far short of infallibility, though they would not use the word. Our text gives the principal mark of the true guidance of the Lord. *"Led* by the Spirit" means that He *deals,* and does not drive or force, therefore the soul must take heed not to force itself to any course of action which is repugnant to it, that is, *pre-supposing that the will is surrendered to God, as ready to take any course unmistakably shown to be His will.*

Then let us understand, too, that as the life of Christ matures in the believer, the Spirit leads more from *within* by the working of *life*, which manifests itself as simply and naturally as the life of nature. When the believer becomes a "full grown man" (Heb. 6:1, R. V. *m.*), with heart and will under the complete control of the Spirit, the new life will increasingly work in him with less and less *perceived action* to his consciousness. As many as are led by the Spirit, in this way, are indeed sons of God, with spirit, soul, and body, working out His will with ease and spontaneity. (1) They are "guided by the skilfulness of His hands" (Psa. 78:72), leading them hour by hour into the path prepared for them. (2) They are guided by their faithfulness to God: "The integrity of the upright shall guide them" (Prov. 11:3)—for they know what to do by the very instinct of right and wrong which God has planted within them. (3) The "meek will He guide in judgment" (Psa. 25:9), for He uses their renewed minds (Rom. 12:2), yea, giving them the very mind of Christ, which led Him to empty Himself, and be obedient unto death —the death of the Cross. The soul that knows this principle of sacrifice and self-effacement as the characteristic of the life of Christ, *needs no inner voice nor special guidance, to tell him what course he is to take while walking in this present evil world!*

The wiles concerning "liberty." "Ye have been called unto liberty; only use not liberty for an occasion to the flesh" (Gal. 5:13, A. V.). The believer who has emerged into the life in the Spirit finds himself free in a way he has never known before. It is just now that the evil one is ready with new wiles to ensnare the freed one, suggesting to him (1) "You have liberty now to do anything, for you are free"; or (2) "You are under no man's control now, especially those who are in the flesh." And the adversary now does his best to counterfeit the true freedom in Christ by inciting rebellion to those in authority, and fleshly zeal under the name of the liberty of the Spirit. But the Word of God shows that the liberty wherewith Christ makes us free is really freedom from slavery to sin, and to the evil one. The freed soul passes under *law to Christ,* under the perfect law of liberty, which is liberty to do right, instead of *seeing* what is right, and *doing* what is wrong. Liberty to obey God intsead of disobeying Him.

The law of Christ comes in here, and shows that there is a limitation placed to liberty by the conscience of the weak brother. The freed one is not only to be subject to others in authority for the Lord's sake, but is to take heed lest his liberty of action become a "stumbling block to the weak" (1 Cor. 8:9). The Apostle Paul sets the example to the believer, and he wrote, "I have not used my right, but forego every claim, lest I should by any means hinder the course of Christ's glad-tidings" (1 Cor. 9:12, C. H. and note). The meaning of the word "claim" is "to hold out against." He would not "hold out" for his rights, but forego everything for himself rather than hinder the Gospel.

CONCLUSION

These wiles of the devil are those which will meet every believer who enters the sphere of the Spirit, and they are wiles which cease to a great extent as he progresses in the knowledge of God, and learns to know his foe.

The preaching of the Cross is therefore the supreme need in this day of contact with the supernatural forces of the unseen world, and conformity to the death of Christ (Phil. 3:10), rather than the craving for signs and wonders, is the safest objective for all who desire to press on in the fullest knowledge of the upward calling of God in Christ Jesus our Lord.

CHAPTER VII

THE HOLY SPIRIT AND THE SONS OF GOD

BY REV. W. J. ERDMAN, D. D.,

GERMANTOWN, PENNSYLVANIA

It is evident from many tracts and treatises on the Baptism of the Holy Spirit that due importance has not been given to the *peculiar characteristic* of the Pentecost gift in its relation to *the sonship of believers.*

Before considering this theme a few brief statements may be made concerning the personality and deity of the Holy Spirit and His relation to the people of God in the dispensations and times preceding the Day of Pentecost.

1. *The Holy Spirit, the Comforter, another Person, but not a different Being.*

In general it may be said, He is not an "influence" or a sum and series of "influences," but a personal Being with names and affections, words and acts, interchanged with those of God.

He is God as Creator. (Gen. 1:2; Psa. 104:30; Job 26:13; Luke 1:35.) He is one with God as Jehovah (Lord) in providential leading and care, and susceptible of grief on account of the unholiness of His chosen people. We cannot grieve an "influence," but only a person, and a person, too, who *loves us.* (Psa. 78:40; Eph. 4:30.) He is one with God as Adonai (Lord), whose glory Isaiah beheld and John rehearses, who commissioned the prophet and sent forth the apostle. (Isa. 6:1-10; John 12:37-41; Acts 13:2; 20:15-18.) In these Scriptures one and the same act is that of Jehovah and of Jesus and of the Holy Spirit.

Besides the clear evidence of personality and equality in the baptismal words and in the benediction (Matt. 28:19;

2 Cor. 13:14), the promise of Jesus affirms the presence and the abiding of the Spirit to be one with His own and with the Father's in this Word. "If a man love Me he will keep My words, and My Father will love him, and we will come unto him and make our abode with him" (John 16:23). Above all, the name "another Comforter" (Paraclete) suggests a Person who would do for the disciples what Jesus the other Comforter (Luke 2:25) had been doing for them. He speaks, testifies, teaches, reminds, reproves, convicts, warns, commands, loves, consoles, beseeches, prays, intercedes, (often the word is "paracletes"); in brief, all these and other acts and dealings are not those of an impersonal medium or influence, but of a person, and One who in the nature of the case cannot be less than God in wisdom, love and power, and who is one with the Father and the Son; *another Person indeed, but not a different Being.*

2. *The spiritual, Divine life in the people of God is the same in kind in every age and dispensation,* but *the relation* to God in which *the life was developed of old* was *different* from that which now exists between believers as sons and God as Father, and in accordance with that relationship the Holy Spirit acted.

He was of old the Author and Nourisher of all spiritual life and power in righteous men and women of past ages, in patriarch and friend of God, in Israelites as minors and servants, in pious kings and adoring psalmists, in consecrated priests and faithful prophets; and whatever truth had been revealed, He employed to develop the Divine life He had imparted. From the beginning, He used promise and precept, law and type, Psalm and ritual to instruct, quicken, convince, teach, lead, warn, comfort and to do all for the growth and establishment of the people of God.

The Psalms run through the gamut of the spiritual experience possible for those, who while waiting for the consolation of Israel and the future out-pouring of the Holy Spirit, were "apart from us" not to be "made perfect" as sons and as "worshipers." More than one prayed, "Teach me to do Thy will, for Thou art my God; let Thy good Spirit lead me into the land of uprightness" (Psa. 143:10). But there was then still lacking among men the consummate Reality and perfect Illustration of a Son of God.

When at last, all righteousness and holy virtues appeared in a Life of filial love and obedience, even in Christ "the first-born of many brethren," then the Mold and Image of the spiritual life of the saints of the old covenant, who were waiting for sonship, was seen perfect and complete.

It was pre-eminently the life of a Son of God and not only of a righteous man; of a Son ever rejoicing before the Father, His whole being filled with filial love and obedience, peace and joy. In ways Godward and manward, in self-denial and in full surrender to His Father's will, in hatred of sin and in grace to sinners, in purity of heart and forgiveness of injuries, in gentleness and all condescension, in restful yet ceaseless service, in unity of purpose and faultless obedience—in a word, in all excellencies and graces, in all virtues and beauties of the Spirit, in light and in love, the Lord Jesus set forth the mold and substance of the life spiritual, divine, eternal.

3. *Redemption must precede both the sonship and the gift of the Spirit.*

This is very clearly seen in the Apostle's argument on the great subject: "God sent forth His Son, born of a woman, born under the law, that He might redeem them that were under the law, that we might receive the adoption of sons. And because ye are sons God sent forth the Spirit of His Son into our hearts, crying, Abba, Father" (Gal. 4:4-6). The word "adoption" signifies the placing in the state and relation of a son. It is found in Romans 9:4; 13:15, 23; Gal. 4:5; Eph. 1:5.

In the writings of John believers are never called sons, but "children" ("born ones"), a word indicating nature, kinship.

Sonship relates not to nature, but to legal standing; it comes not through regeneration, but by redemption. The disciples of Jesus had to wait until the Son of God had redeemed them; and then on the redeemed disciples the Spirit of God was poured at Pentecost, not to make believers sons, but because they had become sons through redemption. In brief, sonship, though ever since redemption inseparable from justification, does in the order of salvation succeed justification. Justification in Rom. 5:1 precedes the "grace" of sonship in 5:2. This "access" or "introduction" is of the justified into the presence of God as Father; and it is through Christ and by the Spirit. (Eph. 2:18; 3:12.)

We were "predestined" to be sons of God, and to be "conformed to the image of His Son" (Eph. 1:5; Rom. 8:29). In Eph. 1:5 the "sonship" is rather corporate; all believers are viewed as one "son," one "body," just as Jehovah said of Israel, "My son," "My first born." This corporateness is really to be understood in Gal. 3:28, which may read, "Ye are all one son in Christ Jesus," instead of "one man." (See also Eph. 4:13; 1 Cor. 12:12.)

And this image is His as glorified, so that until we have been conformed to His body of glory, our "adoption" or sonship is not complete nor our experience of redemption finished. (Rom. 8:23.)

And special emphasis should be laid upon the truth that sins were before God only *pretermitted* until the atonement was made; "propitiation for the pretermission [passing over] of sins that are past" (Rom. 3:25); "for the redemption of the transgressions that were under the first testament" (Heb. 9:15).

Remission came through the great offering for sin, just as sonship came through this redemption; and as the Spirit was given because believers had become sons, so also He could be given because believers had received the remission of their sins. This is the invariable order; faith in Christ, remission of sins, gift of the Holy Spirit.

Yea, more, as without the gracious power of the Spirit of God *the new birth* would be impossible, so without the redeeming blood of Christ the estate of sonship would have been unattainable; the Spirit and the blood are equally necessary to the full accomplishment of the eternal purpose of God.

In brief, through redemption the new dignity of sonship was conferred, the new name "sons" was given to them as a new name "Father" had been declared of Him; a new name was given to the life in this new relation, "the life eternal," and a new name, "Spirit of His Son," was given to the Holy Spirit, who henceforth, with new truth and a new commandment, would nourish and develop this life and illumine and lead believers into all the privileges and duties of the sons of God.

These facts are then all related to and dependent upon each other; Jesus must first lay the ground of the forgiveness of sins of past and future times in His work of redemption and reconciliation; as risen and glorified, not before, He is "the first-born of many brethren," to whose image they are predestined to be conformed; as the Son, He declared to them the name of God as Father, the crowning name of God corresponding to their highest name, sons of God. As His "brethren" in this high and peculiar sense, He did not call them until He had first suffered, died, and risen again from the dead, but that name is the first word He spoke of them on the morning of resurrection, as if it were the chiefest joy of His soul to name and greet them as His brethren, and sons of God, being in and with Him "sons of the resurrection;" and because they were sons, the Father, through the Son, sent forth the Spirit of His Son into their hearts, crying, "Abba, Father!"

It is the marvelous dignity of a sonship in glory, like that of our Lord Jesus, with all its attendant blessings and privileges, service and rewards, suffering and glories, to which the gift of the Holy Spirit is related in this present dispensation.

Accordingly when the disciples were baptized with the Spirit on the Day of Pentecost they were not only endued with ministering power, but they also then entered into the experience of sonship. Then they knew as they could not have known before, though the Book of the Acts records but little of their inner life, that through the heaven-descended Spirit the sons of God are forever united with the heaven-ascended, glorified Son of God. Whether they at first fully realized this fact or not, it is seen as in the Gospel of John, they were in Him and He in them. Was Jesus begotten of the Spirit, so were they; was He not of the world as to origin and nature, neither were they; was He loved of the Father, so were they, and with the same love; was He sanctified and sent into the world to bear witness to the truth, so likewise He sent them; did He receive the Spirit as the seal of God to His Sonship, so were they sealed; was He anointed with power and light to serve, so they received the unction from Him; did He begin to serve when there came the attesting Spirit and confirming word of the Father, so they began to serve when the Spirit of the Son, the Witness, was sent forth into their hearts, saying Abba, Father; was He, after service and suffering, received up in glory, so shall they obtain His glory when He comes again to receive them unto Himself. Verily, "we are as He is in this world." (1 John 4: 17; John 10: 36; 17: 1-26; Rom. 5: 5.)

In view of these truths of Divine revelation how foolish the wisdom of the natural man and how sadly misleading the doctrine which makes the "fatherhood of God and the brotherhood of man," which are by nature and creation, identical and co-extensive with that which is by grace and redemption; for not only does the imperative word, "Ye must be born again," sweep away all the merit and glory of man as he is by the first birth, but also, the predestination to a sonship like that of the Son of God in glory lifts the "twice-born" to a height and dignity never conceived of by the natural man.

4. In the *gift of the Holy Spirit on the Day of Pentecost all gifts* for believers in Christ were contained and were *related* to them as *Sons of God* both individually and cor-poratively as the Church the Body of Christ.

In kind, as can be seen on comparison, there was no dif-ference in His gifts and acts before and after that day, but the new Gift was now to dwell in the hearts of men as sons of God and with more abundant life and varied manifesta-tions of power and wisdom.

But by the Spirit the one Body was formed and all gifts are due to His perpetual presence. (1 Cor. 12:14.) Also, it is to be understood that such a word of Jesus, "If ye then being evil know how to give good gifts unto your children, how much more shall your Heavenly Father give the Holy Spirit to them that ask Him," could not have been fulfilled until a later hour, for repeating His promise at another time it is said of Jesus, "But this spake He of the Spirit which they that believed on Him should receive, for the Holy Ghost was not yet given, because Jesus was not yet glorified" (John 3:7-39). These are some of the *anticipative sayings* of our Lord, not to be made good until He had died and risen again. The good things could not be given until "transgression had been forgiven and sin covered." The water could not pour forth until the Rock had been smitten. And as to the use of the words, "baptize" and "pour," they afterwards, in later Scriptures, imply the original incorporating act.

It is significant that after Pentecost only the words, "filled with the Spirit," are used. Nothing is said of an individual receiving a new or fresh "baptism of the Spirit." It would imply that the baptism is one for the whole Body until all the members are incorporated; one the outpouring, many the fillings; one fountain, many the hearts to drink, to have in turn a well of water springing up within them.

The disciples were indeed endued with power for service according to promise; on *that* especially their eyes and hearts had been fixed; that was the chief thing for them; but in the light of later Scriptures it is seen that the chief thing with God was not only to attest the glory of Jesus by the gift of the Spirit, but also *"in one Spirit to baptize into one body"* the "children of God," who until then were looked upon as "scattered abroad," as unincorporated members. (1 Cor. 12:13; John 11:52; Gal. 3:27, 28.) And the Gift, whether to the Body or to the individual member, is once for all. As the Christian is once for all in Christ, so the Holy Spirit is once for all in the Christian; but the intent of the presence of the Spirit is often but feebly met by the believer, just as his knowledge of what it is to be "in Christ" is often most defective.

5. *The Holy Spirit is given at once on the remission of sins* to them that believe in Christ Jesus as their Lord and Saviour.

It is, however, to be observed that as the Spirit acts according to the truth known, or believed and obeyed, *an interval* unspiritual or unfruitful *may come* between the remission of sins and the *marked manifestation* of the Spirit, either in relation to holiness of life, or to power for service, or to patience in trials. It certainly is the divine ideal of a holy life, that the presence of the Spirit should at once be *made manifest* on the forgiveness of sins, and continue in increasing light and power to the end. (Rom. 5:1-5; Titus 3:4-7.)

And this steady onward progress more and more unto the perfect day has been and is true of many, who from early childhood, or from the day of conversion, in the case of adults, were led continuously by the Spirit and never came to one great crisis. With others it is not so, for it is the confession of a large number of men and women, afterward eminent for holiness, devotion, endurance, that their life previous to such crisis had been hardly worth the name of Christian. Whatever explanation or "philosophy" of such experience may be given, the following is true of the majority.

The full truth of the sonship and salvation of believers may not have been taught them when they first believed; the life may have begun under a yoke of legal bondage; the freedom of filial access may have been doubted, even though their hearts often burned within them because of the presence of the unknown Spirit; and thus weary, ineffective years passed, attended with but little growth in grace or fruitful service, or patient resignation, until a point was reached in various ways, and through providences often unexpected and most marvelous, when at last the Holy Spirit made Himself manifest in the fulness of His love and power.

That there is *with God* an interval between justification and the giving of the Spirit (an interval such as certain theories contend for), cannot be proved. The unsatisfactory experience of the ignorant Christian may lead him to think he never had the Spirit.

There are, however, certain intervals recorded in the New Testament which should be considered. The one between the ascension and Pentecost was for a peculiar preparation through prayer and waiting on the Lord; that of the forty days between the resurrection and the ascension was a continuation of the presence of Jesus the other Comforter, and of whom it is written, "He opened their understanding that they understand the Scriptures," so doing what His Holy Spirit was to do when He came; and during the previous days of His public ministry not only did Jesus teach, but as attested at the confession of Peter, also the Father was revealing truth to men: "Flesh and blood hath not revealed it unto thee, but My Father who is in heaven."

In the light of this word to Peter it may be said that up to Pentecost the Spirit of God was at work in the world in the modes of the old dispensation, but that when the Day of

Pentecost came His peculiar work began in relation to believers as sons of God. Even the breathing of Christ upon the disciples on the evening of the day of His resurrection was, in accordance with the many symbolic acts and sayings recorded in the Gospel of John, symbolic of the Mighty Breath of Pentecost, for both the symbol and the reality were associated with the enduement of power for the service which began at Pentecost. Besides, they were told forty days later to tarry in Jerusalem for such enduement. They could not already have received it and yet be told to wait for it. And Thomas was not present on the evening of that breathing.

As to other intervals; that in case of the converts on the Day of Pentecost was doubtless for the confirmation of the apostolic authority; that of the Samaritans when Philip preached may be accounted for by remembering the religious feud between Jew and Samaritan which now must be settled for all time and the unity of the Church established. Also seeing "salvation is from the Jews," the authority of Jewish apostles must be affirmed, for to them Christ had committed the founding of the Church. (Acts 8: 14-17.)

In regard to Paul, it is evident from the narrative, he knew not the full import of the appearing of Jesus, until Ananias came. The recovery of sight, the forgiveness of sins, the filling of the Holy Spirit, all took place during this interview. He received the Spirit, as was befitting the Apostle to the Gentiles, in a Gentile city, far away from the other apostles, for his apostleship was to be "not from men, neither through a man" (Acts 9: 10-19; 22: 6-16).

But the case of Cornelius proves that *no interval at all need exist,* for the moment Peter spoke this word, received by faith by Cornelius and those present, the Holy Spirit who knew their hearts fell on them: "To Him give all the prophets witness that through His name whosoever believeth in Him shall receive *the remission of sins.*" Peter intended to say more, but God showed by the sudden outpouring of the Spirit that Peter had said enough, for from Peter's report to the church in Jerusalem we learn that he intended to say more, and not only say more but probably do more, so making an interval even as in the case of the Samaritans through baptism, prayer and laying on of his hands that they might receive the Holy Ghost. (Acts 8:14-17; 10:43-44; 11:15, 16.)

It is especially to be noted in this connection that the text of Eph. 1:13, so often quoted as proving a long interval between faith in Christ and "the sealing of the Spirit," "In whom also *after* that ye believed, ye were sealed with that Holy Spirit of promise," lends no authority for such long interval of time, for the word "after" implies more than the Greek participle warrants, and accordingly the Revision reads, "In whom having also believed, ye were sealed with the Holy Spirit of promise;" *but the very same participle,* "having believed," used by Paul in Ephesians, is used by Peter in the Acts in rehearsing the interview with Cornelius, who received the Spirit *immediately.* (Acts 2:17.)

Neither does the remaining instance of the twelve disciples of John the Baptist whom Paul found in Ephesus, prove that such an interval is necessary or inevitable today; for they had not even heard that Jesus had come, and that redemption had been accomplished, and the Spirit given; but as soon as remission of sins in the name of Jesus was preached to them, they believed, were baptized, and through prayer and the laying on of Paul's hands, received the Holy Spirit. (Acts 19:1-6.)

The question Paul addressed to them, "Have ye received the Holy Ghost since ye believed?" (or in the Revision, "Did ye receive the Holy Ghost when ye believed?") has been most strangely applied in these days to Christians, whereas it was pertinent to these disciples of John only. *To address it to Christians now is to deny a finished redemption, the sonship of believers and the once-for-all out-pouring of the Holy Spirit.*

And it is implied in the case of Cornelius* with which the Apostle Peter had nothing to do except to preach the word, that when the apostles had passed away *the mold of experience* common for all succeeding centuries would be *that of these Gentile converts* wherever in Christendom or heathendom the Gospel of Christ might be preached.

6. The *conditions of the manifestation* of the presence and power of the Spirit are *the same,* at conversion or at any later, deeper experience of the believer, whether in relation to fuller knowledge of Christ, or to more effective service, or to more patient endurance of ill, or to growth in likeness to Christ.

The experience, in each case, is run in the same mold; *each part, each word or fact of Christ, must be received in the same attitude and condition of mind as the first,* when He was seen as the Bearer of our sins, even *by faith alone.*

Negatively, it may be said that the conditions are confessed weakness and inability to help oneself; the end of nature's wisdom, power, righteousness has been reached; utter despair of there being any good thing *"in the flesh"* settles over the soul, a willingness to look to God alone for help begins to stir in the heart. Convictions of unfaithfulness and self-seeking mingle with a hunger and thirst for righteousness and a life worthy of the name of Christian.

It is not, however, as consciously sinless in themselves that the Spirit is given to them who "seek the blessing," but to them as sinless "in Christ." Believers in Christ begin their life in the very standing of the Son of God Himself. Neither do the Scriptures teach, as implied or expressed in certain theories, that there is an interval between the remission of sins and "the sealing of the Spirit," and that "justified" believers may die during such interval having never been "sealed," and so never been "in Christ," and never been attested sons of God.

*Acts 10.

Such belief contradicts the very grace of God and implies that sonship depends upon the gift of the Spirit and not upon redemption and the remission of sins, and would read, "Because ye have the Spirit ye are sons," instead of, "And because ye are sons, God sent forth the Spirit of His Son into your hearts, crying, Abba, Father." It also follows that such justified ones devoid of the Spirit are not Christ's nor Christians, for it is plainly written, "But if any man hath not the Spirit of Christ, he is none of His;" and also, "No man can say, Jesus is Lord, but in the Holy Spirit." And as to the proof of the presence of the Spirit at such times, whatever emotions or high raptures may attend the discoveries of the love and power of God in the case of some, they are not to be the tests and measures for all. Conversions are not alike in all, neither are the manifestations of the Spirit. He may come like the sun at high noon through rifted clouds or like a slowly deepening dawn; like a shower or like the dew; like a great tide of air or like a gentle breathing; but "all these worketh the one and self-same Spirit." But more than all, the proof is seen in growth in holiness, in self-denials for Christ's sake, in the manifold graces and abiding fruit of the Spirit.

As in the apostolic day so now the desire exists for the manifestation of the Spirit in marvelous ways; but a life sober, righteous, holy, lived in the hope of the glory to come, is the more excellent way of the Spirit's manifestation and undeniable proof of His indwelling.

Positively, the requirements or inseparable accompaniments of the manifestation of the indwelling Spirit, whether for holy living or faithful service, must be drawn from the example of the Son of God our Lord Jesus. And they are *prayer, obedience, faith,* and above all *a desire and purpose to glorify Christ.* All, indeed, may be summed up in one condition, and that is, *to let God have His own will and way with us.*

If, then, it is to believers as sons of God, to whom and in whom and through whom the Holy Spirit manifests His presence and power, it would follow that whatever Jesus did in order to fulfil His mission in the power of the Spirit, believers must do; and we find His life to have been a life of *prayer* for all the gifts and helps of God, a life of *obedience,* always doing the things that pleased the Father; and so, never left alone, a life of *faith* in the present power of God, a life of *devotion* to the glory of God, so that at its close He, through the eternal Spirit, offered Himself without blemish unto God.

But the chief and all-including condition and proof is the desire and purpose to glorify Christ.

The prayer should not be so much for this or that gift, or this or that result, as for Christ Himself to be made manifest to us and through us. The Apostle who was most filled with the Spirit sums all up in that one great word, "For me to live is Christ." As Jesus the Son of God glorified the Father, so the sons of God are to glorify Christ.

The Spirit cannot be where Christ is denied as Redeemer, Life and Lord of all. Christ is "the Truth," and the Spirit is "the Spirit of the Truth;" all is personal, not ideal, for the sum and substance of material wherewith the Spirit works is Christ. The Spirit cannot be teaching if Christ is not seen in "the law of Moses, and in the prophets, and in the Psalms," as well as in the Gospels, or if Christ is not acknowledged to have continued "to do and to teach" in the Acts and in the Epistles what He began in the Gospels.

If Christ is indeed the wisdom of God unto salvation, the Holy Spirit alone can demonstrate it unto the minds and hearts of men; and He has *no mission* in the world separable from Christ and His work of redemption. The outer work of Christ and the inner work of the Spirit go together. The work *for* us by Christ is through the *blood*, the work *in* us by the Spirit is through the *truth;* the latter rests upon the former; and without the Spirit, substitutes for the Spirit and

His work will be accompanied by substitutes for Christ and His work. The importance, therefore, of the presence and work of the Holy Spirit should be estimated according to that far-reaching and all-touching word of Christ, "He shall glorify Me" (John 16:13-15).

To glorify Christ is to manifest Him as supremely excellent; to blind the eyes of men to that glory is the purpose of the god of this world; therefore, which spirit is at work in a man or in a church can easily be told.

7. In conclusion, the sum of all *His mission is to perfect in saints the good work He began, and He molds it all according to this reality of a high and holy sonship:* He establishes the saints in and for Christ. (2 Cor. 1:21.) According to this reality their life and walk partake of thoughts and desires, hopes and objects, unworldly and heavenly. Born of God and from above, knowing whence they came and whither they are going, they live and move and have their being in a world not realized by flesh and blood.

Their life is hid with Christ in God; their work of faith is wrought out in the unseen abode of the Spirit; their labor of love is prompted by a loyal obedience to their Lord, who is absent in "a far country" to which both He and they belong; their sufferings are not their own but His, who, from out of the Glory could ask, "Why persecutest thou Me?" Their worship is of the Father "in spirit and in truth" before the mercy seat, "in the light which no man can approach unto;" their peace is "the peace of God," which can never be disturbed by any fear or trouble which eternal ages might disclose; their joy is "joy in the Lord," its spring is in God and ever deepening in its perpetual flow; their hope is the coming of the Son of God from heaven and the vision of the King in His beauty amidst the unspeakable splendors of His Father's house; and through all the way, "thorn and flower," by which they are journeying to the heavenly country; it is the good Spirit who is leading them. (Isa. 63:7-14.)

CHAPTER VIII

CONSECRATION

(Exodus 28:40-43)

BY REV. HENRY W. FROST, DIRECTOR FOR NORTH AMERICA OF THE
CHINA INLAND MISSION, GERMANTOWN, PA.

Some years ago, when I resided in Toronto, I went one
Sabbath morning to attend service at Knox Church, of which
the Rev. Dr. Henry M. Parsons was pastor. I went to the
service in a very comfortable state of mind, longing of course,
for a new blessing, but without any special sense of the kind
of blessing which I needed. God, however, understood my real
need, and before the sermon was done that morning my comfort was past and I was in distress of mind and spirit. The
sermon had been upon a theme connected with the new life
in Christ, and the Lord had made such a personal application
of it to me that I felt wholly undone. My situation was
similar to that of the bride in Solomon's Song who cried:
"Look not upon me, because I am black, because the sun
hath looked upon me!" And in that state of heart, I returned to my home.

Immediately after dinner that day, I found a quiet place
in our home where I might be alone with myself and God, for
I needed to understand myself, and above all, to know God's
purpose for me. And so I meditated and prayed, and prayed
and meditated. Thus, there was brought to me, at last, the
consciousness that I was wrong at the center of my life. Not
that I doubted that I was saved, for I knew that I was a
Christian; nor that I doubted God's acceptance of me as
His servant, for I was being daily blessed and used in my
work for Him; but that my life was an up and down one,
sometimes in fellowship with God, and sometimes out of fel-

lowship with Him; sometimes praising Him for victory won, and more often confessing sin as a result of deplorable defeat. Thus it was that I saw that what I needed was a new consecration.

When I reached this point, I took up my Bible to study the subject of consecration. But not knowing where to turn, I sought the aid of the concordance, with the intention of working out a Bible reading on the subject. Here, however, I met with difficulty. There were few passages which referred to consecration. But I thought to myself that this did not matter, as consecration and sanctification are the same thing, and what I could not obtain under one word I should obtain under the other. But when I looked at the word sanctification, I was in the opposite difficulty, for there were so many passages that I knew not what to do with them. It was in this way that I turned to a passage which I had noticed, which spoke both of consecration and sanctification, namely,   Exodus 28: 40-43, and it was thus that I shut myself up to it and prayerfully meditated upon it. And I wish to say, that God taught me something from this portion of Scripture, that Sabbath afternoon, which has never been unlearned, and which has revolutionized my life. Not that since then I have never known spiritual inequality, and have ever walked blamelessly before God. Alas! my life has often been marred by failure and sin. Nevertheless, I say it to the praise of Christ, that things have been different from what they were, and that I have possessed a blessed secret of living which I had never possessed before. And it is because I have a longing to pass on to you the secret which God gave to me that I am writing thus personally, and that now, I shall beg to lead you in the study of the passage of Scripture referred to.

The first thing that I noticed in my study is, that consecration and sanctification are not one and the same thing. We are dealing, as I believe, with a verbally inspired Scripture, and I observe that the Spirit says, "consecrate and sanctify." This signifies to me that consecration and sanctification—I speak from an experimental standpoint—are separate things. It is clear that they are closely connected, that one precedes the other and leads to the other, and that the other follows the one and results from that one. Indeed, one may truly say that they are inseparable. At the same time, consecration comes first and sanctification comes second. To put it in the form of a picture, consecration is the initial act of going through the outer door of a palace, and the subsequent acts of passing through other doors in the palace in order to occupy the whole and to reach the throne-room of the king; and sanctification is the palace itself, the whole of which is the home of the king, and where the king may be seen face to face. Or, to put it more simply and plainly, consecration is an initial act and many subsequent, similar acts; and sanctification is the consequent and resultant state.

The second thing which I noticed is, that the one who was to be consecrated had to belong to the right family. There were many orders of people in the world at that time. First, there were the great nations without; then, there were the Israelites in an inner circle; then, there were the Levites at large in a more inner circle; then, there were the sons of Aaron still nearer the center; and, finally, there was Aaron himself at the very center. Now, consecration—in the sense used in this passage—was not for the nations, nor for the Israelites, nor for the Levites at large. It was only for Aaron and Aaron's sons, and the only way, therefore, that a person could reach the experience of consecration was by being born into that particular family. This suggests, of course, the idea of exclusiveness. At the same time, it is more inclusive than it appears. For who are the successors of Aaron and Aaron's sons? The answer comes from Rev. 1: 5, 6, in John's ascription of praise: "Unto Him that loveth us, and loosed us from our sins by His blood, and He made us to be a kingdom, to be priests unto His God and Father." Aaron and his sons were priests. We who believe in Christ are likewise priests. Thus we also may be consecrated.

The third thing which I noticed is, that the person who was to be consecrated had to have the right dress on. Moses, before he came to the act of consecration, was commanded to make linen under and outer garments, and to put these upon Aaron and Aaron's sons. These were called the "garments for glory and for beauty." And notice the order of the words. If Moses, as a mere man, had been writing, he would have said, garments for beauty and for glory; but as a Spirit-inspired man, he said, "garments for glory and for beauty." This is important, for the order of words gives us the clue as to what the garments signify. Man ever seeks to put the beauty before the glory, for he argues that a person must become beautiful in order that he may become glorious. But God, as it were, says no, for it is impossible for a man to become beautiful, and, therefore, it is impossible for him to become glorious, and hence, that he must become glorious in order that he may become beautiful. In other words, God sees only one beauty in this world; it is the glory of His Christ; and, therefore we must be clothed upon with His glory if we are to appear beautiful in His holy presence. These thoughts are amply confirmed by a comparison of Rev. 19:8, and 2 Cor. 5:21: "And to her [the bride] was granted that she should be arrayed in fine linen, clean and white, for the fine linen is the righteousness of saints." "For He [God] hath made Him [Christ] to be sin for us who knew no sin that we might be made the righteousness of God in Him." In short, if we have faith in Christ, we are clothed with the priestly garments, and hence, we may be consecrated.

The fourth thing which I noticed is, that Aaron and his sons, before they were consecrated, had to be anointed. From the following chapter, the 20th and 21st verses, we learn what this anointing was. First, there was a ram of consecration, which was slain in sacrifice. Then, its blood was put upon the priest's right ear, thumb and toe. And, finally, oil was put upon the blood. Note the emblems and the order. It was not oil, and no blood; it was oil and blood. And it was not oil and then blood; it was first blood and then oil. In other words, there was first the sign of ownership through redemption, and after this there was the sign of acceptance for priestly service and empowering for that service. But once more, the one who believes in Christ has gone through this process. The believer is sprinkled with precious blood, and he is anointed with holy oil, for we have been bought with a price, even with the precious blood of Christ, and we have all been baptized by one Spirit into one body.

Having observed these preliminary conditions, I came at last, that Sabbath day, to the thought of consecration itself. And here I met with a great surprise. I had, as I thought, a fairly clear conception of what consecration was. It was going to a consecration meeting and there joining with others in giving one's self to God. Or, if that was not enough, it was shutting one's self into one's room, and there making resolutions and taking vows to put away this and that and to take on this and that and so forever be the servant of God. But I had glanced at the margin of my Bible and had seen opposite the word "consecrate" the three words, "fill their hands," and what filling the hands had to do with consecration I did not know. Thus it was that I read the context of the passage and came to the 29th chapter, the 22nd-24th verses. And thus it was that I learned what true consecration meant, and what it must ever mean. This was what I found. Moses, after clothing and anointing Aaron and Aaron's sons, took the inward parts of the ram and its right shoulder, and also a loaf of bread, a cake of oiled bread, and a wafer out of the basket of unleavened bread, and laid all of these in the hands of Aaron and Aaron's sons. Then Aaron and his sons stood and waved these in the presence of the Lord. And as they did this—nothing more and nothing less—

they were consecrated. Do you wonder, when I read this, that I was surprised? How different it was from what I had imagined. And yet how simple it was. But, simple as it is, it is profoundly deep. That ram of consecration symbolized Christ, for those rich inward parts and that strong, right shoulder set forth His eternal deity, and those various portions of bread, made from wheat into fine flour, manifested His matchless humanity. In other words, as those priests stood there holding up these several tokens before God, they declared—whether they fully understood it or not—that their only right in holy presence was through the redemption and eternal merit of Another; and that it was in that Person's life and glory that they appeared and dedicated themselves to priestly ministry. And as God looked down from heaven and saw, not them, but the uplifted and interposed symbols of that Other, of the Christ, He accepted Aaron and His sons and consecrated them to holy service. And this is what is necessary now. Anything else is high presumption and sin, for this is the Divine way of acceptance, power and glory. In other words, the watchword of every act of consecration is this: "Jesus only!" And do you ask, what is the watchword of sanctification? It is still, "Jesus only!" only this time, it is longer drawn out and it covers the whole of life. Paul put it thus: "For me to live is Christ!" It is for us to put it in the same way.

But I almost hear some one say: This is old-time doctrine, containing old-time ideals; but as for me, I live face to face with new-time conditions, where such doctrines and ideals are not possible of fulfillment. My reader, I will not argue with you. But I beg to suggest to you that you are wrong. For first, our passage says: "It shall be a statute forever unto him, and his seed after him," and, since, as Christians, we are in the priestly line we are also within the privileges of the priestly succession. And also, God never repents of His gifts and callings, and what He has done once and of old

He is able and ready to do again and now. Moreover, I have seen lives, in our own day, lived out wholly for Christ, and in the midst of most untoward circumstances, so that I am persuaded that such consecration as has been spoken of is quite possible for any saint of these present days, even amid the undoubtedly difficult conditions which the present times have produced. In closing, then, let me speak of some consecrated lives which I have personally known.

Mr. Hudson Taylor, while once traveling in China, came to a river, and hired a boatman to ferry him across it. Just after he had done this, a Chinese gentleman, in silks and satins, reached the river and not observing Mr. Taylor, asked the boatman to hire the boat to him. This the man refused to do, saying that he had just engaged the boat to the foreigner. At this the Chinese gentleman looked at Mr. Taylor, and without a word, dealt him a heavy blow with his fist between the eyes. Mr. Taylor was stunned and staggered back, but he presently recovered himself, and, looking up, saw his assailant standing between himself and the river's brink. In an instant Mr. Taylor raised his hands to give the man a push into the stream. But in an instant more, he dropped his arms at his side. Mr. Taylor then said to the gentleman: "You see I could have pushed you into the stream. But the Jesus whom I serve would not let me do this. You were wrong in striking me, for the boat was mine. And since it is mine, I invite you to share it with me and to go with me across the river." The Chinese gentleman dropped his head in shame, and without a word, he stepped into the boat to accept the hospitality thus graciously offered to him. Mr. Taylor was a man of naturally quick temper, but evidently, for him to live was Christ.

The well-known Rev. James Inglis was pastor of a large church in Detroit. He was a graduate of Edinburgh University and Divinity School, was very learned—he was afterwards requested to act with the American New Testament

Revision Committee—he was unusually eloquent, and he was having a most successful ministerial career. Indeed, he was the most popular preacher in Detroit, if not in Michigan, having large audiences on Sundays, with people seated in the aisles and upon the pulpit stairs of his church, and with his listeners hanging upon his words. One week day, at this period, he sat in his study, preparing one of his sermons for the following Sunday, when a voice seemed to say to him: "James Inglis, whom are you preaching?" Mr. Inglis was startled, but he answered: "I am preaching good theology." But the Voice seemed to reply: "I did not ask you what you are preaching, but whom are you preaching?" My uncle answered: "I am preaching the Gospel." But the Voice again replied: "I did not ask you what you are preaching; I asked you whom are you preaching?" Mr. Inglis sat silent and with bowed head for a long time before he again replied. When he did, he raised his head and said: "O God, I am preaching James Inglis!" And then he added: "Henceforth I will preach no one but Christ, and Him crucified!" Then my uncle arose, opened the chest in his study which contained his eloquent sermons and deliberately put them one by one into the fire which was burning in his study stove. From that time on he turned his back upon every temptation to be oratorical and popular, preached simply and expositionally, and gave himself in life and words to set forth Jesus Christ before men. Later he became the editor of two widely read religious papers, and the teacher in the Scripture of such men as Dr. Brooks of St. Louis, Dr. Erdman of Philadelphia, Dr. Gordon of Boston, and Mr. Moody of Northfield. He died in 1872; but his name is still held in reverent and grateful remembrance by many of the most spiritual of God's saints in America and Europe. Mr. Inglis was by nature a man of proud and ambitious disposition; but it is manifest that it became true in his life that for him to live was Christ.

A friend of mine—whose name I will not give—was a business man in one of our great American cities. He was an able financier and had become wealthy. Thus it came to pass that he was living in a beautiful brown stone house, situated on a prominent avenue, and in luxury. At the same time he was a Christian, being an elder in a Presbyterian church and generally active in good works. It was thus, when Mr. Hudson Taylor visited his city in 1888, that my friend offered to entertain him. The arrangement was brought to pass, and Mr. Taylor was in his home for about a week. My friend was thus brought into close contact with a man of God, the like of whom he had never before seen. As the days went by he was increasingly impressed by the godliness and winsomeness of the life before him. Finally, after Mr. Taylor had departed to another place, my friend knelt down and said to God: "Lord, if Thou wilt make me something like that little man I will give Thee everything I've got." And the Lord took him at his word. From that time onward his spiritual life visibly deepened and developed. At last one day he said to his wife: "My dear, don't you think we can do with a less expensive house than this, so that we may reduce our living expenses and give more money to the Lord?" He then proposed that they should sell the property, build a cheaper house, and give what might thus be gained to foreign missions. Happily, he had a wife who was a true "helpmeet" to him, and she heartily agreed to the proposal. So the old property was sold, the new house was built, and the sum gained was given to God for His cause abroad. About two years later my friend spoke again to his wife on this wise: "Dear, I feel badly about this house. The architect got me in for more money than I intended to spend on it. What do you say to selling it? I have got a lot on an adjacent street, and we can build there a cheaper house than this, and then we can give the difference to foreign missions." My friend's wife was not a woman who liked changes. However.

she loved the Lord, and again she gave a ready assent to the proposal. So the first transaction was repeated, a plainer, cheaper house was built, and all that was made by the change was given to missions. Meanwhile, my friend's general business continued to prosper. Indeed, everything he touched seemed to turn into gold. But his personal and family expenses, by his deliberate choice, were constantly being reduced. He never lived meanly. At the same time he lived more and more simply. Thus he made money, and thus he saved money. Yet all the time he gave and gave to causes at home and abroad. And this continued until his death. At the time of his death he and his wife were supporting some thirteen missionaries, and previously, they had sent to the foreign field, providing for outfits and passages, over one hundred new and older workers. Now my friend, by nature, was a man who loved money. It had a fascination for him, both in the making of it and in the selfish spending of it. But it is manifest that such greediness had been taken out of his life. His heart was where his treasure was, and his real treasure was in heaven. In other words, he too was able to say: "For me to live is Christ!"

Dear reader, whoever you are, the consecrated life is possible and practical. It was for the first century; it is also for the twentieth century. It was for early apostles and disciples; it is also for present day missionaries, ministers, lay workers and business men. In truth, it is for anybody and everybody who is the Lord's. As for you, therefore, but one thing is needed. Empty your hands of whatever you have taken up from the world, and then hold up these emptied hands to God. And as surely as God is holy, as surely as He is loving, as surely as He is gracious, He will fill your, even *your*, hands with Christ. And when you find yourself standing thus, holding up Jesus between yourself and God, hiding yourself beneath Him, confessing Him to be your only merit, glory and power, you too will be consecrated.

CHAPTER IX

THE APOLOGETIC VALUE OF PAUL'S EPISTLES

BY REV. E. J. STOBO, JR., B. A., S. T. D.,
SMITH'S FALLS, ONTARIO, CANADA

"Paul is the greatest literary figure in the New Testament; round him all its burning questions lie." "There is nothing more certain in ancient literature than the authorship of the more important of the Pauline epistles." These utterances of Dr. Fairbairn in his "Philosophy of the Christian Religion" bring us face to face with the apologetic value of the writings of the Apostle to the Gentiles. The oldest Pauline epistle is divided by little more than twenty years from the death of Christ, and by a still shorter interval from the Epistle to the Hebrews and Apocalypse; so that Paul's interpretation of the Christ has a distinct bearing upon the Gospels and later Christian literature.

In this paper we shall deal only with four epistles which are acknowledged by Biblical critics of *all* schools as undoubtedly genuine; viz., Galatians, 1 and 2 Corinthians and Romans. The four epistles in question have the advantage of being more or less controversial in their nature. Debate leads to clearness of statement, and we have the advantage of hearing the words of Paul as well as of understanding the views of those against whom he contends. The controversy in these epistles concerns the nature and destination of Christianity, and consequently we may expect to learn what Paul deemed central and essential in the Christian faith. There is enough Christology in these epistles to show us what Paul thought concerning the Great Founder of Christianity. Moreover there are, in these writings, references to the solemn crisis-experience in his spiritual history, and these of necessity have a bearing upon

Luke's letters to Theophilus, which are popularly known as the Gospel of Luke and The Acts of the Apostles. With such clues to follow we are able to argue for the credibility of the other New Testament documents, and also for the accuracy of the portrait painted of its central figure, the Lord Jesus Christ.

Our first argument has to do with *The Apologetic Value of the References, in Paul's Epistles, to his Christian Experience.*

His theology is an outgrowth of his experience. His thinking is remarkably autobiographical. He resembles Luther in this respect as a religious teacher. His thinking is colored by the age in which he lives, and in such words as law, righteousness, justification, adoption, flesh, spirit, there is undying interest, if we remember the intense, tragic, moral struggle lying behind Paul's theology.

The passages in these four epistles, which exhibit most conspicuously the autobiographical character, occur in the first chapter of the Epistle to the Galatians and the seventh chapter of the Epistle to the Romans. From the former we learn that he belonged to a class which was thoroughly antagonistic to Jesus. His religion was Judaism. He was an enthusiastic in it. He says: "I advanced in the Jew's religion beyond many of mine own age among my countrymen, being more exceedingly zealous for the traditions of my fathers." In other words he was a Pharisee of the most extreme type. His great aim in life was to become legally righteous, and thus all his prejudices were most strongly opposed to the new teaching. In the seventh chapter of Romans we learn that Paul in time made a great discovery. One of the commandments, the tenth, forbids coveting; and so he learned that a mere feeling, a state of the heart, is condemned as sin. In that hour his Pharisaism was doomed. "When the commandment came sin revived and I died." He discovered a world of sin within of which he had not dreamed, and legal righteousness seemed unattainable. That was a great step towards Christianity. He had been trying to satisfy the hunger of his soul with legal ordinances; he found them chaff, not wheat, and so he sought for true nourishment. Eventually he became a convert to Christianity. The Pauline letters give no detailed account of the memorable event like the narratives contained in the Book of the Acts. The main feature of the story is referred to in 1 Cor. 15:8 where the Apostle enumerates the different appearances of the risen Christ: "Last of all He was seen of me also."

Paul's conversion is one of the hard problems for those who undertake to give a purely naturalistic solution of the origins of Christianity. All attempts to explain it without recognizing the hand of God in it must be futile. He himself says devoutly concerning it: "It was the good pleasure of God . . . to reveal His Son in me." This argues that Christianity is a supernatural religion.

When a religious crisis comes to a man of Paul's type it possesses deep significance. For him to become a Christian meant everything. It meant to leap into a large cosmopolitan idea of Christianity, its nature and destination. He saw that all was over with Judaism and its legal righteousness, all over with the law itself as a way of salvation; that salvation must come to man through the grace of God, and that it might come through that channel to all men alike on equal terms, and that therefore the Jewish prerogative was at an end. These consequences are all borne out in the biographical notice in the first chapters of Galatians.

It can easily be seen that if the accounts of Paul's conversion in the epistles be accepted, they lend support and give value to the accounts in the Acts of the Apostles; that the consequences of that conversion as previously indicated are in entire harmony with the teaching of the latter part of the Acts, and so we must come to the conclusion that the contents of that book are trustworthy whether Luke be the author

or not. And since the Acts of the Apostles purports to be a
continuation of the Gospel of Luke, we are led to conclude
that the Gospel must be trustworthy also, and that all the
Synoptists set forth real facts. Such a conclusion involves
the historicity of Jesus Christ.

Our second argument is concerned with *The Apologetic
Value of the References in Paul's Epistles to the Person of
Christ.*

The conversion of Paul admitted as a fact, we have seen
that it leads back by degrees to the fact of Christ. But what
sort of a Christ? The reader will be struck with the fact that,
in these Epistles,

*The Earthly Life of the Christ is Represented as Singularly
Free from the Miraculous.*

He is born of a woman, born under the law (Gal. 4:4);
He springs from Israel, and is, according to the flesh, from
the tribe of Judah and the seed of David (Rom. 9:5; 1:3);
He is unknown to the princes of this world (1 Cor. 2:8);
He is poor, hated, persecuted, crucified (2 Cor. 8:9; Gal.
6:14; 1 Cor. 1:23-25; 2:2); He is betrayed at night just
after He has instituted the supper (1 Cor. 15:23); He dies
on the cross, to which He had been fastened with nails, and
is buried (1 Cor. 15:3, 4). This account it will be seen is at
one with that of the Synoptists, with the exception that we
do not hear of a supernatural birth, nor is there any emphasis
placed upon supernatural works. In its main outlines the portrait of the man Jesus agrees perfectly with that of the Synop-
tic Gospels, and lends credence to the history of the Galilean
Prophet. On the other hand

Christ is Represented as a Being of Ideal Majesty.

The doctrine of Christ's person as found in these four
great epistles is no mere theological speculation; it is the outgrowth of religious experience. Jesus was, for Paul, the Lord
because He was the Saviour. Four leading truths with reference to Christ are brought into prominence in his writings:

A. In Relation to Time. He is God's Son who was "born of the seed of David according to the flesh". On the side of His humanity our Lord "was born." (Rom. 1:2.) That nature begins only then. He is possessed of another nature that dates back long before the incarnation. He is in a peculiar sense God's "own Son" (Rom. 8:32), belonging to Him above all others, or as Alford well says, "His νὸς μονογενής, the only one of God's Sons who is one with Him in nature and essence, begotten of Him before all worlds. This Son was delivered up for us all. This idea is hinted at in 2 Cor. 8:9: "Ye know the grace of our Lord Jesus Christ, that though He was rich, yet for your sakes He became poor," and finds full expression in the Epistle to the Philippians (2:5-9), concerning which there is very little controversy. The straggling hints we have in the four great epistles confirm the teaching of the Letter to the Philippians, and above all the classic statement of the Fourth Gospel: "In the beginning was the Word."

B. In Relation to Man.. Paul says Christ was "made of a woman" (Gal. 4:4), and that He was sent into the world "in the likeness of sinful flesh" (Rom. 8:3); that is, He came into the world by birth and bore to the eye the aspect of any ordinary man. But though Christ came in the likeness of sinful flesh, He was not a sinner. He "knew no sin" (2 Cor. 5:21). The mind that was in Him before He came ruled His life after He came. However, Paul regards the resurrection as constituting an important crisis in the experience of Christ. Thereby He was declared to be the Son of God with power (Rom. 1:4), "the man from heaven" (1 Cor. 15:47); and yet to Paul, Jesus is a real man, a Jew with Hebrew blood in His veins, a descendant of David. The portrait thus painted agrees perfectly with that of the Evangelists who depict Him as a real man, but, in some strange fashion, different from other men. "His soul was like a star and dwelt apart."

The Son of David was, for Paul, moreover, "The second man" (1 Cor. 15:47). This title points out Christ as one who has, for His vocation, to undo the mischief wrought by the transgression of the first man. Hence He is called, in sharp contrast to the first man Adam, "a quickening spirit" (1 Cor. 15:45). As the one brought death into the world, so the other brings life (1 Cor. 15:22); and this teaching agrees with the declaration of the Synoptists: "The Son of Man is come to seek and to save that which was lost;" "Thou shalt call His name Jesus, for He shall save His people from their sins."

C. In Relation to the Universe. He is represented in the Epistle to the Colossians as the Firstborn of all creation, as the Originator of creation as well as its final cause, all things in heaven and on earth visible and invisible, angels included, being made by Him and for Him (Col. 1:15-16). This goes beyond anything found in the four great epistles, yet we may find rudiments of a cosmic doctrine even in these letters. For Paul it was an axiom that the universe has its final aim in Christ its King. (See 1 Cor. 8:6.)

D. In Relation to God. Paul applies two titles to Christ, "the Son of God" and "the Lord." Both of these titles are combined in the introduction of the Epistle to the Romans, "His Son, Jesus Christ, our Lord." He is "declared to be the Son of God with power, according to the Spirit of holiness, by a resurrection of the dead" (Rom. 1:4). The most convincing proof of the divinity of Christ Paul found in the resurrection. Writing to the Corinthians he says: "If Christ hath not been raised then is our preaching vain—your faith is vain, ye are yet in your sins" (1 Cor. 15:14-17). He submits to them the proof of his Apostleship in the fact that he has seen "Jesus our Lord" (1 Cor. 9:1). He tells the Galatians that his gospel came "through revelation of Jesus Christ" (Gal. 1:12), and that Gospel, according to 1 Cor. 15:3-8, contains five elementary facts: 1, Christ died for our sins; 2, He was buried; 3, He rose on the third day; 4, He appeared to many disciples, and 5, Last of all, He appeared to Paul himself. These are the things that are vital in Paul's preaching. When we remember that, as a Pharisee, his prejudices were all against the Gospel, we must come to the conclusion that Paul's testimony argues most strongly for the historicity of the resurrection and the truths involved therein.

It may not be out of place to re-iterate what has already been stated regarding Paul's use of the expression, "His own Son," in Rom. 8:3. This passage deals with the brotherhood of sons. Jesus, amid the multitudes having the right to call themselves sons of God, is an unique figure, towering above them all. In 2 Cor. 4:4 it is stated that Christ is the image of God, and in Rom. 8:29 it is said that the destiny of believers is to be conformed to the image of God's Son. The ideal for Christians is to bear the image of Christ. For Christ Himself is reserved the distinction of being the image of God. This throws a side light upon Paul's idea of Christ's sonship.

He is represented as the one Lord by whom or on account of whom are all things (1 Cor. 8:6). According as δι οὖ or δι ὄν is accepted as the reading, Jesus is the Creator of all things or furnishes the Divine reason for creation. The groaning of the creation in labor for the brnging forth of a new redeemed world is a graphic picture of the relation of Christ's redemptive work to the physical universe. (Rom. 8:22.) It is true that this teaching goes beyond that of the Gospels in some particulars, but it agrees with John's Gospel when it teaches the creatorship of the Logos. (John 1:3.)

In 1 Cor. 8:5, 6, the term "Lord" gains equal significance to that of "Son". In view of pagan polytheism, the Apostle sets one real θεὸς over against the many θεοί λεγόμενοι of paganism, and one real Lord over against its κύριοι πολλοί. It would seem by this inscription that the Apostle desired to introduce Christ into the sphere of the truly Divine.

The famous benediction at the close of the Second Epistle to the Corinthians implies a very high conception of Christ's person and position. One could scarcely believe that Paul would use such a collocation of phrases as the grace of the Lord Jesus, the love of God and the fellowship of the Holy Spirit, unless Christ had been for him a Divine Being, even God. Now all this simply adds force to John's prologue: "In the beginning was the Word, and the Word was with God, and the Word was God."

The four great Pauline epistles agree, in the most important details, with the portraiture given us of Jesus in the Gospels. The conception of the person of Christ, as we have already shown, was not natural to Paul. He was a bitter opponent of Christianity. It was not the result of gradually changing convictions regarding the claims of Jesus Christ—all the testimony which bears upon the subject implies the contrary. It was not due to extreme mysticism, for Paul's writings impress us as being remarkably sane and logical. No endeavor to account for it upon merely natural grounds is satisfactory, and so we must accept his own statement of the case. The truth of the Messiahship of Jesus was a matter of revelation in the experience of his conversion, and if we accept that, we must necessarily accept all that it involves. The Gospels and Epistles do not contradict, but only supplement this protraiture. They add lines of beauty to the rugged outline painted by Paul, and are inextricably connected with the four great epistles. Accepting these letters as genuine and Paul's explanation of his doctrine as true, we must accept the whole of the New Testament documents as credible, and the portraiture of the Christ as that of a real person— Son of man and Son of God, the God-Man.

CHAPTER X

WHAT THE BIBLE CONTAINS
FOR THE BELIEVER

BY REV. GEORGE F. PENTECOST, D. D.,
DARIEN, CONNECTICUT

I. *The Bible is the Only Book That Can Make Us Wise unto Salvation.*

The Bible is not a book to be studied as we study geology and astronomy, merely to find out about the earth's formation and the structure of the universe; but it is a book revealing truth, designed to bring us into *living union* with God. We may study the physical sciences and get a fair knowledge of the facts and phenomena of the *material* universe; but what difference does it make to us, as *spiritual* beings, whether the Copernican theory of the universe is true, or that of Ptolemy? On the other hand, the eternal things of God's Word do so concern us. Scientific knowledge, and the words in which that knowledge is conveyed, have no power to change our characters, to make us better, or give us a living hope of a blessed immortality; but the Word of God has in it a vital power, it is "quick and powerful"—living and full of Divine energy (Heb. 4:12)—and when received with meekness into our understanding and heart is able to save our souls (Jas. 1:18, 21), for it is the instrument of the Holy Spirit wherewith He accomplishes in us regeneration of character. The Word of God is a living seed containing within itself God's own life, which, when it is received into our hearts, springs up within us and "brings forth fruit after its kind;" for Jesus Christ, the eternal Word of God, is the living germ hidden in His written Word. Therefore it is written, "The words that I speak unto you, they are spirit and they are life" (John

6:63), and so it is that "he that heareth My words"—that is, receiveth them into good and honest hearts—that heareth the Word and understandeth it, *"hath everlasting life"* (John 5:24). Of no other book could such things as these be said. Hence we say, the Word of God is the instrument in His hand to work in us and for us regeneration and salvation; "for of His own will begat He us with the Word of truth, the engrafted Word, which is able to save your souls" (Jas. 1:18, 21).

This leads us to say that we are related to God and the eternal verities revealed in this Book, not through intellectual apprehension and demonstration, but by *faith*. Not by reasoning, but by simple faith, do we lay hold on these verities, resting our faith in God, who is under and in every saving fact in the Book. (See 1 Pet. 1:21.) It seems to me, therefore, to be the supreme folly for men to be always speculating and reasoning about these spiritual and revealed things; and yet we meet constantly even good people who are thus dealing with God's Word. First of all, they treat the revelation as though it were only an *opinion* expressed concerning the things revealed, and so they feel free to dissent from or receive it with modification, and deal with it as they would with the generalizations and conclusions, more or less accurate, of the scientists, and the theories, more or less true, of the philosophers. If the Word commends itself to their judgment they accept it; thus making *their judgment* the criterion of truth, instead of submitting their opinions to the infallible Word of God. It is not seldom that we hear a person say they believe the Word of God to be true; and then the very next instant, when pressed by some statement or declaration of that Word, they say, "Ah! but then *I* believe so and so"— something entirely different from what God has declared. Then again, many people who profess to believe God's Word seem never to think of putting themselves into practical and saving relation to it. They believe that Jesus Christ is the

Saviour of the world, but they never believe *on* Him or *in* Him; in other words, that He is a Saviour to *them*.

God's Book is full of doctrines and promises. We declare them, and some one says, "You must prove that doctrine or that promise to be true." The only way to prove a doctrine to be true is by a personal experience of it through faith in Jesus Christ. Jesus Christ says, "Ye must be born again." Should you attempt to master the meaning and power of that doctrine by mere speculation, you would presently land just where Nicodemus did, and say, "How can these things be?" Instead of doing so, suppose you attend further to what is said, namely, "Whosoever believeth is born of God" (1 John 5:1; John 1:12, 13). In obedience to this Divine teaching, not knowing how it is to be done in us, we take that Word and yield ourselves to Jesus Christ; and lo! there dawns upon us an experience that throws light upon all that which before was a mystery. We have experienced no *physical shock,* but a great change is wrought in us, especially in our relation to God. "Old things are passed away, and behold all things are become new" (2 Cor. 5:17). Thus we come into an experimental understanding of the doctrine of the new birth. So every other doctrine pertaining to the spiritual life is by God's grace transmuted into experience. For just as a word stands for an idea or thought, so the doctrines of God stand for experiences; but the doctrine must be received before the experience can be had. And, moreover, we are to receive all doctrines, all truth, through faith in Him, for Christ and His Word are inseparable, just as a man's *note* is only current and valuable because the *man* is good. A bank-note is received in the faith of the *bank* it represents. Should the bank fail, the note instantly becomes worthless.

But there are some things revealed in the Word of God which we believe without experience. For instance, we believe that this "vile body" (Phil. 3:21), dishonored by sin and upon the neck of which death will soon put his foot, will in the day of "His appearing and kingdom" (2 Tim. 4:1; 1 Thess. 4:15) be raised, changed and fashioned like unto His glorious body (Phil. 3:21). Do you know how we can so surely believe these things? We answer, because God has proved to us so much of His Word that when He announces something *yet to be made true*, on the basis of past experience we reach out toward and accept as true the promise of the future things. Indeed, He already makes it true in our hearts, for "faith is the substance of things hoped for" (Heb. 11:1). For even here we have a present spiritual experience which is as an earnest to us of the culmination yet future; for we are already risen with Christ. (Col. 2:13; 3:1; Eph. 2:5, 6; Rom. 8:11.)

2. *The Bible Contains in Itself the Absolute Guarantee of Our Inheritance in Christ.*

Suppose we should come to you some day and call in question your ownership of your house, and demand that you give it up—a homestead bequeathed to you by your father. "Why do you make such a demand upon me?" you ask. "Because," we reply, "it is not your house; you have no right to it; at least you do not know that it is yours." "Oh, yes," you reply, "I am quite sure it is my house." "How do you know? What is your reason for believing it is your house?" "Why, because my father lived here before me." "That is no good reason." "Well, I have lived here undisputed for five years myself." "It does not hence follow that the house is yours." "But I am very happy in it; I enjoy myself here." "Well, but my dear sir, that you may do, and still have no right to it." At last, pushed to the wall, you take us with you down to the court-house, and show us your father's will, duly written, signed, sealed and recorded. This may serve to illustrate the point. A great many Christians are at a loss where and how to ground their "title." It is not in the fact that you are a descendant of a saintly father, a child of believing parents, for, as old Matthew Henry says, "Grace

does not run in the blood;" nor is it that you have membership in the visible Church of Christ; nor is it to be found in
delightful frames and feelings—in a word, not even a genuine
Christian experience constitutes your "title-deed." Where
then are we to bottom our hope? Why, just in the naked
bare Word of God. It is written, "Verily, verily, I say unto
you, he that heareth My words, and believeth on Him that
sent Me *hath* everlasting life," etc. (John 5:24). Straight
to the record do we appeal for a final test as to our possession
in God. "This is the record, that God hath given to us eternal
life, and this life is in His Son. He that hath the Son hath
life; and he that hath not the Son of God hath not life"
(1 John 5:11, 12). Our faith lays hold on the Son of God,
in whom we have redemption (Eph. 1:7) by means of and
through the recorded Word of promise, for this record was
"written, that ye might believe that Jesus is the Christ, the
Son of God; and that believing ye might have life through
His name" (John 20:31). The Scriptures are the covenants,
old and new, in which God has guaranteed to us, by word
and oath (Heb. 6:17, 18), sealed with the blood of Jesus
Christ (Matt. 26:28), an inheritance among the saints. We
do not emphasize this point in any wise to underrate Christian
experience (for it is most blessed and true), or undervalue
the blessing of believing parents, or the Church and her
ordinances, but only to draw your attention to "the more sure
Word of prophecy" (2 Pet. 1:19), which is better to us for
confirmation than visions and voices, frames and feelings,
parental benedictions, and church sacraments.

3. *The Word of God is the Means Appointed for the
Culture of Our Christian Life.*

James tells us (1:18) that the Word of truth is the instrument of our regeneration, and Jesus tells us that the truth
not only "makes us free," but prays the Father that we may
be "sanctified through the truth" (John 6:32-36; 17:17-19).
And Paul tells us, in words which the Holy Ghost teacheth,

that "Christ loved the church, and give Himself for it, that
He might sanctify and cleanse it with the washing of water
by the Word," etc. (Eph. 5:25, 27). "This is the will of
God, even your sanctification" (1 Thess. 4:3), for God hath
not called us to uncleanness, but unto holiness (1 Thess. 4:7).
After regeneration, nothing can be more important than this.
We are told in the Bible and we believe it—that by and by we
shall be in another state of existence—in heaven in the presence of the loving and glorified Jesus; that we shall see His
face, and His name shall be on our foreheads (Rev. 22:4),
that we shall be with the angels, an innumerable company,
and with the spirits of just men made perfect, the saints of
all ages (Heb. 12:23), that we shall know them and be in
their society (Matt. 17:3; 1 Cor. 13:12), that we shall be
absolutely untainted with sin, as glorious as the uncreated
light of God. (Rev. 21:4, 27; Matt. 13:45.) This being the
place and the company toward which we are being borne
along so rapidly, we want to be prepared for both place and
society.

Ah, friends, you are anxious to be cultured for this world
and its "best society," in its knowledge, in its customs, and in
its manners. Yes, you lavish time and money upon yourself
and your children, in order that they may be furnished with
the accomplishments and culture of this world. You say
when you appear in good society you want to be at ease, to
be a peer among the most accomplished, and you wish the
same for your children. Were you invited to go six months
hence to take up your abode at the Court of St. James, as
the guest of England's noble king, you would ransack all the
books at your command that treated of court etiquette and
manners; you would brush up in English history, so that you
might not be taken unawares either in your knowledge of the
affairs of the country, or in court ceremonial. But in a little
while we are going to the court of the King immortal, eternal,
in the kingdom of glory. We know not the day nor the hour

when the Lord will come, or call us hence; and we want to be ready, both as to purity of character and the courtly culture of the heavenly city. We wish to be familiar with the history of redemption, and with the mysteries of the kingdom. We should not want to appear as an awkward stranger in our Father's house of light. We can only get this sanctification of character and culture of life and manner by constant familiarity and communion with God and the saints through the Word.

Men of the world are anxious that they, or, it may be, that their children, should appear well in the society of this world. To this end they devote themselves and them to the schools of the world and fashion; the dancing-school and the academy, they fancy, is the only place where polite manners and courtly grace may be acquired. Believers, too, are anxious that their children should be cultured and accomplished in every way worthy of being the King's sons or daughters, as by grace they are. But they should not think of seeking for them the *entrée* of what is called in this world the "best society", or sending them to fashionable finishing-schools and dancing-academies, in order to such end. If they may have their hearts filled with the dear, great love of God, and the sweet grace of Christ; if they hang on the chamber walls of their souls as pictures, "Whatsoever things are honest, just, pure, lovely and of good report, and *think* on these things" (Phil. 4:8); if they journey through this world in companion-ship with Him; if the Holy Spirit guides them through the Word, as Bunyan's Pilgrim was led through the "house of the interpreter," and shows them wonderful and beautiful things out of His law; if the fruit of the Spirit, which "is love, joy, peace, long-suffering, gentleness, goodness, faith, meekness, and temperance" (Gal. 5:22, 23), adorns their lives and characters—Christians are not then afraid that their children will be a whit behind the foremost society people in the land in culture of mind and heart, and grace of manner.

Ah! there is a heavenly culture and a Divine grace of manner
that far transcend anything found in the schools of this world.
Only a Christian could think of saying with Paul, standing
before his judge, "except these bonds" (Acts 26:29).

John Bunyan, locked up for twelve years in Bedford Jail,
with his Bible and concordance for his constant companions,
produced and sent forth to the world his immortal dream,
written with such beauty of style and in such chaste and
simple manner, as to make it classic in English literature. So
perfect and matchless was the intellectual and spiritual culture
of this unlearned "tinker of Elstow," that the scholarly John
Owen testified before the King, "Your Majesty, if I could
write as does that tinker in Bedford Jail I would gladly lay
down all my learning." Where did John Bunyan get his
culture? In glorious fellowship with Moses in the Law, with
David in the Psalms, with Isaiah and the prophets and holy
men of God, who wrote as they were moved by the Holy
Spirit; with Matthew, Mark, Luke and John; with Paul, Peter
and all the rest who wrote and spoke not the thoughts, nor
in the words, of man's wisdom, but God's thoughts, and in
words which the Holy Spirit giveth. Read Homer and Milton,
Shakespeare and Dante; read Bacon, Macaulay, Addison and
Carlyle; go through all the best literature of all ages, and it
will fall infinitely short of the purity, beauty and grandeur
of thought and expression found in God's Word.

Goethe, who said he was "not Christian," has declared of
the canonical Gospels: "The human mind, no matter how
much it may advance in intellectual culture, and in the extent
and depth of the knowledge of nature, will never transcend
the high moral culture of Christianity as it shines and glows
in the canonical Gospels." Renan, the French infidel author,
concludes his life of Jesus with these remarkable words
"Whatever may be the surprises of the future, Jesus will never
be surpassed; His worship will grow young without ceasing;
His legend will call forth tears without end; His suffering

will melt the noblest hearts; all ages will proclaim that among
the sons of men there is none born greater than Jesus." And
Strauss, the rationalistic German author of the "Life of
Jesus," says: "Jesus presents within the sphere of religion
the culminating point, beyond which posterity can never go;
yea, which it cannot even equal. He remains the highest
model of religion within the reach of our thought, and no
perfect piety is possible without His presence in the heart."
Thus the power of the "Book and the Person" for the highest
culture of the highest nature of man, is affirmed by the great
apostle of modern culture, and by those who do not admit the
Divine origin of the Scriptures, or the deity of Him of whom
they are from first to last the witness. If, then, you want to
know how to serve God and do His will on the earth, and be
thoroughly prepared and cultured for heaven hereafter, take
His Word, and make it the rule and companion of your life.

4. *The Bible is the Christian's Armory.*

The Christian's calling in the world is that of a soldier.
He must fight the good fight of faith. (1 Tim. 6:12; 2 Tim.
4:7.) Sinners are to be won from the power of the devil
to God. Their intelligence, their wills, and their affections,
are to be stormed and carried for Him; they are to be turned
from the power of darkness to light; their prison-houses of
sin are to be broken into; their chains knocked off and the
captives set free (Acts 26:16-18). We also, in our own
Christian life and pilgrimage, are set upon by the powers of
darkness; by the fiery darts of the devil. Doubts, infidelity,
temptations, evil imaginations, unclean, unholy, and vain
thoughts assail us, poured in upon our souls by Satan, the
lusts of the flesh being thus set on fire of hell, if by this
means the child of God may be overtaken in a fault or overcome by sin. But this warfare is not carnal, or after the
manner of the flesh. "For though we walk in the flesh [have
our lives as other men do in fleshly bodies] we do not war
after the flesh: (for the weapons of our warfare are not

carnal, but mighty through God to the pulling down of strongholds) ; casting down imaginations [reasonings] and every high thing [lofty edifice] which is being raised against the knowledge of God, and bringing into captivity every thought in obedience to Christ" (2 Cor. 10:3-5). Just as Joshua went up against Jericho, and took its strongholds and high towers, and cast them down and made captive the city, not with carnal weapons, but with trumpets of rams' horns (Josh. 6), so we, proceeding against the strongholds, imaginations, and infidel arguments of men, are to take the Gospel trump. The sword we are to wield is the "Word of God, the sword of the Spirit" (Eph. 6:17) which makes him who wields it invincible. The Bible itself must be brought out, not only as the best defense against all the assaults of infidelity from the lofty towers of human reasonings, but also as the mighty weapon to overcome and bring the enemies of God into captivity to Christ. "They overcame by the blood of the Lamb and the word of their testimony" (Rev. 12:11). "Wherefore take unto you the whole armor of God; having your loins girt about with truth; and having on the breatsplate of righteousness, and your feet shod with the preparation of the Gospel of peace; and above all, taking the shield of faith, whereby ye shall be able to quench all the fiery darts of the wicked; and take the helmet of salvation and the sword of the Spirit, *which is the Word of God*" (Eph. 6:13-17). We have only to recall how our Saviour overcame the devil with the all-prevailing weapon, "It is written," in order that we may be furnished with the secret of successful warfare for Him.

Very often Christians, young and old, come to us in the "inquiry room" and say, "Won't you come and talk with this friend of mine?" "Why don't you talk with him (or her) yourself?" we reply. "Because I don't know what to say to him, and, besides, you know more of the Bible." "Well, why don't *you* know more of the Bible?" To this, various answers are given. At any rate we meet here one grave mistake. An ignorance of the Bible, which not only furnishes us with our spiritual weapons, but "thoroughly furnishes us unto all good works" (2 Tim. 3:17), leads many earnest Christians to the doubtful use of their own argumentation in dealing with their own and others' souls. It is a hopeless task to pull down the strongholds of the unregenerated mind and heart with anything less than these Divine weapons. But all may equip themselves from this great armory. The Bible contains ideas which no philosophy or human theory can furnish, and therefore puts us in possession of weapons which the enemy cannot withstand when hard pushed by them, re-inforced as they are by the invisible and mighty presence of the Holy Spirit, and which renders us impregnable to the assaults of the adversary. Of this mighty power of the Word and Spirit of God we have a splendid example in the case of Stephen, and other early disciples, whose words, drawn from the Scripture, the Jews could not withstand. We have never yet met an infidel or atheist whose arguments we could not turn aside when depending simply on the Word of God. Nay, more, we have never yet met one in the "inquiry rooms" who has been able to withstand God's Word and the mighty facts of the Bible, when, in humble dependence upon God we have set them in array before him. If you know God's thoughts and seek to be guided by the Holy Spirit, He will say out of your mouth the right word at the right time, both to ward off an assault and to strike a telling blow for the truth. And amidst all this warfare, the light and love and gentleness of Jesus Christ will so shine out in your bearing and manner that they will be convinced of your sincerity, and God will give you the victory.

5. *The Bible is a Perfect Map and Chart to the Christian on Pilgrimage Through the World.*

With God's Word in hand and heart you may tread your way with perfect safety and confidence through all the labyrinths of this world. The straight and narrow way is so clearly and sharply marked that he who runs may read. It is a highway (unseen, it may be, by the worldling) in which a wayfaring man, though a fool, need not err (Isa. 35:8), for it is everywhere marked by His commandments. More than that, we have an unseen Guide, even the Spirit of Truth, who leads us, and says to us, in places of doubt or uncertainty, "This is the way, walk ye in it" (Isa. 30:21). Thus, a pilgrim and a stranger, you may keep your onward way to the city of God in safety and confidence, following in the light of the Word, which is "a lamp to your feet, and a light unto your path" (Psa. 119:105), the path that no one knoweth save He that leadeth thee. Yea, and you will find that the way, over hills and through valleys, shines more and more unto the perfect day. (Prov. 4:18.) The Word of God is a chart that marks all the rocks and reefs in the sea of life; if we heed, and sail our frail bark by it, we shall come safely into the haven of rest at last. But if we are heedless and proud, and self-sufficient in our own conceits, we shall make shipwreck of our faith. A young lieutenant in the English navy discovered a small but dangerous rock in the Mediterranean, never before known, and reported it to the admiralty. It was telegraphed to all the stations, and ordered to be put down on all the charts. The first ship to sail over the spot was under command of an old captain, who, noting the warning newly placed on his chart, desired to know by whom the rock was reported. On being informed he replied: "There is no such rock there. I have sailed over this sea for twenty years, and if such a rock had been there I would have found it." And then in his pride and conceit he gave orders to his sailing-master to steer directly over the spot indicated. The gallant ship was driven over the danger spot under full sail. There was a tremendous crash, and the noble vessel went down with all hands. Many a Christian suffers shipwreck through un-heeding conceit or neglect of his infallible chart. May the

Holy Spirit incline us to study diligently our Divine chart, and sail closely by it!

6. *The Bible Reveals Things to Come.*

It contains not only the history of the past, of God's dealings with nations, but it also contains much unfulfilled prophecy. Revelation is a book devoted to things that "must shortly come to pass." Prophecy has been called unacted history, and history is but fulfilled prophecy. It is a mistake to suppose that God's hand in history has been limited to those nations mentioned in the Bible. Could we have the story of God in history, it would be seen that His providence has been in and over all the great and small events of all nations. Daniel in his great prophecy has given a rapid and graphic sketch of the course of history from the golden-headed Babylonian Empire down to the end of time, when the "Son of man shall come with the clouds of heaven" . . . when there "shall be given Him dominion and glory, and a kingdom, that all nations and languages should serve Him." When He comes, "His dominion will be an everlasting dominion which shall not pass away, and His kingdom one which shall not be destroyed" (Dan. 2:44; 7:13-27). Meantime God among nations will be overturning, and "overturning, and overturning until He comes whose right it is" (Ezek. 21:27). The Book of Revelation is a detailed exposition of the second and seventh chapters of Daniel, and the two books should be read together.

Emperors and kings and cabinets are rapidly bringing to pass things that God has marked out in prophecy ages ago. But they know not what they do. There are "signs in the heavens," and on the earth there is "distress of nations with perplexity; and the sea and the waves roaring; men's hearts failing them for fear, and for looking after those things which are coming on the earth; for the powers of the heavens shall be shaken. And then shall they see the Son of man coming in a cloud, with power and great glory" (Luke 21:25-27).

Of the day and hour when the flaming heavens shall reveal the "appearing and kingdom" of our Lord Jesus Christ (2 Tim. 4:1), no man knoweth; but we are bidden to wait and be ready, lest we be surprised by the great and notable day of the Lord. To this end the Scriptures are also written, that the loving student of them may live in advance of history, and be overtaken by no untoward event. If His prophetic Word dwell richly in our hearts and minds, there will be no great surprise for us as time goes on. We shall discern through the prophetic telescope, dimly, it may be, the approaches of those things out of which history is made. Should it be our blessed lot to be "alive, and remain unto the coming of the Lord" (1 Thess. 4:15) we shall see the sign of Him in the heavens (Matt. 24:30) before the startled and amazed world, lying in sin and mocking unbelief (2 Pet. 3:3; Luke 18:8), are overwhelmed in that "everlasting destruction from the presence of the Lord and from the glory of His power" (2 Thess. 1:7-9). We know that there is a growing disposition on the part of many excellent Christians to make light (they know not what they do) of all prophetic study; but our risen Lord, in His last revelation to John concerning things to come, caused him to write at the very outset: "Blessed is he that readeth and they that hear the words of this prophecy; and keep those things which are written therein; for the time is at hand;" and at the close of the book to add: "These sayings are faithful and true; and the Lord God of the holy prophets sent His angel to show unto His servants the things which must shortly be done. Behold I come quickly; *blessed is he that keepeth the sayings of the prophecy of this book*" (Rev. 22:6, 7).

May the Spirit of God give us a mind to study His Word reverently and believingly, with a prepared heart, as did Ezra (7:10), in the light and under the guidance of the Holy Spirit. Then will He "show us things to come" (John 16:13).

CHAPTER XI

MODERN SPIRITUALISM
BRIEFLY TESTED BY SCRIPTURE*

BY ALGERNON J. POLLOCK,
WESTON-SUPER-MARE, ENGLAND

I. ORIGIN AND GROWTH

Modern Spiritualism claims as its birthday March 31, 1848, and the place of its birth Hydesville, Wayne County, New York, U. S. A.; but it is in reality almost as old as the world's history, and will go on to its close.

That the number of adherents of Modern Spiritualism is amazingly large is borne out by Dr. F. Maack, of Hamburg, writing so recently as 1910. As an antagonist of Spiritualism, he is not likely to overstate the numbers. In Berlin alone, he says, there are probably 10,000 Spiritualists, among them exalted and court personages; 400 mediums, and from fifteen to twenty societies. In North America there are said to be 16,000,000 adherents; while in the whole world it was computed that in 1894 there were 60,000,000 Modern Spiritualists, with 200 journals exclusively devoted to the propaganda of this awful system. The number has grown considerably since. Add to these the demonized races of the heathen world; the millions of China, Japan and India; the countless tribes of Africa; the savage hordes of the Sudan; the cannibal inhabitants of the South Sea Islands; and you complete roughly the picture of Spiritualism covering the earth with darkness—Ancient Spiritualism in the East, and Modern Spiritualism in the West, bringing in its train wickedness of every hideous kind.

*Condensed for the Fundamentals.

II. ATTRACTIONS OF SPIRITUALISM

Spiritualism, like all systems of error, works to a large extent underground. It does not present itself in its true colors to the uninitiated. Once a dupe is caught in its toils he is drawn farther and farther away from God.

Some are attracted to it through sheer curiosity. The love of the unknown allures them. Some, believing it to be mere trickery, think they can detect the fraud, and so get entangled in the *real* thing. That there is trickery in it is certain; but with full allowance for all this, there are effects produced which can be attributed only to the influence of personating demons. Others again are drawn into it by the deep desire to fill the aching void made by the death of a loved one. When David, after agonizing prayer for the life of Bathsheba's child, heard of his death, he asked, *"Can I bring him back again? I shall go to him, BUT HE SHALL NOT RETURN TO ME"* (2 Sam. 12:23). David evidently knew nothing of intercourse with the spirits of the departed.

III. REFUSES TEST OF SCRIPTURE

A well-known spiritualistic author, writing under the *nom de plume*, *"Oxford, M. A.,"* says: "So long as you reply to our arguments with a *text*, we cannot teach you. Any one who can so reply is beyond reach of reasonable teaching" ("Spirit Teachings," p. 198).

The author of *"Outlines of Spiritualism for the Young,"* says: "To assert that it [the Bible] is a holy and Divine book, that God inspired the writers to make known His Divine will, is a gross outrage on, and misleading to, the public. . . . The truth is, the Old Testament is neither more nor less than Jewish history. . . . The New Testament is made up of traditions and theological speculations by unknown persons. A book so full of errors . . . requires to be read with care" (*"Outlines,"* pp. 13, 14).

Refusal of the Bible could not be more explicit.

IV. MODERN SPIRITUALISM FORETOLD

The rise and progress of Modern Spiritualism is clearly indicated in Holy Scripture: "Now the Spirit speaketh expressly, that in the latter times some shall depart from the faith, giving heed to seducing spirits and doctrines of devils; speaking lies in hypocrisy; having their conscience seared with a hot iron; forbidding to marry, and commanding to abstain from meats" (1 Tim. 4:1-3). The gravity of the warning is emphasized by the way it is introduced, *"Now the Spirit speaketh expressly."*

"SEDUCING SPIRITS"

So crafty is the enemy that the spirits often advise the uninitiated to pray and to read the Bible. While the *immediate* purpose of such advice is to gain the victim's confidence, the *ultimate* object is to undermine faith in the Scriptures. The spirits giving such advice are well described as *"seducing spirits."*

A lady, a Christian worker, was persuaded to attend a Spiritualistic meeting. She was advised to read the Bible and pray. This led her to believe that the spirit of a Christian was speaking to her. When the "seducing spirits" had thus gained her confidence, they led her to question certain parts of the Bible. The result was that she became a complete infidel, going absolutely to the bad, not only spiritually but morally. "By their fruits ye shall know them."

In the temptation in the wilderness we see how Satan quoted Scripture, leaving out an essential part for his evil purpose; and we see how a *text* of Scripture sufficed for his defeat. Scripture clearly indicates deceitfulness as his chief characteristic. (2 Cor. 2:11; 2 Cor. 11:14, 15.)

V. THE BIBLE OPPOSED TO SPIRITUALISM

Before quoting a few texts, so dreaded by *"Oxford, M. A."* and his *confrères*, it would be well to clear the ground by

stating that Spiritualists affirm their belief in God as Creator
and Sustainer; deny that the Lord Jesus was and is Divine;
deny the existence of the devil, demons and angels. They
affirm their belief in the existence of an impersonal God, and
of human beings, either incarnate—that is, in their human
bodies in this world; or discarnate—that is, disembodied in
the spirit-world, as they term it. The system is simplicity
itself. If there be no devil, Spiritualism cannot be Satanic.
If there be no demons, there can be no truth in the charge
that the spirits that communicate with the living, claimed by
them to be the spirits of departed friends, are in reality personating demons, or "seducing spirits." Thus the way is
cleared for Modern Spiritualism.

Under the heading of *"Biblical Spiritualism,"* if you please,
the author of "Outlines" quotes a number of passages of
Scripture in the vain endeavor to prove that the Bible is not
opposed to Spiritualism. In every passage he quotes except
one (the well-known case of the witch of Endor), we are
given instances of *angelic* visitation. Mark well: in no instance
does he quote the plain condemnations of Spiritualism the
Bible contains. Is this honest? But since he appeals to the
Bible, to the Bible we are well content to turn.

1. OLD TESTAMENT CONDEMNATION

"And the soul that turneth after such as have familiar
spirits, and after wizards, to go a whoring after them, I . . .
will cut him off from among his people" (Lev. 20:6; also
19:31).

"A man also, or woman that hath a familiar spirit, or
that is a wizard, shall surely be put to death; they shall stone
them with stones" (Lev. 20:27).

"There shall not be found among you any one . . .
that useth divination, or an observer of times, or an enchanter,
or a witch, or a charmer, or a consulter with familiar spirits,
or a wizard, or a necromancer" (Deut. 18:10, 11).

"They shall no more offer their sacrifices unto devils" (Lev. 17:7; Deut. 32:17; Psa. 106:37).

"And when they shall say unto you, Seek unto them that have familiar spirits, and unto wizards that peep and that mutter; should not a people seek unto their God? for the living to the dead? [See R. V.] To the law and the testimony: if they speak not according to this word, it is because there is no light in them" (Isa. 8:19, 20).

From the foregoing we see in the Old Testament, that

1. *Spiritualism is sternly forbidden by God.*

2. *It is defiling.*

3. *Its followers GOD would destroy.*

4. *Its mediums, THE PEOPLE were commanded to stone to death.*

5. *It is no new thing. Satan and his myriads of demons have been busy at their work of deception ever since the Fall.*

6. *It is not an advance on Christianity, as some affirm, but a backward movement to the worst features of heathenism.*

Isaiah 8:19, 20 is especially conclusive; plainly showing that it is wrong for the living to seek the dead, rather than God Himself. Spiritualism is the setting aside of God Himself, hence of morality, uprightness, and every true principle.

2. NEW TESTAMENT CONDEMNATION

"Then was Jesus led up of the Spirit in the wilderness to be tempted of the devil" (Matt. 4:1). This proves that there is a personal devil. Indeed, only one person is called in Scripture *the devil,* the Greek word meaning *the accuser.* Demon is really the correct description of the myriad fallen spirits who own Satan as their prince. (Matt. 12:24.)

"They brought unto Him all sick people that were taken with divers diseases and torments, and those which were possessed [Greek: daimonizomai—demonized or demon-possessed] with devils, and those which were lunatic, and those that had the palsy; and He healed them" (Matt. 4:24).

This passage is most important, as from it and other Scriptures it is plain that demon-possession is distinct from disease, though the two are often, and naturally, present together; for disease is the product of sin. It has been contended that demon-possession and lunacy are the same, but this Scripture shatters that contention, as it differentiates between them:

"There met Him two possessed with devils . . . and, behold, they cried out, saying, . . . Art Thou come hither to torment us before the time? . . . So the devils besought Him, saying, If Thou cast us out, suffer us to go away into the herd of swine. And He said unto them, Go. And when they were come out, they went into the herd of swine; and, behold, the whole herd of swine ran violently down into a steep place into the sea, and perished in the waters" (Matt. 8:28-32).

"And there was in their synagogue a man with an *unclean* spirit; and he cried out, saying, Let us alone; what have we to do with Thee, Thou Jesus of Nazareth? Art Thou come to destroy us? I know Thee who Thou art, the Holy One of God" (Mark 1:23, 24).

These passages prove that demons know and recognize the authority of the Lord Jesus as the Son of God; that they are aware of their future, and dread it.

"Jesus . . . rebuked the *foul* spirit, saying unto him, Thou dumb and deaf spirit, I charge thee, come out of him, and enter no more into him. And the spirit cried, and rent him sore, and came out of him" (Mark 9:25, 26; Rev. 18:2).

From these Scriptures and the preceding one (Mark 1:23, 24) we learn the unclean character of these seducing spirits. Further, that they are strong, sullen and vicious, and can hurt their victims physically to a dangerous degree.

The case is cited of a minister who took up automatic writing. At first the communications were pure, and expressed in beautiful language. After a time they became mixed with obscene language. Then he heard voices, and things so preyed upon his mind that he became insane, and died in three months, raving mad.

The following well-known passage from Spiritualistic literature is very significant: *"They come, THE DOOR ONCE OPEN, in crowds, in riotous invasion. They run, they leap, they fly, they gesticulate, they sing, they whoop, and they curse. . . . Mind, body, soul, memory and imagination—nay the very heart—are polluted by the ghostly canaille."*

May God preserve the writer and reader from ever opening the door to such diabolical wickedness; or if already opened, may he or she seek the power of Him, who is stronger than the strong man armed, even of the Lord Jesus Christ.

"Mary called Magdalene, out of whom went *seven* devils" (Luke 8:2).

"And Jesus asked him saying, What is thy name? And he said, Legion, because many devils were entered into him" (Luke 8:30).

Here is evidence that more than one demon may take possession of the human body. Mediums admit that at times several spirits control them, and hence the incoherency of the messages.

"A certain damsel possessed with a spirit of divination met us . . . the same followed Paul and us, and cried, saying, These men are the servants of the most high God, which show unto us the way of salvation. . . . But Paul being grieved, turned and said to the spirit, I command thee in the name of the Lord Jesus to come out of her. And he came out the same hour" (Acts 16:16-18).

"Then certain of the vagabond Jews, exorcists, took upon them to call over them which had evil spirits the name of the Lord Jesus, saying, We adjure you by Jesus, whom Paul preacheth. And there were seven sons of one Sceva, a Jew, and chief of the priests, which did so. And the evil spirit answered and said, Jesus I know and Paul I know; but who are ye? And the man, in whom the evil spirit was, leaped on them, and overcame them, and prevailed against them, so that they fled out of the house naked and wounded" (Acts 19:13-16).

The contrast between these passages is deeply instructive. The damsel, possessed by the evil spirit, advertises Paul and his companions as "servants of the most high God, which show unto us the way of salvation." Her conduct, very like that of modern mediums, who advise the reading of the Bible and prayer, did not deceive the Apostle. Observe how the Apostle uses the name of One whom he knew; whereas the exorcists, mere imitators, said, "We adjure thee by Jesus whom Paul preacheth," that is, One of whom *they* knew nothing for themselves. The consequences were disastrous; for instead of resisting the devil, and the devil fleeing, as in Paul's case of exorcism, the demon urged his victim to deeds of violence.

"The things which the Gentiles [heathen] sacrifice, they sacrifice to devils, and not to God" (1 Cor. 10:20, 21).

This passage proves that behind heathendom, idol worship, sun worship, etc., there is demon power; that heathendom with its frightfully wicked, base, voluptuous customs, is a vast system of Spiritualism. Missionaries in India and heathen lands are able to confirm what I allude to here.

"And the rest of the men which were not killed by these plagues, yet repented not of the works of their hands, that they should not worship devils, and idols of gold, and silver, and brass, and stone and of wood. . . . neither repented they of their murders, nor of their sorceries, nor of their fornication, nor of their thefts" (Rev. 9:20, 21).

"They are the spirits of devils, working miracles" (Rev. 16:14).

Rev. 9:20, 21 clearly identifies the worship of devils with

that of idols of gold, etc., and shows how violence and immorality are its accompaniments; while Rev. 16: 14 adds the power of working miracles.

The reader now has before him most ample testimony from Scripture as to the source of Spiritualism, its wickedness and powers, and of the utter condemnation meted out to it by God.

3. THE ONE POSSIBLE EXCEPTION

There is possibly one solitary instance in Scripture in which God permitted the spirit of one departed to revisit the earth for a specific purpose. (See 1 Sam. 28: 3-25.) We have here either a piece of skilful acting on the part of the witch of Endor; or, what seems more natural, there was a real appearance of Samuel at the behest, not of the witch, but of God Almighty Himself. King Saul, after a long course of evil, was in sore straits. In his dilemma he enquired of the Lord, but He did not answer him, "neither by dreams, nor by Urim nor by prophets." Disguised, Saul asked the witch to bring up Samuel. God then intervened. He restrained the personating demon from appearing at the medium's behest, and, judging from the matter-of-fact narration, allowed the spirit of Samuel to appear. The medium was evidently astonished beyond measure. "When the woman saw Samuel, she cried with a loud voice," charging Saul with deception.

This is the only case on record in the Scriptures where, apparently, the spirit of one departed has been permitted to revisit the earth for a specific purpose, whereas Spiritualists claim that there is continual intercourse between living persons and departed spirits. And note, Samuel did not come at the call of the medium of Endor, and God will not allow the spirits of the departed to be at the beck and call of any medium, who may be of questionable character. 1 Chron. 10: 13, 14 specifically tells us that Saul died for his transgressions, including his invoking the demon's aid: "So Saul died for his transgressions, . . . *and also for asking counsel of one that had a familiar spirit, to enquire of it;* and enquired not of the Lord."

VI. CONCEPTION OF CHRIST

We have seen how the blessed Saviour went about "healing all that were oppressed of the devil," showing what He thought of Spiritualism. Yet, in spite of such plain testimony, Dr. Wisse, a noted Spiritualist, said: "All testimony received from advanced spirits only shows that Christ was a *medium* or reformer in Judea; that He is now an advanced spirit in the sixth sphere; but that *He* never claimed to be God and does not at present."

The late Gerald Massey, poet, and Spiritualist, wrote: "I do not find that Christ claimed for Himself more than He held out as possible for others. When He identified Himself with the Father, it was in the oneness of *mediumship.* He was the great *Medium* or *Mediator.*"*

Could profanity go farther? The Lord Jesus again and again claimed for Himself that which He could share with none other. *"For there is one God, and ONE MEDIATOR between God and man, the Man Christ Jesus; who gave Himself a ransom for all, to be testified in due time"* (1 Tim. 2:5, 6), shatters the whole of his contention. The daring of confounding *medium* with *Mediator* is awful. A blow against redemption is thus aimed. It is not scholarship or philosophy, but profanity and knavery. We may well ask, Why cannot Spiritualism leave Christ's name alone? They seem impelled to endeavor to get His support for their system. It only proves most conclusively that Spiritualists feel the reality of Christianity and of Christ, and are forced to these attentions. They are not continually fighting against Mohammedanism and Brahminism and the like.

*Another noted Spiritualist, Dr. J. M. Peebles, wrote, "The Apostle (Paul) with a singular clearness of perception pronounced the Nazarene a Mediator, i. e., a Medium, between God and man."

VII. THE DENIALS OF MODERN SPIRITUALISM

Modern Spiritualism denies—
1. The inspiration of the Bible.
2. The fall of man.
3. The Deity of the Lord Jesus.
4. The atoning value of His death.
5. The existence of a personal devil.*
6. The existence of demons.
7. The existence of angels.
8. The existence of heaven.
9. The existence of hell.*

Enough has been written to prove the above statements, but it is as well to place it in clear tabulated form, so that the reader may see that Spiritualism is the absolute negation of Christianity. In 1866 at a Spiritualistic conference held at Providence, Rhode Island, U. S. A., at which eighteen states and territories were represented, the following daring resolutions were passed:
1. To abandon all Christian ordinances and worship.
2. To discontinue all Sunday Schools.
3. To denounce sexual tyranny.
4. To affirm that animal food should not be used.

We have so far had ample Biblical proof that 1 Tim. 4: 1-3 applies to Spiritualism in its prediction that in the latter times some would depart from the faith and would pay heed to seducing spirits and doctrines of devils. To this Nos. 3 and 4 resolutions carry us on to "forbidding to marry" and "commanding to abstain from meats."

And yet with all this negation of Christianity Spiritualists continue in many cases to be members and ministers of churches, calling themselves Christian Spiritualists. For instance, the late Rev. H. R. Haweis, M. A., Incumbent of St. James', Marylebone, a special preacher in Westminster

---

"All spirit people of wisdom, knowledge and love say there is no burning hell . . . no fearful devil."—"Outlines,"* p. 15.

Abbey, and Royal Institution Lecturer, said in 1900 in an address:

"Spiritualism fitted very nicely on to Christianity; it seemed to be a legitimate development, not a contradiction, not an antagonist. . . . Spiritualism had rehabilitated the Bible. . . . They [spiritualistic phenomena] occur every day in London as well as in the Acts of the Apostles."

VIII. "THREE BLACK I'S" OF SPIRITUALISM.

The Rev. Frank Swainson in his addresses on Spiritualism speaks of its "three black I's—Infidelity, Insanity and Immorality."

1. INFIDELITY

In a Spiritualistic book, *"Whatever Is, Is Right,"* circulating among a certain section of advanced Spiritualists, we read the following:

"What is evil? Evil does not exist, evil is good."

"What is a lie? A lie is the truth intrinsically; it holds a lawful place in creation; it is a necessity."

"What is vice? Vice and virtue, too, are beautiful in the eyes of the soul."

"What is virtue? Virtue is good and sin is good. The woman who came to the well of Sychar was just as pure in spirit before she met Christ, even though she was a harlot, as she was afterwards when she went to live a different life. There's no difference between Herod the murderer of the babies in Bethlehem, and Christ the Saviour of men."

"What is murder? Murder is good. Murder is a perfectly natural act."

"What are evil spirits? There are no evil spirits. There is no devil and no Christ. Christ and the devil are both alike."

> " 'For not a path on earth is trod
> That does not lead the soul to God.'

"No matter how bad that path may be, whether it be the

path of the liar, the murderer; it is the path of Divine Ordination and Divine Destiny."

2. INSANITY

Dr. Forbes Winslow, Oxford Lecturer on Mental Diseases, of Charing Cross Hospital, said the prevalence of madness *owing to Spiritualism* was on the increase. The late Reader Harris, K. C., wrote: "The most remarkable case of mediumship I have met with was that of a lady, who commenced with a little seemingly innocent table-turning at a children's party, and finished up by death in a madhouse."

Sir William Crookes, claimed by the Spiritualists as a strong sympathizer, wrote: "After witnessing the painful state of nervous and bodily prostration in which many of the experiments have left the medium fainting, pale, breathless, I cannot doubt but that the violence of psychic forces means a corresponding drain on the vital forces."

Is this the high and holy substitute for Christianity? Is this the glorious effect of truth?

3. IMMORALITY

Mr. T. L. Harris, once a Spiritualistic medium, testifies that the marriage vow imposes no obligation on the Spiritualistic husband. They have been known to abandon their own wives, and prefer the company of those of whom the spirits told them that they had a closer spiritual affinity to them. Mrs. Woodhull, elected three years in succession as president of the Spiritist Societies in America, often lectured in favor of free love; and advocated the abolition of marriage ("forbidding to marry"), stigmatizing virtue and responsibility as the two thieves on the cross. She said: "It was the sublime mission of Spiritism to deliver humanity from the thraldom of matrimony, and to establish sexual emancipation." Rev. F. Swainson, writing of a lady of his acquaintance, says: "Up to the time that her husband came into contact with

Spiritism he was all that could be desired. When he took to Spiritism he came in touch with a certain Spiritist woman, who claimed affinity. The result was this, that the man cruelly deserted his wife, and left her to die, as she is dying today, of a broken heart. That man today is passing as a leading official of a Spiritist circle in England."

The charge against the "three black I's" of Modern Spiritualism is well proved.

IX. WHAT SPIRITUALISM OFFERS

I shall now describe what Spiritualism offers in place of the Bible as our guide, Christ as our Saviour, heaven as our eternal home. According to the author of *"Outlines,"* man is made up of a soul, a spiritual body, and a physical body.

"There is something more than the nerves which we cannot see, because it is as fine in its nature as the perfume of flowers. This fine something is called 'nerve-aura' . . . All above what is required for daily use is thrown off like perfume from flowers. . . .   Our spiritual bodies are formed of this fine nerve-aura, which is *spiritualized matter.* . . . When our spiritual friends and guardians visit us, they . . . look . . . at our spiritual bodies, and by their purity or otherwise, they can see at a glance what kind of lives we live. . . . People who indulge in evil habits, such as opium or tobacco smoking, and laudanum and intoxicating drink, carry the appetite with them at death; it is because some of the narcotic and alcohol from these things help to compose the spiritual body, that they crave or hunger for their kind. So that these spirit people seek those in the body who still indulge in these bad habits, and get their craving satisfied through other people" (*"Outlines,"* pp. 30-32).

So we read on: "I have explained to you how the spirit-body is formed—that it is the *spiritualized* or *refined* particles of our physical body: so that you will understand me when I tell you that the spirit world is made up of refined or *spir-*

itualized particles given off by the earth. Every blade of grass, every tiny flower, shrub and tree, insect and animal, by their lives cause matter to become refined and spiritualized, which then ascends high above the clouds, and there spreads out in a broad belt, and surrounds the earth, like the rings of Saturn surround that planet. There are a great number of these rings or zones, one beyond the other, which may be called spirit worlds" (*"Outlines,"* p. 33).

Then we are told in *"Outlines"* that in the spirit-world souls may do wrong there, as they do here. When they do, they reap what they sow, and are punished, and thus they are gradually purified and blessed—they become their own saviours, though why they should need to be saved seems a mystery.

We read also that after death, if the spiritual life is kind, and gentle and good, the grosser elements of the spiritual body are eliminated, leaving the body more refined and spiritual; so that it can rise into a higher zone, which, in its turn, is composed of the more refined and spiritualized elements eliminated from this higher zone, and the third zone is composed of the still more refined and spiritualized elements from the second, and so on. And yet people who are too "clever" to believe the Bible are so foolish as to believe such bombastic nonsense put forward without one atom of proof.

X. SHIRKS AWFUL PROBLEMS

In *"Outlines,"* while there is a stout refusal of the doctrine of total depravity, and the fall of man is denied,* there is no attempt whatever to adequately explain the awful sorrow and suffering in this world, and the still more awful sorrow of death. We are told God is too good to allow man's fall or the existence of what is malevolent, like Satan and his demons; but the present awful state of things, which God has

---

"Thus, by his [man's] intellectual faculties, moral powers, and spiritual nature, he is 'God manifest in the flesh.' "—"Outlines."*

allowed for His own wise and inscrutable purpose, the author of *"Outlines"* shirks and must shirk. He throws away the only lamp of truth—the Word of God. Can we wonder that he walks in darkness, and that his wisdom is folly indeed, fraught with awful consequences?

We have now had ample proof from Scripture that Spiritualism is in reality demonism. Nay, more; in some way or other every form of evil has its origin, I believe, in this cult. Heathendom in its nameless horrors is Spiritualism. All false religions bear features of their common parent. They may vary as to details, and contradict each other (for Satan must have many baits for many minds), but the essence of all evil teaching is Satanic, and therefore Spiritualism in its essence.

XI. THE POWER OF CHRIST'S NAME

While it is well that we should be aware of the awful power of Satan, the believer has no need to be *personally* afraid, if only he keeps near to the Lord and cleaves to His Word. "Resist the devil, and he will flee from you" (James 4:7). "Be sober, be vigilant; because your adversary the devil, as a roaring lion, walketh about, seeking whom he may devour; whom resist, steadfast in the faith" (1 Pet. 5:8, 9). "For we wrestle not against flesh and blood, but against principalities, against powers, against the rulers of the darkness of this world, against spiritual wickedness in high places. Wherefore take unto you the whole armor of God, that ye may be able to withstand in the evil day, and having done all, to stand" (Eph. 6:10-13). "Ye are of God, little children, and have overcome them [that is, *spirits* that confess not that Jesus Christ is come in the flesh]; because greater is He that is in you [that is, the Holy Ghost], than he that is in the world [that is, the devil]" (1 John 4:4).

We may walk serenely through this evil world, conscious of the Lord's protecting hand, just as Elisha was calm, conscious that he was protected by the mountain being full of horses and chariots of fire. With all the glittering rewards of divination within the reach of the covetous Balaam, if only he would curse God's people, he was obliged to cry out, *"Surely there is no enchantment against Jacob, neither is there any divination against Israel"* (Num. 23:23).

A friend has just given me an authentic instance of the power of Christ's name. A Spiritualist in Bradford invited a Christian neighbor to one of their meetings. The Christian, wearied by her neighbor's importunity, made a compact with her, that if she attended once she would never again be invited. They went to the meeting. After a little while the medium, who had no previous knowledge of her, declared there was a Christian present, and until that Christian left the room they could not proceed. The Christian kept her seat. After a few minutes the medium again said there was a Christian present and insisted that the person should leave the meeting. The Christian lady thereupon retired. When her neighbor returned home, she informed her that the meeting proceeded after she left without any further difficulty. Such is the power of Christ's name.

A SCRIPTURAL TEST

Amidst all the abounding evil, the uninstructed believer might well be bewildered. But Scripture furnishes a simple but thorough test of every system of teaching. It will be seen that the Person of Christ is the test. "Every spirit that CONFESSETH NOT that Jesus Christ is come in the flesh, is not of God; and this is that spirit of antichrist" (1 John 4:3). "He is antichrist, that denieth the Father and the Son" (1 John 2:22). "Wherefore I give you to understand, that no man speaking by the Spirit of God calleth Jesus accursed: and that no man can say that Jesus is the Lord, but by the Holy Ghost" (1 Cor. 12:3).

PUBLISHERS' NOTICE

Particular attention is hereby called to the following points:

1. All English-speaking Protestant pastors, evangelists, missionaries, theological professors, theological students, Y. M. C. A. secretaries, Y. W. C. A. secretaries, Sunday School superintendents, religious lay workers, and editors of religious publications throughout the earth, who so desire, are entitled to a free copy of each volume of "THE FUNDAMENTALS." Any person, belonging to one of these classes, who has not received the earlier volumes, may obtain them upon application to the undersigned. *State plainly* which volumes are wanted, and *state also the line of Christian work engaged in* and the denominational affiliation. After an order is sent in, allow at least two weeks (and more if from a distance) for filling it.

2. Changes of address should be promptly reported. *Write plainly* both the old and the new addresses *in full.*

3. In case any person receives two or more copies of any one volume, *kindly notify us.* These books are too valuable and the demand for them too great to permit waste through duplication. However, where extra copies have been received, they need not be returned, but may be loaned or otherwise placed in circulation.

4. To meet the demand on the part of the laity each volume is being furnished postpaid at a cost of fifteen cents per copy, eight copies for one dollar, or one hundred copies for ten dollars. (In Great Britain, 8d; 4s 2d; and £2 1s 1d, respectively.) These prices will be applied to the cost of issuing future volumes.

5. Do not send currency or personal checks. *Remit by post office money order, or by bank draft* on Chicago, New York, or London, making the same payable to the Testimony Publishing Company.

6. Foreign correspondents should be careful to prepay card and letter postage *in full.* Otherwise we are compelled to pay *double* the amount of the deficiency.

7. Please bear in mind that we publish nothing except "THE FUNDA- MENTALS," and do not issue any catalogue.

In conclusion, we would emphasize once more the *great importance* of writing plainly and briefly, and always giving *full address*—street (or rural route) number, post office, state, and (if outside of the United States) country.

Much time and delay will be saved by carefully reading and comply- ing with the foregoing directions.

TESTIMONY PUBLISHING COMPANY,

808 La Salle Avenue,

Chicago, Illinois, U. S. A.

The Fundamentals

A Testimony to the Truth

Volume XI

Compliments of
Two Christian Laymen

TESTIMONY PUBLISHING COMPANY
(Not Inc.)
808 North La Salle Street
Chicago, Ill., U. S. A.

"To the Law and to the Testimony"
Isaiah 8:20

FOREWORD

There has been much unavoidable delay in connection with the issue of this volume of "THE FUNDAMENTALS," Volume XI. This was occasioned by the very serious illness of the former Executive Secretary of "THE FUNDAMENTALS" Committee. This illness lasted for many months, only terminating in his death. He bore up very bravely and it was not thought wise to put the work in other hands lest he should be discouraged, feeling that there was no hope. Further delay was occasioned by the necessity of going over his manuscripts and papers and selecting such as had already been passed upon by the Committee for Volume XI and in passing upon other manuscripts in his possession.

We have been greatly cheered by the letters that have come to us from all parts of the world, from ministers, missionaries, editors, college presidents, Sunday School superintendents and others, speaking of the great personal blessing which they have received from "THE FUNDAMENTALS," and of the good accomplished by the various volumes in the lives of others to whom they have been passed on.

The present volume will go to about one hundred thousand English-speaking Protestant pastors, evangelists, missionaries, theological professors, theological students, Y. M. C. A. secretaries, Y. W. C. A. secretaries, Sunday School superintendents, religious editors, and lay workers throughout the earth. May we ask the prayers of every reader that it may be abundantly blessed, as its predecessors have been, unto the strengthening of the faith of Christians, unto the defense of the truth against the various forms of error so prevalent at the present day, and unto the conversion of a multitude of the unsaved.

There is a large circle of prayer formed of men and women in all parts of the earth who know God and who are upholding before Him the work of "THE FUNDAMENTALS" and of the Committee to which the Two Christian Laymen have entrusted the editing and publishing of these volumes. We earnestly request other men and women who know God to join this circle of prayer in order that in answer to believing and united prayer the truth may have new power and that a world-wide revival of religion may be begun and grow.

It was the original plan of the Two Laymen who gave the money for this work that there should be twelve volumes of "THE FUNDAMENTALS" issued: so there remains but one volume to be issued. Prayer is desired that wisdom may be given to the Committee in the selection of the material for the final volume. A wide desire is manifested that "THE FUNDAMENTALS" be continued in some way after the issue of the twelve volumes. Probably essentially the same work will be continued in some form, but that form has not yet been decided upon.

All editorial correspondence should be addressed to the Executive Secretary of The Fundamentals, 1945 La France Avenue, South Pasadena, California. There is no desire, however, for the submission of manuscripts by anybody unless specific request for such manuscript is made. We can use but few more manuscripts, and some are already in hand.

All business correspondence should be addressed to the Testimony Publishing Company, 808 North La Salle Street, Chicago, Illinois, U. S. A.

(See Publishers' Notice, Page 127.)

CONTENTS

THE FUNDAMENTALS

VOLUME XI

CHAPTER I

THE BIBLICAL CONCEPTION OF SIN

BY REV. THOMAS WHITELAW, M. A., D. D.,
KILMARNOCK, AYRSHIRE, SCOTLAND

Holy Scripture undertakes no demonstration of the reality of sin. In all its statements concerning sin, sin is presupposed as a fact which can neither be controverted nor denied, neither challenged nor obscured. It is true that some reasoners, through false philosophy and materialistic science, refuse to admit the existence of sin, but their endeavors to explain it away by their respective theories is sufficient proof that sin is no figment of the imagination but a solid reality. Others who are not thinkers may sink so far beneath the power of sin as to lose all sense of its actuality, their moral and spiritual natures becoming so hardened and fossilized as to be "past feeling," in which case conviction of sin is no more possible, or at least so deteriorated and unimpressible that only a tremendous upheaval within their souls, occasioned perhaps by severe affliction, but brought about by the inward operation of the Spirit of God, will break up the hard crust of moral numbness and religious torpor in which their spirits are encased. A third class of persons, by simply declining to think about sin, may come in course of time to conclude that whether sin be a reality or not, it does not stand in any relation to them and does not concern them—in which case once more they are merely deceiving themselves. The truth is that it is extremely doubtful whether any intelligent person whose moral intuitions have not been completely destroyed and whose mental perceptions have not been largely blunted by indulgence in wickedness, can successfully persuade himself, at least permanently, that sin is a myth, an illusion of the mind, a creature of the imagination, and not a grim reality. Most men know that sin is in themselves a fact of consciousness they cannot deny, and in others a fact of observation they cannot overlook. As Chesterton expresses it, the fact of sin any one may see in the street: the Bible assumes that any man will discover it who looks into his own heart.

Accordingly the Bible devotes its efforts to imparting to mankind reliable knowledge about the nature and universality, the origin and culpability, but also and especially about the removableness of sin; and to set forth these in succession will be the object of the present paper.

I. THE NATURE OF SIN

It scarcely requires stating that modern ideas about sin receive no countenance from Scripture, which never speaks about sin as "good in the making," as "the shadow cast by man's immaturity," as "a necessity determined by heredity and environment," as "a stage in the upward development of a finite being," as a "taint adhering to man's corporeal frame," as a "physical disease," "a mental infirmity," "a constitutional weakness," and least of all "as a figment of the imperfectly enlightened, or theologically perverted, imagination," but always as the free act of an intelligent, moral and responsible being asserting himself against the will of his Maker, the supreme Ruler of the universe. That will the Bible takes for granted every person may learn, either from the law written on his own heart (Rom. 1:15); or from the revelation furnished by God to mankind, first to the Hebrew Church in the Old Testament Scriptures, and afterwards to the Christian Church and through it to the whole world in the New Testament

Gospels and Epistles. Hence, sin is usually described in the Sacred Volume by terms that indicate with perfect clearness its relation to the Divine will or law, and leaves no uncertainty as to its essential character.

In the Old Testament (Ex. 34: 5, 6; Psa. 32: 1, 2) three words are used to supply a full definition of sin. (1) "Transgression" (pesha'h) or a falling away from God and therefore a violation of His commandments; with which exposition John agrees when he says that "sin is a transgression of the law" (1 John 3:4), and Paul when he writes (Rom. 4:15), "Where no law is, there is no transgression." (2) "Sin" (chataah) or a missing of the mark, a coming short of one's duty, a failure to do what one ought, for which reason the term is fittingly applied to sins of omission; with which again John agrees when he states (1 John 5:17) that "all unrighteousness [or defect in righteousness] is sin," or Paul when he affirms (Rom. 3:23), that "all have sinned and *come short* of the glory of God," and Christ when He charges the Scribes and Pharisees with "leaving undone the things they ought to have done" (Matt. 23:23; Luke 11:42). (3) "Iniquity" ('avōn) or a turning aside from the straight path, curving like an arrow, hence perversity, depravity and inequality—a conception which finds an echo in the words of a later psalmist (78:5) who complained that Israel had "turned aside from Jehovah like a deceitful bow," and in those of the prophet Isaiah (53:6) who confessed that "all we like sheep have gone astray, and have turned every one unto his own way," and in those of his countryman Hosea (7:16) who lamented that Israel "like a deceitful bow had returned, but not to the Most High." The words employed in the New Testament to designate sin are not much, if at all, different in meaning—*hamartia,* a failure, fall, a false step, a blunder; and *anomia,* or lawlessness. Hence the Biblical conception of sin may be fairly summed up in the words of the Westminster Confession: "Sin is any want of conformity unto or transgression of the law of God;" or in those of Melancthon: "Pecatum recte definitur 'ανομία, seu discrepantia a lege Dei, h. e. defectus naturae et actionum pugnans cum lege Dei."

II. THE UNIVERSALITY OF SIN

According to the Bible, sin is not a quality or condition of soul that has revealed itself only in exceptional individuals like notorious offenders—prodigals, profligates, criminals, and vicious persons generally; or in exceptional circumstances, as for instance in the early ages of man's existence on the earth, or among half developed races, or in lands where the arts and sciences are unknown, or in civilized communities where the local environment is prejudicial to morality; but different from this sin is a quality or condition of soul which exists in every child of woman born, and not merely at isolated times but at all times, and at every stage of his career, though not always manifesting itself in the same forms of thought, feeling, word and action in every individual or even in the same individual. It has affected *extensively* the whole race of man in every age from the beginning of the world downward, in every land beneath the sun, in every race into which mankind has been divided, in every situation in which the individual has found himself placed; and *intensively* in every individual in every department and faculty of his nature, from the circumference to the center, or from the center to the circumference of his being.

Scripture utters no uncertain sound on the world-embracing character of moral corruption, saying in the pre-diluvian age of the world that "all flesh had corrupted its way upon the earth" (Gen. 6:12); in David's generation, that all mankind had "gone aside and become filthy," so that "there was none that did good, no, not one" (Psa. 14:3); in Isaiah's time, that "all we like sheep had gone astray and turned every one to his own way" (53:6); in the opening of the Christian era, that "all had sinned and come short of the glory of God" (Rom.

3:23); and generally Solomon's verdict holds goods of every day, "There is no man that sinneth not" (1 Kings 8:46), not even the best of men who have been born again by the Spirit and the incorruptible seed of the Word of God, renewed in their minds and created anew in Christ Jesus. Even of these one writer says: "If we say we have no sin, we deceive ourselves, and the truth is not in us" (1 John 1:8); while another counsels Christians to mortify the deeds of the body, and to put off the old man which is corrupt according to the deceitful lusts of the flesh (Rom. 7:13; Col. 3:5-10); and a third asserts that "in many things we all offend" (James 3:2). How true this is may be learned from the fact that Scripture mentions only one person in whom there was no sin, viz., Jesus of Nazareth, who not only challenged His contemporaries (in particular His enemies) to convict Him of sin, but of whom those who knew Him most intimately (His disciples) testified that He "did no sin, neither was guile found in His mouth" (1 Pet. 2:22; 1 John 3:5). Of this exception of course the explanation was and is that He was "God manifest in the flesh" (1 Tim. 3:16). But besides Him not a single person figures on the page of Holy Writ of whom it is said or indeed could have been said that he was sinless. Neither Enoch nor Noah in the ante-diluvian age; neither Abraham nor Isaac in patriarchal times; neither Moses nor Aaron in the years of the Israelitish wanderings; neither David nor Jonathan in the days of the undivided monarchy; neither Peter nor John, neither Barnabas nor Paul, in the Apostolic age, could have claimed such a distinction; and these were some of the best men that have ever appeared on this planet.

Nor is it merely extensively that the reign of sin over the human family is universal, but intensively as well. It is not a malady which has affected only one part of man's complex constitution: every part thereof has felt its baleful influence. It has darkened his understanding and made him unable, without supernatural illumination, to apprehend and appreciate spiritual things. "The natural man receiveth not the things of the Spirit of God, neither can he know them, because they are spiritually discerned" (1 Cor. 2:14); and again, "The Gentiles walk in the vanity of their minds, having the understanding darkened, being alienated from the life of God through the ignorance that is in them, because of the blindness of their hearts" (Eph. 4:17, 18). It defiles the heart, so that if left to itself, it becomes deceitful above all things and desperately wicked" (Jer. 17:9), so "full of evil" (Eccl. 9:3) and "only evil continually" (Gen. 6:5), that out of it proceed "evil thoughts, murders, adulteries, fornications and such like" (Matt. 15:19), thus proving it to be a veritable cage of unclean birds. It paralyzes the will, if not wholly, at least partially, in every case, so that even regenerated souls have often to complain like Paul that when they would do good evil is present with them, that they are carnal sold under sin, that what they would they do not, and what they hate they do, that in their flesh, i. e., their sin-polluted natures, dwelleth no good thing, and that while to will is present with them, how to perform that which is good they know not (Rom. 7:14-25). It dulls the conscience, that vicegerent of God in the soul, renders it less quick to detect the approach of evil, less prompt to sound a warning against it and sometimes so dead as to be past feeling about it (Eph. 4:19). In short there is not a faculty of the soul that is not injured by it. "Sin when it is finished bringeth forth death" (James 1:5).

III. THE ORIGIN OF SIN

How a pure being, possessed of those intellectual capacities and moral intuitions which were needful to make him justly responsible to Divine law, could and did lapse from his primitive innocence and fall into sin is one of those dark problems which philosophers and theologians have vainly endeavored to solve. No more reliable explanation of sin's entrance into the universe in general and into this world in particular has ever been given than that which is furnished by Scripture.

According to Scripture sin first made its appearance in the angelic race, though nothing more is recorded than the simple fact that the angels sinned (2 Pet. 2:4) and kept not their first estate (or principality) but left their own (or proper) habitation (Jude 6), their motive or reason for doing so being passed over in silence. The obvious deduction is that the sin of these fallen spirits was a free act on their part, dictated by dissatisfaction with the place which had been assigned to them in the hierarchy of heaven and by ambition to secure for themselves a loftier station than that in which they had been placed. Yet this does not answer the question how such dissatisfaction and ambition could arise in beings that must be presumed to have been created sinless. And inasmuch as external influence in the shape of temptation from without, by intelligences other than themselves, is by the supposition excluded, it does not appear that other answer is possible than that in the creation of a finite personality endowed with freedom of will, there is necessarily involved the possibility of making a wrong, in the sense of a sinful, choice.

In the case of man, however, sin's entrance into the world receives a somewhat different explanation from the sacred writers. With one accord they ascribe the sinful actions, words, feelings and thoughts of each individual to his own deliberate free choice, so that he is thereby with perfect justice held responsible for his deviation from the path of moral rectitude; but some of the inspired penmen make it clear that the entrance of sin into this world was effected through the disobedience of the first man who stood and acted as the representative and surety of his whole natural posterity (Rom. 5:12), and that the first man's fall was brought about by temptation from without, by the seductive influence of Satan, the lord of the fallen spirits already mentioned, the prince of the power of the air, the spirit that now worketh in the children of disobedience (Gen. 2:1-6; John 8:44; 2 Cor.

11:3; Eph. 2:2). Whatever view may be taken of the origin and authorship, literary form and documentary source of the Genesis story of the fall (on these points this paper does not enter) its teaching unmistakably is, to this effect: That the first man's lapse from a state of innocence entailed disastrous consequences upon himself and his descendants. Upon himself it wrought immediate disturbance of his whole nature (as already explained), implanting in it the seeds of degeneration, bodily, mental, moral and spiritual, filling him with fear of his Maker, laying upon his conscience a burden of guilt, darkening his perceptions of right and wrong, (as was seen in his unmanly attempt to excuse himself by blaming his wife,) and interrupting the hitherto peaceful relations which had subsisted between himself and the Author of his being. Upon his descendants it opened the floodgates of corruption by which their natures even from birth fell beneath the power of evil, as was soon witnessed in the dark tragedy of fratricide with which the tale of human history began, and in the rapid spread of violence through the pre-diluvian world.

This is what theologians call the doctrine of "Original Sin," by which they mean that the results of Adam's sin, both legal and moral, have been transmitted to Adam's posterity, so that now each individual comes into the world, not like his first father, in a state of moral equilibrium—"born good," as Lord Palmerston of England used to say, or in the words of Pelagius—"born without virtue and without vice, but capable of both" (capaces utriusque rei, non pleni nascimur, et sine virtute ita et sine vitio procreamur), but as the inheritor of a nature that has been disempowered by sin.

That this doctrine, though frequently opposed, has a basis in science and philosophy, as well as in Scripture, is becoming every day more apparent. The scientific law of heredity by which not only physical but mental and moral characteristics are transmitted from parent to child seems to justify the Scripture statement, that "by one man's disobedience sin entered into the world and death by sin, and so death passed upon all men, because that all have sinned" (Rom. 5:12). The following words of the late Principal Fairbairn in his monumental work, "The Philosophy of Religion" (p. 165), go to support the Scriptural position: "Man is to God a whole, a colossal individual, whose days are centuries, whose organs are races, whose being as corporate endures immortal amid the immortality (mortality?) of its constituent units. . . . Hence there must be a Divine judgment of the race as a race, as well as of the individual as an individual." But in any case, whether confirmed or contradicted by modern thought, the doctrine of Scripture shines like a sunbeam, that man is "conceived in sin and shapen in iniquity" (Psa. 51:5), that children are "estranged from the womb and go astray" (Psa. 58:3), that all are by nature "children of wrath" (Eph. 2:3), that "the imagination of man's heart is evil from his youth" (Gen. 8:21), and that everyone requires to have "a new heart" created in him (Psa. 51:10), since "that which is born of the flesh is flesh" (John 3:6), and "no man can bring a clean thing out of an unclean" (Job 15:14). If these passages do not show that the Bible teaches the doctrine of original, or transmitted and inherited, sin, it is difficult to see in what clearer or more emphatic language the doctrine could have been taught. The truth of the doctrine may be challenged by those who repudiate the authority of Scripture; that it is a doctrine of Scripture can hardly be denied.

IV. THE CULPABILITY OF SIN

By this is meant not merely the blameworthiness of sin as an act, inexcusable on the part of its perpetrator, who, being such a personality as he is, endowed with such faculties as are his, placed under a law so good and holy, just and spiritual, simple and easy as that prescribed by God, and having such motives and inducements to keep it as were offered to him—to the first man and also to his posterity,—ought never to have committed it; nor only the heinousness of it, as an act done against light and love bestowed upon the doer of it, and in flagrant opposition to the holiness and majesty of the Lawgiver so that He, the Lawgiver, cannot but regard it with abhorrence as an act abominable in His sight, and repel from His presence as well as extrude from His favor the individual who has become chargeable with it; but over and above these representations of sin which are all Scriptural, by the culpability of sin is intended its exposure to the penalty affixed by Divine justice to transgression.

That a penalty was affixed by God in the first instance when man was created, the Eden narrative in Genesis declares: "The Lord God commanded the man, saying, Of every tree of the garden thou mayest freely eat, but of the tree of the knowledge of good and evil thou shalt not eat of it, for in the day thou eatest thereof thou shalt surely die" (Gen. 2:16); and that this penalty still overhangs the impenitent is not only distinctly implied in our Saviour's language, that apart from His redeeming work the world, i. e., every individual therein, was in danger of perishing and was indeed already condemned (John 3:16-18); but it is expressly declared by John who says, that "the wrath of God abideth" on the unbeliever (3:16), and by Paul who asserts that "the wages of sin is death" (Rom. 6:23).

Without entering on the vexed question as to how far Adam's posterity are legally responsible for Adam's sin, in the sense that apart from their own transgressions they would be adjudged to spiritual and eternal death, it is manifest that Scripture includes in the just punishment of sin more than the death of the body. That this does form part of sin's penalty can hardly be disputed by a careful reader of the Bible; but equally that that penalty includes what theologians call spiritual and eternal death, Scripture unmistakably implies. When it affirms that men are naturally "dead in trespasses and in sins," it obviously purposes to convey the idea that until the soul is quickened by Divine grace it is incapable, not of thinking upon the subject of religion, or reading the Word of God, or of praying, or of exercising faith, but of doing anything spiritually good or religiously saving, of securing their legal justification before a Holy God, or of bringing about their spiritual regeneration. When Scripture further asserts that the unbeliever shall not see life (John 3:36), and that the wicked shall go away into everlasting punishment (Matt. 25:46), it assuredly does not suggest that on entering the other world the unsaved on earth will have another opportunity of accepting salvation (Second Probation), or that extinction of being will be their lot (Annihilation), or that all mankind will eventually attain salvation (Universalism). (On these three modern substitutes for the doctrine of future punishment see next section.) Meanwhile it suffices to observe that the words just quoted seem to teach that the penalty of sin continues beyond the grave. Granting that the words of Christ about the worm that never dies and the fire that shall not be quenched are figurative, they unquestionably signify that the figures stand for some terrible calamity,— on the one hand, loss of happiness, separation from the source of life, exclusion from blessedness, and, on the other, access of misery, suffering, wretchedness, woe, which will be realized by the wicked as the due reward of their impenitent and disobedient lives, and which no revolving years will relieve. The pendulum of the great clock of eternity, as it swings through the ages, will seem to be ever saying: "He that is unjust, let him be unjust still, and he that is filthy, let him be filthy still; he that is righteous, let him be righteous still, and he that is holy, let him be holy still."

V. THE REMOVAL OF SIN

Heinous and culpable as sin is, it is not left in Scripture for the contemplation of readers in all the nakedness of its loathsome character in God's sight, and in all the heaviness of its guilt before the law, without hope of remedy for either; but in a cheering and comforting light it is set forth as an offence that may be forgiven and a defilement that will or may be ultimately cleansed.

As for *the pardonableness* of sin, that indeed constitutes the pith and marrow of the "Good News" for the publication of which the Bible was written. From the first page in Genesis to the last in Revelation an undertone, swelling out as the end approaches into clear and joyous accents of love and mercy, proclaiming that the God of heaven, while Himself holy and just, of purer eyes than to behold iniquity, and unable to clear the guilty, is nevertheless merciful and gracious, long-suffering and slow to wrath, abundant in goodness and truth, keeping mercy for thousands, forgiving iniquity, transgression and sin (Ex. 34:6); announcing that He has made full provision for harmonizing the claims of mercy and justice in His own character by laying help upon One that is mighty, (Psa. 89:19), even His only begotten and well-beloved Son, upon whom He had laid the iniquity of us all (Isa. 53:6), that He might once for all, as the Lamb of God, take away the sins of the world (John 1:29), intimating that the whole work necessary for enabling sinful men to be forgiven has been accomplished by Christ's death and resurrection, and that now God is in Him "reconciling the world unto Himself, not imputing unto men their trespasses" (2 Cor. 5:19), inviting men everywhere to repent and be converted, that their sins may be blotted out (Acts 3:19); telling men that nothing more is required of them in order to be freely and fully justified from all their transgressions than faith in the propitiation of the cross (Rom. 3:25); and declaring that nothing will shut a sinner out from forgiveness except refusal to believe in the great redemption and accept the freely offered forgiveness— though that will, since it is written that he who believeth not on the Son of God "shall not see life" (John 3:36).

The ultimate *removal* of sin from the souls of the believing and pardoned is left by Scripture in no uncertainty. It was foretold in the name given to the Saviour at His birth: "Thou shalt call His name Jesus, because He shall save His people from ["out of," not "in"] their sins." It was implied in the object contemplated by His incarnation: "He was manifested to take away our sins." It is declared to have been the purpose of His death upon the cross: "He gave Himself for us, that He might redeem us from all iniquity and purify unto Himself a peculiar people zealous of good works." It is held up before the Christian as his final destiny "to be conformed to the image of His [God's] Son," to be presented "faultless before the presence of His glory with exceeding joy," and to be a dweller in the heavenly city "into which there can enter nothing that defileth."

Whether sin will be ultimately extirpated if not from the universe, then from the family of man, is a different question, upon which the pronouncement of Scripture is thought by some to be less explicit. Its complete and permanent removal from the race is considered by certain interpreters to be taught in Scripture. That texts can be cited which seem to lend support to the theories of Annihilation, Second Probation, and Universal Salvation need not be denied; but a close examination of the passages in question will show that the support derived from them is exceedingly precarious.

That those who depart this life in impenitence and unbelief will be *annihilated* either at death or after the resurrection is deemed a legitimate deduction from the use of the word death as the punishment of sin. But as "applied to man death does not necessarily mean extinction of being." Bishop Butler long ago drew attention to the fact that various organs of the body might be removed without extinguishing the indwelling spirit, and argued that it was at least probable that the immaterial part of man would not be destroyed though the entire material frame were reduced to dust; and only recently Sir Oliver

Lodge from the presidential chair told the British Association that the best science warranted belief in the continuity of existence after death. Solely on the assumption that mind is merely a function of matter can the dissolution of the body be regarded as the extinction of being. Such an assumption is foreign to Scripture. In the Old Testament David expected to "dwell in the house of the Lord forever;" Asaph at the end of life hoped to be "received into glory;" and Solomon wrote: "Then shall the dust return to the earth as it was, and the spirit shall return to God who gave it." In the New Testament Christ took for granted that Abraham, Isaac and Jacob, though long dead were still living, and in His parable assumed that Dives and Lazarus still existed in the unseen world, although their bodies were in the grave. He also assured the dying robber that when the anguish of the cross was over they would pass together into Paradise, and counselled men generally to be afraid of "him who could destroy both soul and body in hell." Paul, too, had no hesitation in writing that to be "absent from the body" meant to be present with the Lord," nor had Stephen any doubt in praying as he closed his eyes in death: "Lord Jesus, receive my spirit." None of these citations suggest that the soul is simply a function of the body, or that it ceases to be when the body dies.

But now, conceding that the souls of the impenitent are not annihilated at or after death, may it not be that another opportunity of accepting the Gospel will be afforded them, and that in this way sin may be removed even from them. This theory of *a Second Probation,* is commonly thought to derive countenance from two passages of Scripture of doubtful interpretation—1 Pet. 3:19; 4:6. Were the best scholars agreed as to the exact import of the two statements that Christ "by the Spirit went and preached to the spirits in prison" and that "the Gospel was preached also to them that are dead," it might be possible to make these texts the basis of a theological doctrine. But scholars are not agreed; and well informed students of the Bible are aware that both statements can be explained in such a way as to render them useless as a basis for the doctrine of a second probation. In judging concerning this, therefore, dependence must be placed on texts which admit of no dubiety as to their meaning. Such texts are Matt. 12:32: "Whosoever speaketh a word against the Holy Ghost it shall not be forgiven him, neither in this world, nor in that which is to come"—no second chance in this case. Matt. 25:48: "These shall go away into everlasting punishment, but the righteous into life eternal." Not much hope here of the ultimate destruction of sin through a second probation. Every attempt to find room for the idea shatters itself on the unchallengeable fact that the words "everlasting" and "eternal" are the same in Greek (*aionion*) and indicate that the punishment of the wicked and the blessedness of the righteous are of equal duration. 2 Cor. 6:2: "Behold, now is the day of salvation"—not hereafter in a future state of existence, but here in this world. Nor is it merely that the doctrine of a second probation is devoid of support from Scripture, but, contrary to all experience, it takes for granted that every unsaved soul would accept the second offer of salvation, which is more than any one can certainly affirm; and, if all did not, sin would still remain. It may be argued that all would accept because of the fuller light they would then have as to the paramount importance of salvation, or because of the stronger influences that will then be brought to bear upon them; but on this hypothesis a reflection would almost seem to be cast on God for not having done all He might have done to save men while they lived, a reflection good men will be slow to make.

The third theory for banishing sin from the human family if not from the universe is that of *Universalism*, by which is signified that through reformatory discipline hereafter the souls of all will be brought into subjection to Jesus Christ. That the universal headship of Christ is taught in Scripture is true: Paul declares that all things will yet be subdued unto Christ

(1 Cor. 15:28) and that it was God's purpose in the fulness of the times "to gather all things into one in Christ" (Eph. 1:10). But these statements do not necessarily demand the inference that all will surrender in willing subjection to Christ. Subject to Him must every power and authority be, human and angelic, hostile and friendly, believing and unbelieving. "He must reign till all His enemies have been placed beneath His feet"—not taken to His heart, received into His love and employed in His service. This does not look like universal salvation and the complete extinction of moral evil or sin in the universe. Solemn and sad as the thought is that sin should remain, if not in many, yet in some of God's creatures, it is the teaching of Scripture. In the resurrection at the last day, it is written, "All who are in their graves shall come forth, they that have done good unto the resurrection of life; and they that have done evil unto the resurrection of damnation," or "judgment" (R. V.) (John 5:29).

A dark and insoluble mystery was the coming of sin into God's universe at the first: as dark a mystery is its remaining in a race that was from eternity the object of God's love and in time was redeemed by the blood of God's Son, and graciously acted on by God's Spirit. Happily we are not required to understand all mysteries: we can leave this one confidently in the Divine Father's hand.

CHAPTER II

AT-ONE-MENT BY PROPITIATION

BY DYSON HAGUE,

VICAR OF THE CHURCH OF THE EPIPHANY, TORONTO, CANADA;
PROFESSOR OF LITURGICS, WYCLIFFE COLLEGE, TORONTO;
CANON OF ST. PAUL'S CATHEDRAL, LONDON, ONT., 1906-1912

The importance of the subject is obvious. The Atonement is Christianity in epitome. It is the heart of Christianity as a system; it is the distinguishing mark of the Christian religion. For Christianity is more than a revelation; it is more than an ethic. Christianity is uniquely a religion of redemption. At the outset we take the ground that no one can clearly apprehend this great theme who is not prepared to take Scripture as it stands, and to treat it as the final and authoritative source of Christian knowledge, and the test of every theological theory. Any statement of the atonement, to satisfy completely the truly intelligent Christian, must not antagonize any of the Biblical viewpoints. And further; to approach fairly the subject, one must receive with a certain degree of reservation the somewhat exaggerated representations of what some modern writers conceive to be the views of orthodoxy. We cannot deduce Scriptural views of the atonement from non-Biblical conceptions of the Person of Christ; and the ideas that Christ died because God was insulted and must punish somebody, or that the atonement was the propitiation of an angry Monarch-God who let off the rogue while He tortured the innocent, and such like travesties of the truth, are simply the misrepresentations of that revamped Socinianism, which is so widely leavening the theology of many of the outstanding thought-leaders of today in German, British, and American theology.

The subject will be dealt with from four viewpoints: the Scriptural, the Historical, the Evangelico-Ecclesiastical, the Practical.

1. THE ATONEMENT FROM THE SCRIPTURAL VIEWPOINT

THE OLD TESTAMENT WITNESS

As we study *the Old Testament* we are struck with the fact that in the Old Testament system, without an atoning sacrifice there could be no access for sinful men into the presence of the Holy God. The heart and center of the Divinely revealed religious system of God's ancient people was that without a propitiatory sacrifice there could be no acceptable approach to God. There must be acceptance before there is worship; there must be atonement before there is acceptance. This atonement consisted in the shedding of blood. The blood-shedding was the effusion of life; for the life of the flesh is in the blood—a dictum which the modern science of physiology abundantly confirms (Lev. 17:11-14). The blood shed was the blood of a victim which was to be ceremonially blemishless (Ex. 12:5; 1 Pet. 1:19); and the victim that was slain was a vicarious or substitutionary representative of the worshipper (Lev. 1:4; 3:2, 8, 13; 4:4, 15, 24, 29; 16:21, etc.). The death of the victim was an acknowledgment of the guilt of sin, and its exponent.

In one word: the whole system was designed to teach the holiness and righteousness of God, the sinfulness of men, and the guilt of sin; and, above all, to show that it was God's will that forgiveness should be secured, not on account of any works of the sinner or anything that he could do, any act of repentance or exhibition of penitence, or performance of expiatory or restitutionary works, but solely on account of the undeserved grace of God through the death of a victim guilty of no offence against the Divine law, whose shed blood represented the substitution of an innocent for a guilty life. (See

"Lux Mundi," p. 237. The idea, in p. 232, that sacrifice is essentially the expression of unfallen love, is suggestive, but it would perhaps be better to use the word "also" instead of "essentially." See also, the extremely suggestive treatment in Gibson's "Mosaic Era," of the Ritual of the Altar, p. 146.) It is obvious that the whole system was transitory and imperfect, as the eighth chapter of Hebrews shows. Not because it was revolting as the modern mind objects, for God intended them thereby to learn how revolting sin was and how deserving of death; but because in its essence it was typical, and pro- phetical, and intended to familiarize God's people with the great idea of atonement, and at the same time to prepare for the sublime revelation of Him who was to come, the despised and rejected of men Who was to be smitten of God and afflicted, Who was to be wounded for our transgressions and bruised for our iniquities, Whose soul was to be made an offering for sin (Isa. 53:5, 8, 10, 12).

THE NEW TESTAMENT WITNESS

When we come to *the New Testament* we are struck with three things:

First. The unique prominence given to the death of Christ in the four Gospels. This is unparalleled. It is with- out analogy, not only in Scripture, but in history, the most curious thing about it being that there was no precedent for it in the Old Testament (Dale, "Atonement," p. 51). No particular value or benefit is attached to the death of anybody in the Old Testament; nor is there the remotest trace of any- body's death having an expiatory or humanizing or regenera- tive effect. There were plenty of martyrs and national heroes in Hebrew history, and many of them were stoned and sawn asunder, were tortured and slain with the sword, but no Jewish writer attributes any ethical or regenerative importance to their death, or to the shedding of their blood.

Second. It is evident to the impartial reader of the New Testament that the death of Christ was the object of His incarnation. His crucifixion was the main purport of His coming. While His glorious life was and is the inspiration of humanity, after all, His death was the reason of His life. His mission was mainly to die. Beyond thinking of death as the terminus or the inevitable climax of life, the average man rarely alludes to or thinks of death. In all biography it is accepted as the inevitable. But with Christ, His death was the purpose for which He came down from heaven: "For this cause came I to this hour" (John 12:27). From the outset of His career it was the overshadowing event. 'It was distinctly foreseen. It was voluntarily undergone, and, in Mark 10:45, He says: "The Son of Man came to give His life a ransom for many." We are not in the habit of paying ransoms, and the metaphor nowadays is unfamiliar. But, to the Jew, ransom was an everyday custom. It was what was given in exchange for the life of the first-born. It was the price which every man paid for his life. It was the underlying thought of the Mosaic and prophetical writings (Lev. 25:25, 48; Num. 18:15; Psa. 49:7; Isa. 35:10; 51:11; 43:14; Ex. 13:13; 30:12, 16; 34:20; Hos. 13:14; etc., etc.); and so, when Christ made the statement, it was a concept which would be immediately grasped. He came to give His life a ransom, that through the shedding of His blood we might receive redemption, or emancipation, both from the guilt and from the power of son. (The modernists endeavor to evacuate this saying of Christ of all meaning. The text, unfortunately for them, is stubborn, but the German mind is never at a loss for a theory; so it is asserted that they are indications that Peter has been Paulinized, so reluctant is the rationalizer to take Scripture as it stands, and to accept Christ's words in their obvious meaning, when they oppose his theological aversions.)

Third. The object of the death of Christ was the forgiveness of sins. The final cause of His manifestation was remission. It would be impossible to summarize all the teaching of the New Testament on this subject. (The student is referred to Crawford, who gives 160 pages to the texts in the New Testament, and Dale's "Summary," pp. 443-458.)

It is clear, though, that, to our Saviour's thought, His cross and passion was not the incidental consequence of His opposition to the degraded religious standards of His day, and that He did not die as a martyr because death was preferable to apostasy. His death was the means whereby men should obtain forgiveness of sins and eternal life (John 3:14, 16; Matt. 26:28). The consentient testimony of the New Testament writers, both in the Acts and in the Epistles, is that Christ died no accidental death, but suffered according to the will of God, His own volition, and the predictions of the prophets, and that His death was substitutionary, sacrificial, atoning, reconciling and redeeming (John 10:18; Acts 2:23; Rom. 3:25; 5:6, 9; 1 Cor. 15:3; 2 Cor. 5:15, 19, 21; Heb. 9:14, 26, etc., etc.). In proof, it will be sufficient to take the inspired testimony of the three outstanding writers, St. Peter, St. John, and St. Paul.

ST. PETER'S WITNESS.

To St. Peter's mind, the death of Jesus was the central fact of revelation and the mystery, as well as the climax, of the Incarnation. The shedding of His blood was sacrificial; it was covenanting; it was sin-covering; it was redeeming; it was ransoming; it was the blood of the Immaculate Lamb, which emancipates from sin (1 Pet. 1:2, 11, 18, 19). In all his post-Pentecostal deliverances he magnifies the crucifixion as a revelation of the enormity of human sin, never as a revelation of the infinitude of the Divine love (Dale, p. 115). His death was not merely an example; it was substitutionary. It was the death of the sin-bearer. "Christ also suffered for us," "He bare our sins," meaning that He took their penalty and their consequence (Lev. 5:17; 24:15; Num. 9:13; 14:32, 34; Ezek.

18:19, 20). His death was the substitutionary, the vicarious work of the innocent on behalf of, in the place of, and instead of, the guilty (1 Pet. 3:18). (It is surely an evidence of the bias of modernism to interpret this as bearing them in sympathy merely.)

According to St. John, the death of the Lord Jesus Christ was propitiatory, substitutionary, purificatory. It was the *Hilasmos;* the objective ground for the remission of our sins.

The narrow and superficial treatment of modernism, which, if it does not deny the Johannine authorship of the fourth Gospel and the Revelation, at least insinuates that the death of Christ has no parallel place in the writings of St. John to that which it has in the writings of St. Peter and St. Paul, and the other New Testament authors, is entirely contradicted by the plain statements of the Word itself.

The glory of the world to come is the sacrificed Lamb. The glory of heaven is not the risen or ascended Lord, but the Lamb that was slaughtered (Rev. 5:6-12; 7:10; 21:23, etc.). The foremost figure in the Johannine Gospel is the Lamb of God which taketh away the sin of the world, who lifts the sin-burden by expiating it as the Sin-Bearer. The center of the Johannine evangel is not the teaching Christ, but the uplifted Christ, whose death is to draw as a magnet the hearts of mankind, and whose life as the Good Shepherd is laid down for the sheep. (John 12:32; 10:11-15).

No one who fairly faces the text could deny that the objective ground for the forgiveness of sins, in the mind of St. John, is the death of Christ, and that the most fundamental conception of sacrifice and expiation is found in the writings of him who wrote by the Spirit of God, "He is the propitiation of our sins, and not for ours only" (I John 2:2). "Hereby perceive we the love of God because He laid down His life for us" (1 John 3: 16). "Herein is love," etc. (1 John 4: 10).

The propitiatory character of the blood, the substitutionary character of the atonement, and, above all, the expiating character of the work of Christ on Calvary, clearly are most indubitably set forth in the threefoldness of the historic, didactic, and prophetic writings of St. John.

ST. PAUL'S WITNESS

St. Paul became, in the province of God, the constructive genius of Christianity. His place in history, through the Spirit, was that of the elucidator of the salient facts of Christianity, and especially of that one great subject which Christ left in a measure unexplained—His own death (Stalker's "St. Paul," p. 13). That great subject, its cause, its meaning, its result, became the very fundamentum of his Gospel. It was the commencement, center, and consummation of his theology. It was the elemental truth of his creed. He began with it. It pervaded his life. He gloried in it to the last. The sinner is dead, enslaved, guilty, and hopeless, without the atoning death of Jesus Christ. But Christ died for him, in his stead, became a curse for him, became sin for him, gave Himself for him, was an Offering and a Sacrifice to God for him, redeemed him, justified him, saved him from wrath, purchased him by His blood, reconciled him by His death, etc. To talk of Paul using the language he did as an accommodation to Jewish prejudices, or to humor the adherents of a current theology, is not only, as Dale says, an insult to the understanding of the founders of the Jewish faith, it is an insult to the understanding of any man with sense today. Christ's death was a death for sin; Christ died for our sins; that is, on behalf of, instead of, our sins. There was something in sin that made His death a Divine necessity. His death was a propitiatory, substitutionary, sacrificial, vicarious death. Its object was to annul sin; to propitiate Divine justice, to procure for us God's righteousness; to ransom us, and to reconcile us. Christ's death was conciliating, in that by it men are reconciled to God, and sin's curse and the sinner's slavery and liability to death, and incapability of returning to God, are overcome by the death of the Lamb who was slaughtered as a victim and immolated as a sacrifice (1 Cor. 5:7).

To Paul the life of the Christian emerged from the death of Christ. All love, all regeneration, all sanctification, all liberty, all joy, all power, circles around the atoning work of the Lord Jesus Christ, who died for us, and did for us objectively something that man could never do, and who wrought that incredible, that impossible thing, salvation by the substitution of His life in the place of the guilty.

THE BIBLE SUMMARY

To epitomize, then, the presentment of the Bible: The root of the idea of At-one-ment is estrangement. Sin, as iniquity and transgression, had the added element of egoistic rebellion and positive defiance of God (1 John 3:4; Rom. 5:15, 19). The horror of sin is that it wrenched the race from God. It dashed God from His throne and placed self thereupon. It reversed the relationship of man and God. Its blight and its passion have alienated mankind, enslaved it, condemned it, doomed it to death, exposed it to wrath. The sacrifice of the cross is the explanation of the enormity of sin, and the measure of the love of the redeeming Trinity. Surely it is ignorance that says God loves because Christ died. Christ died because God loves. Propitiation does not awaken love; it is love that provides expiation. To cancel the curse, to lift the ban, to inoculate the antitoxin of grace, to restore life, to purchase pardon, to ransom the enslaved, to defeat Satan's work; in one word, to reconcile and restore a lost race; for this, Jesus Christ, the Son of God, and Son of Man, came into this world and offered up His Divine-human Person, body and soul.

Christ's death upon the cross, both as a substitute and as the federal representative of humanity, voluntary, altruistic, vicarious, sinless, sacrificial, purposed not accidental, from the standpoint of humanity unconscionably brutal, but from the standpoint of love indescribably glorious, not only satisfied all the demands of the Divine righteousness, but offered the most powerful incentive to repentance, morality, and self-sacrifice. The Scripture in its completeness thus sets forth the substance of the two great theories, the moral and the vicarious, and we find in the rotundity or allness of the Scriptural presentment no mere partial or antagonistic segments of truth, but the completeness of the spiritual, moral, altruistic and atoning aspects of the death of Christ. (Hodge on the "Atonement," pp. 292-320, and Workman, "At-one-ment and Reconciliation with God," may in different ways be taken as representative of a one-sided way of treating a great subject. The Socinian view that Christ's death was mainly, if not exclusively, to produce a reconciling influence upon the heart of mankind, which Workman espouses, is as narrow, if not narrower, and as partial as Hodge's advocacy of the theory that Christ died for the elect only).

II. THE HISTORICAL

We will discuss this aspect of the subject in four brief sections: The Primitive, the Mediæval, the Reformational, the Modern.

THE PRIMITIVE CHURCH WITNESS

With regard to the writers and writings of the primitive church in the Ante-Nicene and the Post-Nicene era, it may be said, broadly speaking, that the atonement is presented by them as a fact, with its saving and regenerative effects. The consciousness of the primitive church did not seem to be alive to the necessity of the formation of any particular theory of the atonement. It follows the Apostle's Creed, which makes no reference whatever to the miraculous words or marvellous works of Jesus, but significantly passes by them all to focus the confession of the Church upon the great purpose and achievement of the Incarnation; His suffering as the Lamb slain from the foundation of the world. As regards the writers of the post-apostolic age, Clement of Rome, Origen, and Athanasius, may be referred to as outstanding exponents of the Church's thought in the first four centuries. Of the first and third it may be said that they simply amplified the language of the New Testament. There is no trace of the attitude of the modernist, with its brilliant attempts to explain away the obvious. Their doctrine of the atonement is entirely free, as has been said, from the incrusting difficulties of spurious explanation. There were no attempts at philosophy or sophistry, though, as was to be expected, there was more or less of the embroidery of the oriental imagination, and a plethora of metaphor. (Justin Martyr, Chrysostom, and Augustine, may be mentioned also here.)

Origen, following possibly Irenæus, is accredited with the theory that the atonement was a ransom paid to Satan. This was the theory of Gregory of Nyssa, Leo Magnus, and Gregory the Great. It was a weird theory, involving some strange conclusions, and evoked the antagonism of Gregory Nazianzen and John of Damascus.

THE MEDIÆVAL VIEW

As we pass into the mediæval period (broadly speaking, from 500 to 1500 A. D.), we find that, with one or two exceptions, the ransom-paid-to-the-devil hypothesis held sway. It was not a thinking era, and the imprisonment of the Bible meant the reign of ignorance.

In the eleventh century, Anselm appeared. He was an Italian by birth, a Norman by training, and Archbishop of Canterbury by office. Anselm's *Cur Deus Homo* is probably the greatest work on the atonement that has ever been written.

The work is great because it contains great conceptions of God, and great conceptions of sin. Sin is not to render to God His due, and the sinner is bound to pay back the honor of which he has robbed God. It is a debt we are obliged to pay, and failing to do it, we must die. As sin is debt, there are only two ways in which man can be righted with God; either by incurring no debt, or by paying the debt. But this, man cannot do, and herein comes the glory of the Gospel of the atonement, securing at once the honor of God and the salvation of the sinners. No one *ought* to make satisfaction for the sin of man except man, and no one *can* make satisfaction except God Himself. He who makes the satisfaction for human sin must, therefore, be man and God; and so in wondrous love, the God-Man of His own accord offered to the Father what He could not have been compelled to lose, and paid for our sins what He did not owe for Himself.

The Anselmic conceptions of God, of sin, of man, and of the soul are so transcendent that they are altogether too strong and too high for this age. His theory seems fantastic, his reasoning preposterous to the modern mind. Yet, after all, Anselm has never been surpassed. His mind was filled with the august greatness of God, the just penalty of sin, the impossibility of human atonement; and the atoning work of Christ, because of the Person who did the deed, outweighed the sins of all mankind, and bound mankind to the suffering Son of God by bonds of love that eternity will not sever.

Anselm swayed his own and has swayed every succeeding age. The counter theories of Abelard and Duns Scotus (Moberly, p. 372; Dale, p. 285), in which the modern mind is much more interested, and with which it is much more sympathetic, may be regarded as the foregleams of modern Unitarianism.

THE REFORMATION ERA

When we pass to the Reformation era, we find that the Pauline-Augustinian presentment of the subject is almost universal. The reformers, Lutheran and Calvinistic, were practically agreed in representing the death of Christ as an atoning death. Both the Lutheran and the Reformed systems of theology alike, the latter, of course, including all the Anglican reformers, held the forensic idea of the death of Christ, which is so obviously manifest in the Pauline, Petrine, and Johannine presentments of the truth.

Turretin, the most distinguished writer on the subject of the atonement of the Reformation era; Mastricht, a half century later, and Hugo Grotius, the antagonist of Socinius (whose *Defensio fidei Catholicae de satisfactione Christi* appeared in 1617); all of them, with various divergences, held the sacrificial, representative, vicarious theory of atonement (Dale, pp. 290-297; Hodge, Sys, Theol. II., 573-575).

THE NINETEENTH CENTURY

As we pass into the modern world of theology, three outstanding names in the nineteenth century may be selected as the representatives of the so-called orthodox, and three as representatives of the broader school of theology. The works of Crawford of Edinburgh, of Dale of Birmingham, and of Denney of Glasgow, are probably the finest expositions of the subject from the Scriptural and spiritual standpoint. All of them try to set forth the doctrine of the atonement in the language of the New Testament, and according to the mind of the inspired writers, and take their stand upon the vicarious, substitutionary character of the atonement. Professor A. A. Hodge's work is also most able and most scholarly. It is the strongest thing ever written on the subject from the Calvinistic standpoint. Bushnell, the American; Jowett, the Anglican; and McLeod Campbell, the Scotchman; may be taken as representatives of the broader school. All of them are inclined to select a number of the texts which unquestionably favor their theory, and to minimize almost to the point of explaining away those statements of the Old Testament, and of the

New, which emphasize the gravity of the guilt of sin and the necessity of sacrifice as the objective ground of its forgiveness. They all of them incline to represent the sufferings of Christ as sympathetic, rather than vicarious; and, with the Swedenborgians, make the atonement to consist not in what Christ did or offered by dying in our stead, so much as what He accomplished for us in His reconciling love. The atonement was the Incarnation. *That* was the revelation of God's love; and the sufferings of Christ were not a substitute for the penalty of sin, but Christ's expiatory-penitential confession of the sins of humanity. McLeod Campbell, who is followed by Moberly, held the theory that the repentance of Christ, or the penitence of Christ, had in it atoning worth, and was the proper expiation of sin (Moberly, 129, 401; "The Atonement in Modern Religious Thought," p. 375; Clow, 160; Stalker, 135). (This theory, by the way, is becoming very popular nowadays.)

In one word; the object of the death of Christ was the production of a moral impression, the subduement of a revolted world-heart by the exhibition of dying love. This is practically also the Ritschlian view, which, after all, is a re-statement of the old Socinian theory, of the distrust-removing and confidence-re-establishing effect of the cross.

Frederick Maurice and Robertson of Brighton (the noblest spirit of them all) may also be referred to as leaders in this the broader school (Crawford, 303, 348). They were followed by such Church writers as Farrar, Moberly, Freemantle, and by Cave, Adeney, Horton, R. J. Campbell, in the Old Country, and in the United States by Lyman Abbott, Washington Gladden, Munger, and a host of others.

MODERNISM

When we come to the most daring of the present day theories with regard to the atonement, as set forth, for instance, in Sabatier, or the latest work of American modernism, "The Atonement, by Three Chicago Professors of Theology," we are startled with the advance. A very broad space of rationalism intervenes between the broad school of today and the broad school of half a century ago. The present day liberal theology may be traced to two streams of influence:

First. The influence of German rationalism, pre-eminently the Ritschlian theology, and the critical theories of Wellhausen, Kuenen and their school.

Second. The widespread acceptance of the theory of evolution.

To the first may be traced the free and easy way of the modernists of dealing with the Scriptures; and to the second, the revolutionized attitude of theologians with regard to sin, its source, its penalty, and its atonement. Albrecht Ritschl, Professor of Theology at Gottingen, whose magnum opus, "Justification and Reconciliation," was published in 1870, is par excellence, the ruling influence of continental theology.

What Germany thought yesterday, America and Scotland think today, and England will think tomorrow. It is an epigram that has more than a grain of truth in it. The Germanic way of accepting or rejecting what it pleases of the Bible, and opposing its knowledge to the authority of the apostles, is becoming more and more the custom of the leading theologians of the three ruling nations of today, British, American, and German. If a text is inconvenient, modernism disputes it; if a passage is antagonistic, it dismisses it as Pauline or Petrine, not Christian.

Suppose a Christian of the old days was to enter for the first time the class room of one of the extremer modernist professors, addressing a representative body of theologians from Germany, Britain, or the United States. He would be amazed to hear the rankest Socinianism taught. The question the professor would propose would not be the vicarious or the moral theory of the sacrifice of Christ, but did Christ really die, and was there any need of the atoning death? He would state, in the coolest possible manner, that the supposition of God's displeasure or wrath at sin is an archaic concept; that sin is not guilt as traditional theology conceives, nor does it need any propitiation, and that there is no need of salvation, for there never was a fall. (A God who thinks of poor, hard-worked people as miserable sinners, who must account themselves fortunate to be forgiven for Christ's sake, says one of the foremost British modernists, is no God at all. The theologian may call Him a God of love, but in practice He is spiteful and silly!) The doctrine of evolution has washed out of the Bible the existence of such a man as Adam, and biology has taught that death is not due to sin. He would then probably hear the professor going on to show that nobody nowadays thinks of sin as Paul did; that it is impossible for the man of today, familiarized with the doctrine of evolution and the researches of Biblical scholarship, to think of sin as a debt that is due to God; that the God of the Bible is, after all, only the God of traditional theology. In one word, he would hear that what this age not only demands, but requires, is a reconstructed Bible, a re-interpreted Biblical theology, and a presentment of apostolic conceptions in accordance with the modern mind.

But a theology which begins with accepting or rejecting according to its caprice such sections of the Word of God as it pleases, and substituting its own fancies for the New Testament conceptions of sin, of guilt, of wrath, and death, and the idea of punishment, naturally tends to the climax of repudiating the Deity of our Saviour and the teaching of His inspired apostles! A Pelagian hamartology invariably leads to a Socinian Christology; and a Socinian Christology invariably goes hand in hand with a rationalistic soteriology. If there is no objective Deity, there can be no sin. If man is God, there can be no guilt; and if there was no fall, and if it is the rise, not the fall of man with which the study of history makes us acquainted, there is, of course, no need for redemption; and if there is no need for redemption, there could, of course, be no ransom, or Redeemer, and an atonement is theologically and philosophically absurd. If there is no special creation, and man is a mere evolution from some frog or horse or anthropoid, why, of course, there can be no talk of atonement. If there is no storm and nobody is drowning, why on earth should anyone launch a lifeboat! If the wages of sin is not death, what evangel is there in the death of Christ for sin and sinners?

After reading, with every attempt to be sympathetic, the works of the modern theological thought leaders in Great Britain and the United States, we seriously conclude that modernism ·is in essence the sophism of which Paul speaks in 1 Cor. 1:19-22; Rom. 1:22; Col. 2:8, and 1 Tim. 6:20.

III. THE EVANGELICO-ECCLESIASTICAL

THE CONSENSUS OF ALL THE CHURCHES

When we turn to this subject as set forth in the standards of the representatives of the leading Protestant churches, it is refreshing to find what substantial unity there is among them. In all the Creeds and Church Confessions the death of Christ is set forth as the central fact of Christianity; for it ought to be remembered that the Reformed Churches accepted equally with the Roman Church the historic platform of the three great creeds, and that in all these creeds that subject stands pre-eminent. In the Apostles' Creed, for instance, there is not the slightest mention of Christ's glorious example as a man, or of the works and words of His marvelous life. All is passed over, in order that the faith of the Church in all ages may at once be focused upon His sufferings and His death. And as to the various doctrinal standards, a reference to the Articles of the Church of England, or the Westminster Confession of Faith, or the Methodist, or Baptist formularies of belief, at once shows that the atonement is treated as one of the fundamentals of the faith. It may be stated in language that a modern theologian finds difficult to accept and would gladly explain away; but it is unquestionably asserted to be no mere at-one-ment in the Ritschlian sense, but a real vicarious offering; a redemptive death; a reconciling death; a sin-bearing death; a sacrificial death for the guilt and sins of men. His death was the death of the Divine Victim. It was a satisfaction for man's guilt. It propitiated God. It satisfied the justice of the Father. The modern mind sees only one side to reconciliation. It looks at truth from only one standpoint. It fails to take into account the fact of the wrath of God, and that 1 John 2: 1, and Rom. 3: 25 teach that Christ's death does something that can only be expressed as "propitiating." The modern theory ignores one side of the truth, and antagonizes the two complementary sides, and is, therefore, not to be trusted. The Church standards simply set forth, of course, in necessarily imperfect language, the truth as it is in the Scriptures of God. Perhaps no finer summary of their teaching could be found than the language of the Anglican communion service: "Jesus Christ, God's only Son, suffered death upon the cross for our redemption, and made there, by His one oblation of Himself once offered, a full, perfect, and sufficient sacrifice, oblation and satisfaction for the sins of the whole world."

IV. THE PRACTICAL

THE POWER OF HIS DEATH

We finally consider the atonement in its actual power. As we glance through the vistas of history we see it exemplified in innumerable lives. Paul, Augustine, Francis of Assisi, Luther, Latimer, with a myriad myriad of the sinful, struggling, weary, despondent, and sin-sick sons of men, laden with the sin-weight, haunted with the guilt-fear, struggling with the sin-force, tormented with the sin-pain, have found in Him who died their peace. "The atonement," said the great scientist, Sir David Brewster, "Oh, it is everything to me! It meets my reason, it satisfies my conscience, it fills my heart." (See also that fine passage in Drummond, the "Ideal Life," p. 187.)

Or, take our hymns. We want no better theology and no better religion than are set forth in these hymns, says a great theologian (Hodge, Syst. Theol., ii: 591), which voice the triumph, and the confidence, and the gratitude, and the loyalty of the soul, such as:

> "Rock of Ages, cleft for me,
>   Let me hide myself in Thee."

> "My faith looks up to Thee,
>   Thou Lamb of Calvary."

> "When I survey the wondrous cross,
>   On which the Prince of glory died."

Or take the preacher's power. It must be built upon reality as real as life itself; on what the Son of God has done for him. One of the greatest of the nineteenth century preachers said, "Looking back upon all the chequered way, I have to say that the only preaching that has done me good is the preaching of a Saviour who bore my sins in His own body on the tree, and the only preaching by which God has enabled me to do good to others is the preaching in which I have held up my Saviour, not as a sublime example, but as the Lamb of God that taketh away the sins of the world!" And the work of Christ did not end with His death upon the cross. As the risen and ascended One, He continues it. The Crucified is still drawing souls to Himself. He is still applying His healing blood to the wounded conscience. We do not preach a Christ who was alive and is dead; we preach the Christ who was dead and is alive. It is not the extension of the Incarnation merely; it is the perpetuation of the crucifixion that is the vital nerve of Christianity.

But orthodoxy must not be dissevered from orthopraxy. Maclaren, of Manchester, tells us, in one of his charming volumes, that he once heard of a man who was of a very shady character, but was sound on the atonement. But what on earth is the good of being sound on the atonement if the atonement does not make you sound? Anyone who reads his New Testament or understands the essence of apostolic Christianity must understand that a mere theoretic acceptance of the atonement, unaccompanied by a penetration of the life and character of the principles of Jesus Christ, is of no value whatever. The atonement is not a mere formula for assent; it is a life principle for realization. In that we agree with Goldwin Smith. But is it not a fact that, wherever the atonement is truly received, it generates love to God, and love to man; evokes a hatred and horror of sin; and offers not only the highest incentive to self-sacrifice, but the most powerful dynamic for the life of righteousness?

To the soul that beholds the Lamb of God, and finds peace through the blood of the cross, there comes a sense of joyous relief, a consciousness of deep satisfaction, that is newness of life.

Yes, a Christianity that is merely a system of morals, and the best only of natural religions, is not worth preserving. A Christianity without a Christ Divine, an atonement vicarious, and a Bible inspired, will never carry power. A devitalized Gospel, a diluted Gospel, an attenuated Gospel, will conceive no splendid program, inspire no splendid effort. It never did produce a martyr; it never will. It never inspired a reformer, and it never will. The two religious poverties of the day, a lost sense of sin, and a lost sense of God, are simply the result of this attenuated Socinianism that is becoming so prevalent. No minister of Christ has any right to smooth off the corners of the cross. At the same time, a

Christianity that is merely orthodoxy, or an orthodoxy clasped in the dead hand of a moribund Christianity, is one of the greatest of curses. A Church that is only the custodian of the great tradition of the past, and not the expression of a forceful spiritual life; a Christian who is simply conserving a traditional creed, and not exemplifying the life of the living God, is a cumberer of the ground. A dead Church can never be the exponent of the living God, and a dead Church-man can never be the exponent of a living Church, for the test of every religious, political or educational system, after all, as Amiel says, is the man it forms (Amiel, p. 27).

(The chief works on the atonement which have been referred to are the following: Hodge, Dale, Denney, Crawford, Stalker, Van Dyke, Moberly, Clow, Simpson, Sabatier, Champion, Armour, Workman, Cunningham, Van Oosterzee, Ritschl, and Anselm.)

CHAPTER III

THE GRACE OF GOD

BY REV. C. I. SCOFIELD, D. D.,
EDITOR "SCOFIELD REFERENCE BIBLE"

Grace is an English word used in the New Testament to translate the Greek word, *Charis,* which means "favor," without recompense or equivalent. If there is any compensatory act or payment, however slight or inadequate, it is "no more grace"—*Charis.*

When used to denote a certain attitude or act of God toward man it is therefore of the very essence of the matter that human merit or deserving is utterly excluded. In grace God acts out from Himself, toward those who have deserved, not His favor, but His wrath. In the structure of the Epistle to the Romans grace does not enter, could not enter, till a whole race, without one single exception, stands guilty and speechless before God.

Condemned by creation, the silent testimony of the universe (Rom. 1:18, 20); by wilful ignorance, the loss of a knowledge of God once universal (Rom. 1:21); by senseless idolatry (Rom. 1:22, 23); by a manner of life worse than bestial (Rom. 1:24, 27); by godless pride and cruelty (Rom. 1:28, 32); by philosophical moralizings which had no fruit in life (Rom. 2:1, 4); by consciences which can only "accuse" or seek to "excuse" but never justify (Rom. 2:5, 16); and finally by the very law in which those who have the law boast (Rom. 2:17; 3:20), "every mouth" is "stopped, and all the world becomes guilty before God."

In an absolute sense, the end of all flesh is come. Everything has been tried. Innocence, as of two unfallen creatures in an Eden of beauty; conscience, that is, the knowledge of good and evil with responsibility to do good and eschew evil; promises, with the help of God available through prayer; law, tried on a great scale, and through centuries of forbearance, supplemented by the mighty ethical ministry of the prophets, without ever once presenting a human being righteous before God (Rom. 3: 19; Gal. 3: 10; Heb. 7: 19; Rom. 3: 10, 18; 8: 3, 4); this is the Biblical picture. And it is against this dark background that grace shines out.

The New Testament definitions of grace are both inclusive and exclusive. They tell us what grace *is*, but they are careful also to tell us what grace is *not*. The two great central definitions follow:

"That in the ages to come He might show the exceeding riches of His grace in His kindness toward us through Christ Jesus" (Eph. 2: 7).

This is the inclusive, or affirmative, side; the negative aspect, what grace is *not*, follows:

"For by grace are ye saved through faith; and that not of yourselves: it is the gift of God: not of works, lest any man should boast" (Eph. 2: 8, 9).

The Jew, who is under the law when grace comes, is under its curse (Gal. 3: 10); and the Gentiles are "without Christ, being aliens from the commonwealth of Israel, and strangers from the covenants of promise, having no hope, and without God in the world" (Eph. 2: 12).

And to this race God comes to show "the exceeding riches of His GRACE in His kindness toward US," "through CHRIST JESUS."

The other great definition of grace is: "But after that the kindness and love of God our Saviour toward man appeared"—the positive aspect; "Not by works of righteousness which we have done, but according to His mercy He saved us"—the negative aspect.

Grace, then, characterizes the present age, as law characterized the age from Sinai to Calvary. "For the law was given by Moses, but grace and truth came by Jesus Christ." And this contrast between law as a method and grace as a method runs through the whole Biblical revelation concerning grace.

It is not, of course, meant that there was no law before Moses, any more than that there was no grace and truth before Jesus Christ. The forbidding to Adam of the fruit of the tree of the knowledge of good and evil (Gen. 2:17) was law, and surely grace was most sweetly manifested in the seeking, by the Lord God, of His sinning creatures, and in His clothing them with coats of skins (Gen. 3:21)—a beautiful type of Christ "made unto us . . . righteousness" (1 Cor. 1:30). Law, in the sense of *some* revelation of God's will, and grace, in the sense of *some* revelation of God's goodness, have always existed, and to this Scripture abundantly testifies. But "the law" as an inflexible rule of life was given by Moses, and, from Sinai to Calvary, dominates, characterizes, the time; just as grace dominates, or gives its peculiar character to, the dispensation which begins at Calvary, and has its predicted termination in the rapture of the Church.

LAW AND GRACE DIVERSE

It is, however, of the most vital moment to observe that Scripture never, in any dispensation, mingles these two principles. Law always has a place and work distinct and wholly diverse from that of grace. Law is God prohibiting, and requiring (Ex. 20:1, 17); grace is God beseeching, and bestowing (2 Cor. 5:18, 21). Law is a ministry of condemnation (Rom. 3:19); grace, of forgiveness (Eph. 1:7). Law curses (Gal. 3:10); grace redeems from that curse (Gal. 3:1). Law kills (Rom. 7:9, 11); grace makes alive (John 10:10). Law shuts every mouth before God; grace opens every mouth to praise Him. Law puts a great and guilty distance between man and God (Ex. 20:18, 19); grace makes guilty man nigh to God (Eph. 2:13). Law says, "An eye for an eye, and a tooth for a tooth" (Ex. 21:24); grace says, "Resist not evil; but whosoever shall smite thee on thy right cheek, turn to him the other also" (Matt. 5:39). Laws says, "Hate thine enemy;" grace, "Love your enemies, bless them that despitefully use you." Law says, do and live (Luke 10:26, 28); grace, believe and live (John 5:24). Law never had a missionary; grace is to be preached to every creature. Law utterly condemns the best man (Phil. 3:4, 9); grace freely justifies the worst (Luke 23:24; Rom. 5:5; 1 Tim. 1:15; 1 Cor. 6:9, 11). Law is a system of probation; grace, of favor. Law stones an adulteress (Deut. 22:21); grace says, "Neither do I condemn thee"(John 8:1, 11). Under law the sheep dies for the shepherd; under grace the shepherd dies for the sheep (John 10:11).

The relation to each other of these diverse principles, law and grace, troubled the apostolic church. The first controversy concerned the ceremonial law. It was the contention of the legalists that converts from among the Gentiles could not be saved unless circumcised "after the manner of Moses" (Acts 15:1). This demand was enlarged when the "apostles and elders" had come together at Jerusalem to settle that controversy (Acts 15:5, 6). The demand then made put in issue not circumcision merely, or the ceremonial law, but the whole Mosaic system. "That it was needful to circumcise them, *and to command them to keep the law of Moses*" (Acts 15:6).

The decision of the council, as "it seemed good to the Holy Ghost," negatived both demands, and the new law of love was invoked that Gentile converts should abstain from things especially offensive to Jewish believers (Acts 15:28, 29).

But the confusion of these two diverse principles did not end with the decision of the council. The controversy continued, and six years later the Holy Spirit, by the Apostle Paul, launched against the legalistic teachers from Jerusalem the crushing thunderbolt of the Epistle to the churches in Galatia.

In this great letter every phase of the question of the respective spheres of law and of grace comes up for discussion and final, authoritative decision.

The Apostle had called the Galatians into the *grace* of Christ (Gal. 1:6). Now grace means unmerited, unrecompensed favor. It is essential to get this clear. Add never so slight an admixture of law-works, as circumcision, or law effort, as of obedience to commandments, and "grace is no more grace" (Rom. 11:6). So absolutely is this true, that grace cannot even begin with us until the law has reduced us to speechless guilt (Rom. 3:19). So long as there is the slightest question of utter guilt, utter helplessness, there is no place for grace. If I am not, indeed, quite so good as I ought to be, but yet quite too good for hell, I am not an object for the grace of God, but for the illuminating and convicting and death-dealing work of His law.

The law is "just" (Rom. 7:12), and therefore heartily approves goodness, and unsparingly condemns badness; but, save Jesus of Nazareth, the law never saw a man righteous through obedience. Grace, on the contrary, is not looking for good men whom it may approve, for it is not grace, but mere justice, to approve goodness, but it is looking for condemned, guilty, speechless and helpless men whom it may save through faith, sanctify and glorify.

Into grace, then, Paul had called the Galatians. What (1:6) was his controversy with them? Just this: they were "removed" from the *grace* of Christ into "another gospel," though he is swift to add, "which is not another" (Gal. 1:7).

There could not be another "gospel." Change, modify, the grace of Christ by the smallest degree, and you no longer have a gospel. A gospel is "glad tidings"; and the law is not glad tidings. "What things soever the law saith, it saith to them who are under the law; that every mouth may be stopped, and all the world become guilty before God" (Rom. 3:19), and surely that is no good news. The law, then, has but one language; it pronounces " all the world"—"good", bad, and "goody-good"—"guilty".

But you say: What is a simple child of God, who knows no theology, to do? Just this: to remember that any so-called gospel which is not pure unadulterated grace is "another" gospel. If it proposes, under whatever specious guise, to win favor of God by works, or goodness, or "character," or anything else which man can do, it is spurious. That is the unfailing test.

But it is more than spurious, it is accursed—or rather the preachers of it are (Gal. 1:8, 9). It is not man who says that, but the Spirit of God who says it by His apostle. This is unspeakably solemn. Not the denial of the Gospel even, is so awfully serious as to pervert the Gospel. Oh, that God may give His people in this day power to discriminate, to distinguish things which differ. Alas, it is discernment which seems so painfully wanting.

If a preacher is cultured, gentle, earnest, intellectual, and broadly tolerant, the sheep of God run after him. He, of course, speaks beautifully about Christ, and uses the old words—redemption, the cross, even sacrifice and atonement—but what is his *Gospel?* That is the crucial question. Is salvation, perfect, entire, eternal,—justification, sanctification, glory,—the alone work of Christ, and the free gift of God to faith alone? Or does he say: (Dr. Abbott) "Character is salvation," even though he may add that Christ "helps" to form the character?

THE THREE ERRORS

In the Epistle to the Galatians the Holy Spirit through Paul meets and answers the three great errors into which in different degrees, theological systems have fallen.

The course of this demonstration is like the resistless march of an armed host. Nothing can stand before it. The reasonings of ancient and modern legalists are scattered like the chaff of the summer threshing floor.

We have, most of us, been reared and now live under the influence of Galatianism. Protestant theology, alas, is for the most part, thoroughly Galatianized, in that neither law nor grace are given their distinct and separated places, as in the counsels of God, but are mingled together in one incoherent system. The law is no longer, as in the Divine intent, a ministration of death (2 Cor. 3:7), of cursing (Gal. 3:10), of conviction (Rom. 3:19), because we are taught that we must try to keep it, and that by Divine help we may. Nor, on the other hand, does grace bring us blessed deliverance from the dominion of sin, for we are kept under the law as a rule of life despite the plain declaration, "Sin shall not have dominion over you: for ye are not under the law, but under grace" (Rom. 6:14).

THE FIRST ERROR

The Spirit first meets the contention that justification is partly by law-works and partly by faith through grace (Gal. 2:5 to 3:24).

The steps are:

1. Even the Jews, who are not like the Gentiles, hopeless, "and without God in the world" (Eph. 2:12), but already in covenant relations with God, even they, "knowing that a man is not justified by the works of the law, but by the faith of Jesus Christ" (Gal. 2:15, 16), have believed; "for by the works of the law shall no flesh be justified."

2. The law has executed its sentence upon the believer (Gal. 2:19); death has freed him. Identified with Christ's death by faith, he, in the reckoning of God, died with Christ (Rom. 6:3-10; 7:4).

3. But righteousness is by faith, not by law (Gal. 2:21).

4. The Holy Spirit is given to faith, not law-works (Gal. 3:1-9).

5. "As many as are of the works of the law are under the curse"—and the reason is given: "Cursed is every one that *continueth* not in *all things* which are written in the book of the law *to do* them" (Gal. 3:10). The law, then, cannot "help", but can only do its great and necessary work of condemnation (Rom. 3:19, 20; 2 Cor. 3:7, 9; Gal. 3:19; James 2:10).

Elsewhere (Rom. 5:1-5) the Spirit, by the same Apostle, sums up the results of justification by faith with every semblance of human merit carefully excluded. Grace, through faith in Jesus Christ, has brought the believer into *peace with God*, a *standing in grace*, and assured *hope of glory*. Tribulation can but serve to develop in him new graces. The very *love* that saved him through grace now fills his heart; the *Holy Spirit* is given him, and he *joys in God*. And all by grace, through faith!

THE SECOND ERROR

The Spirit next meets and refutes the second great error concerning the relations of law and grace—the notion that the believer, though assuredly justified by faith through grace wholly without law-works, is, after justification, put under law as a rule of life.

This is the current form of the Galatian error. From Luther down, Protestantism has consistently held to justification by faith through grace. Most inconsistently Protestant theology has held to the second form of Galatianism.

An entire section of the Epistle to the Romans, and two chapters of Galatians are devoted to the refutation of this error, and to the setting forth of the true rule of the believer's life. Romans 6, 7, 8, and Galatians 4 and 5, set forth the new Gospel of the believer's standing in grace.

Rom. 6:14 states the new principle: "For sin shall not have dominion over you: for ye are not under the law, but under grace." The Apostle is not here speaking of the justification of a sinner, but of the deliverance of a saint from the dominion of indwelling sin.

In Galatians, after showing that the law had been to the Jew like the pedagogue in a Greek or Roman household, a ruler of children in their nonage (Gal. 3:23, 24) the Apostle says explicitly (ver. 25), "But after that faith has come, we are no longer under a schoolmaster" (pedagogue).

No evasion is possible here. The pedagogue is the law (3:24); faith justifies; but the faith which justifies also ends the rule of the pedagogue. Modern theology says that after justification we are under the pedagogue. Here is a clear issue, an absolute contradiction between the Word of God and theology. Which do you side with?

Equally futile is the timorous gloss that this whole profound discussion in Romans and Galatians relates to the ceremonial law. No Gentile *could* observe the ceremonial law. Even the Jews, since the destruction of the temple, A. D. 70, have not found it possible to keep the ceremonial law except in a few particulars of diet. It is not the ceremonial law which says, "Thou shalt not covet" (*comp.* Rom. 7:7-9).

The believer is separated by death and resurrection from Mosaism (Rom. 6:3-15; 7:1-6; Gal. 4:19-31). The fact remains immutable that to God he is, as to the law, an executed criminal. Justice has been completely vindicated, and it is no longer possible even to bring an accusation against him (Rom. 8:33, 34).

It is not possible to know Gospel liberty, or Gospel holiness, until this great fundamental truth is clearly, bravely
grasped. One may be a Christian and a worthy and useful
man, and be still under bondage to the law, but one can never
have deliverance from the dominion of sin, nor know the
true blessedness and rest of the Gospel and remain under
the law. Therefore, once more, note that it is death which
has broken the connection between the believer and the law.
"The law hath dominion over a man as long as he liveth"
(Rom. 7:1). "But now we are delivered from the law, that
being dead wherein we were held" (Rom. 7:6). Nothing
can be clearer.

But I hasten to add that there is a mere carnal and fleshly
way of looking at our deliverance from the law, which is
most unscriptural, and I am persuaded, most dishonoring
to God. It consists in rejoicing in a supposed deliverance
from the principle of Divine authority over the life—a deliverance into mere self-will and lawlessness.

The true ground of rejoicing is quite other than this. The
truth is, a Christian may get on after a sort under law as a
rule of life. Not apprehending that the law is anything more
than an ideal, he feels a kind of pious complacency in "con-
senting unto the law that it is good," and more or less languidly
hoping that in the future he may succeed better in keeping
it than in the past. So treated, the law is wholly robbed of
its terror. Like a sword carefully fastened in its scabbard,
the law no longer cuts into the conscience. It is forgotten
that the law offers absolutely but two alternatives—exact
obedience, always, in all things, or a curse. There is no third
voice. "Cursed is every one that continueth not in all things
which are written in the book of the law to do them" (Gal.
3:10; James 2:10). The law has but one voice: "What
things soever the law saith, it saith to them who are under the
law; that every mouth may be stopped and all the world may

become guilty before God" (Rom. 3:19). The law, in other words, never says: "Try to do better next time." Of this the antinomian legalist seems entirely unaware.

THE TRUE CHRISTIAN LIFE

And now we are ready to turn from the negative to the positive side to the secret of a holy and victorious walk under grace.

We shall find the principle and the power of that walk defined in Galatians 5:16-24. The principle of the walk is briefly stated:

"Walk in the Spirit, and ye shall not fulfill the lusts of the flesh" (5:16).

The Spirit is shown in Galatians in a threefold way. First, He is received by the hearing of faith (3:2). When the Galatians believed they received the Spirit. To what end? The legalists make little of the Spirit. Though they talk much of "power" in connection with the Spirit, it is power for service which chiefly occupies them. Of His sovereign rights, of His blessed enabling in the inner life, there is scant apprehension. But it is precisely there that the Biblical emphasis falls. In Romans, for example, the Spirit is not even mentioned until we have a justified sinner trying to keep the law, utterly defeated in that attempt by the flesh, the "law in his members," and crying out, not for *help*, but for *deliverance* (Rom. 7:15-24). Then the Spirit is brought in with, Oh, what marvelous results! "The law of the Spirit of life in Christ Jesus hath made me free from the law of sin and death" (Rom. 8:2). Not the Apostle's effort under the law, nor even the Spirit's help in that effort, but the might of the indwelling Spirit alone, breaks the power of indwelling sin (Gal. 5:16-18).

You ask, and necessarily at this point, what is it to walk in the Spirit? The answer is in Gal. 5:18: "If ye be led of the Spirit." But how else may we be led of Him save by yieldedness to His sway?

There is a wonderful sensitiveness in the blessed Spirit's love. He will not act in and over our lives by way of almightiness, forcing us into conformity. That is why "yield" is the great word of Romans 6, where it is expressly said that we are not under the law, but under grace.

The results of walking in the Spirit are twofold, negative and positive. Walking in the Spirit we shall not fulfill the lusts of the flesh (Gal. 5:16). The "flesh" here is the exact equivalent of "sin" in Romans 6:14, "Sin shall not have dominion over you."

And the reason is immediately given (5:17). The Spirit and the flesh are contrary, and the Spirit is greater and mightier than the flesh. Deliverance comes, not by self-effort under the law—that is Romans 7—but by the omnipotent Spirit, who Himself is contrary to the flesh (Gal. 6:7), and who brings the yielded believer into the experience of Romans 8.

CHAPTER IV

FULFILLED PROPHECY A POTENT ARGUMENT FOR THE BIBLE

BY ARNO C. GAEBELEIN,

EDITOR "OUR HOPE," NEW YORK CITY.

"Produce your cause, saith the Lord; bring forth your strong reasons, saith the King of Jacob. Let them bring them forth, and show us what shall happen; let them show the former things, what they be, that we may consider them, and know the latter end of them, or declare us things to come. Show the things that are to come hereafter, that we may know, that ye are gods" (Isa. 41:21-23). "I declare the end from the beginning, and from ancient times the things that are not yet done, saying, My counsel shall stand, and I will do all my pleasure" (Isa. 46:10).

This is Jehovah's challenge to the idol-gods of Babylon to predict future events. He alone can do that. The Lord can declare the end from the beginning, and make known things that are not yet done. The dumb idols of the heathen know nothing concerning the future. They cannot predict what is going to happen. And man himself is powerless to know future events and cannot find out things to come.

Jehovah, who has made this challenge and declaration, has also fully demonstrated His power to do so. He has done it in His holy Word, the Bible. Other nations possess books of a religious character, called "sacred books." Not one of them contains any predictions concerning the future. If the authors of these writings had attempted to foretell the future, they would have thereby furnished the strongest evidence of their deceptions. The Bible is the *only* book in the world which contains predictions. It is pre-eminently that, which no other book could be, and none other is, a book of prophecy. These predictions are declared to be the utterances of Jehovah; they show that the Bible is a supernatural book, the revelation of God.

PROPHECY NEGLECTED AND DENIED

In view of this fact it is deplorable that the professing Church of today almost completely ignores and neglects the study of prophecy, a neglect which has for one of its results the loss of one of the most powerful weapons against infidelity. The denial of the Bible as the inspired Word of God has become widespread.

If prophecy were intelligently studied such a denial could not flourish as it does, for the fulfilled predictions of the Bible give the clearest and most conclusive evidence that the Bible is the revelation of God. To this must be added the fact that the destructive Bible criticism, which goes by the name of "Higher Criticism," denies the possibility of prophecy. The whole reasoning method of this school, which has become so popular throughout Christendom, may be reduced to the following: Prophecy is an impossibility; there is no such thing as foretelling future events. Therefore a book which contains predictions of things to come, which were later fulfilled, must have been written after the events which are predicted in the book. The methods followed by the critics, the attacks made by them upon the authenticity of the different books of the Bible, especially upon those which contain the most startling prophecies (Isaiah and Daniel), we cannot follow at this time. They deny everything which the Jewish Synagogue and the Christian Church always believed to be prophecy, a supernatural unfolding of future events.

PAST, PRESENT AND FUTURE

The prophecies of the Bible must be first of all divided into three classes. 1. Prophecies which have found already their fulfillment. 2. Prophecies which are now in process of fulfillment. Many predictions written several thousand years ago are now being accomplished before our eyes. We mention those which relate to the national and spiritual condition of the Jewish people and the predictions concerning the moral and religious condition of the present age. 3. Prophecies which are still unfulfilled. We have reference to those which predict the second, glorious and visible coming of our Lord, the re-gathering of Israel and their restoration to the land of promise, judgments which will fall upon the nations of the earth, the establishment of the Kingdom, the conversion of the world, universal peace and righteousness, the deliverance of groaning creation, and others.

These great prophecies of future things are often robbed of their literal and solemn meaning by a process of spiritualization. The visions of the prophets concerning Israel and Jerusalem, and the glories to come in a future age, are almost generally explained as having their fulfillment in the Church during the present age. However, our object is not to follow the unfulfilled prophecies, but prophecies fulfilled and in process of fulfillment. At the close of our treatise we shall point out briefly that in the light of fulfilled prophecies, the literal fulfillment of prophecies still future is perfectly assured.

FULFILLED PROPHECY A VAST THEME

Fulfilled prophecy is a vast theme of much importance. It is equally inspiring and interesting. Volumes could be written to show how hundreds of Divine predictions written in the Bible have passed into history. What God announced through His chosen instruments has come to pass. History is bearing witness to the fact that the events which transpired among nations were pre-written in the Bible, even as prophecy is nothing less than history written in advance. As much as space permits we shall call attention to the fulfilled prophecies relating to the person of Christ; to the Jewish people; and to a number of nations, whose history, whose rise and downfall, are divinely predicted in the Bible. Furthermore, we shall mention the great prophetic unfoldings as given in the Book of Daniel, and how many of these predictions have already found a most interesting fulfillment.

MESSIANIC PROPHECIES AND THEIR FULFILLMENT

The Old Testament contains a most wonderful chain of prophecies concerning the person, the life and work of our Lord. As He is the center of the whole revelation of God, the One upon whom all rests, we turn first of all to a few of the prophecies which speak of Him. This also is very necessary. The destructive criticism has gone so far as to state that there are no predictions at all concerning Christ in the Old Testament. Such a denial leads to and is linked with the denial of Christ Himself, especially the denial of His Deity and His work on the cross.

To follow the large number of prophecies concerning the coming of Christ into the world and the work He was to accomplish we cannot attempt in these pages. We point out briefly in a general way what must be familiar to most Christians who search the Scriptures. Christ is first announced in Gen. 3: 15 to be the seed of the woman, and therefore a human being. In Gen. 9:26-27 the supremacy of Shem is predicted. The full revelation of Jehovah God is connected with Shem and in due time a son of Shem, Abraham, received the promise that the predicted seed was to come from him. (Gen. 12: 8.) Messiah was to come from the seed of Abraham.

Then the fact was revealed that He was to come from Isaac and not from Ishmael, from Jacob and not from Esau. But Jacob had twelve sons. The Divine prediction pointed to Judah and later to the house of David of the tribe of Judah from which the Messiah should spring. When we come to the prophecies of Isaiah we learn that His mother is to be a virgin. (Isa. 7: 14.) But the son born of the virgin is

Immanuel, God with us. Clearly the prophetic Word in Isaiah states that the Messiah would be a child born and a Son given with the names, "Wonderful, Counsellor, Mighty God, the Everlasting Father, the Prince of Peace" (Isa. 9:6). The promised Messiah is to be the seed of a woman, of the seed of Abraham, of David, born of a virgin. He is to be Immanuel, the Son given, God manifested in the flesh.

This promised Messiah, the Son of David, should appear (according to Isa. 11:1) after the house of David had been stripped of its royal dignity and glory. And what more could we say of the prophecies which speak of His life, His poverty, the works He was to do, His rejection by His own people, the Jews. In that matchless chapter in Isaiah, the fifty-third, the rejection of Christ by His own nation is predicted. In another chapter a still more startling prophecy is recorded: "Then I said, I have labored in vain, I have spent my strength for naught and in vain." This is Messiah's lament on account of His rejection. Then follows the answer, which contains a most striking prophecy: "It is a light thing that Thou shouldest be My servant to raise up the tribes of Jacob and to restore the preserved of Israel: I also will give Thee for a light to the Gentiles, that Thou mayest be My salvation unto the ends of the earth" (Isa. 49:5, 6). Here the revelation is given that He would not alone be rejected by His own nation, but that He would also bring salvation to the Gentiles. What human mind could have ever invented such a program! The promised Messiah of Israel, the longed-for One, is predicted to be rejected by His own people and thus becomes the Saviour of the despised Gentiles. His sufferings and His death are even more minutely predicted.

In the Book of Psalms the sufferings of Christ, the deep agony of His soul, the expressions of His sorrow and His grief, are pre-written by the Spirit of God. We mention only one Psalm, the twenty-second. His death by crucifixion is prophesied. Yet death by crucifixion was in David's time an unknown mode of death. Cruel Rome invented that horrible form of death. The cry of the forsaken One is predicted in the very words which came from the lips of our Saviour out of the darkness which enshrouded the cross. So are also predicted the words of mockery by those who looked on; the piercing of His hands and feet; the parting of the garments and the casting of the lots. In the fifty-third chapter of Isaiah, the purpose of His death is so blessedly predicted. He was to die the substitute of sinners. There we find also His burial and His resurrection predicted. All this was recorded 700 years before our Lord was born. In the Psalms we find the prophecy that the rejected One would occupy a place at the right hand of God (Psalm 110:1). He was to leave the earth. David's Son and David's Lord was to have a place in the highest glory, even at the right hand of God, to wait there till His enemies are made His footstool. It is indeed a wonderful chain of prophecies concerning Christ. We could give a very few of these predictions. How they all were long ago literally fulfilled in the coming, in the life, in the death, in the resurrection and ascension of our adorable Lord, all true believers know.

THE JEWISH PEOPLE

When Frederick the Great, King of Prussia, asked the court chaplain for an argument that the Bible is an inspired book, he answered, "Your Majesty, the Jews." It was well said. To the Jews were committed the oracles of God. (Rom. 3:2.) These oracles of God, the Holy Scriptures, the Law and the Prophets, are filled with a large number of predictions relating to their own history. Their unbelief, the rejection of the Messiah, the results of that rejection, their dispersion into the corners of the earth, so that they would be scattered among all the nations, the persecutions and sorrows they were to suffer, the curses which were to come upon them, their miraculous preservation as a nation, their future great tribulation and final restoration—all these and much more were over and over announced by their own prophets. All the different epochs of the remarkable history of Israel were predicted long before they were reached. Their sojourn in Egypt and servitude, as well as the duration of that period, was announced to Abraham. The Babylonian captivity of 70 years and the return of a remnant to occupy the land once more was announced by the pre-exile prophets, who also predicted a far greater and longer exile, their present world-wide dispersion and a return which up to 1914 has not yet come. Of the deepest interest and the greatest importance in connection with the predictions of the return from Babylon is the naming of the great Persian king through whom the return was to be achieved. This great prophecy is found in the Book of Isaiah: "That saith of Cyrus, He is My shepherd, and shall perform all My pleasure: even saying of Jerusalem, She shall be built; and of the temple, Thy foundation shall be laid. Thus saith Jehovah to His anointed, to Cyrus, whose right hand I have holden, to subdue nations before him; and I will loose the loins of kings, to open the doors before him, and the gates shall not be shut" (Isa. 44:28; 45:1). This prediction was made about 200 years before Cyrus was born. A careful study of the part of Isaiah where these words are found will show that they are linked with the challenge of Jehovah and the declaration that He knows the end from the beginning; the passages we have already quoted. In naming an unborn king and showing what his work would be, Jehovah demonstrates that He knows the future. The great Jewish historian, Josephus, informs us that when Cyrus found his name in the Book of Isaiah, written about 200 years before, an earnest desire laid hold upon him to fulfill what was written. The beginning of the Book of Ezra gives the proclamation of Cyrus concerning the temple.

When the Prophet Isaiah received the message which contained the name of the Persian king, he wrote it down faithfully, though he did not know who Cyrus was. Two centuries later Cyrus appeared and then issued his proclamation which fulfilled Isaiah's prediction. Higher criticism denies the genuineness of all this. In order to disprove this prophecy as well as others, they declare that Isaiah did not write the book which bears his name. For about 2500 years no one ever thought of even suggesting that Isaiah is not the author of the book. They have invented an unknown person, whom they call Deutero-Isaiah, i. e., a second Isaiah. They claim that he wrote chapters 40-66. With this they have not stopped. They speak now of a third Isaiah, a Trito-Isaiah, as they call him. With their supposed learning they claim to have discovered that some of the chapters of Isaiah were written in Babylon and others in Palestine. However, all the arguments, advanced by the critics for a composite authorship and against one Isaiah who lived and wrote his book at the time specified in the beginning of Isaiah, are disproven by the book itself. One only needs to study this book to find out the unity of the message. One person must be the author of the Book of Isaiah.

A REMARKABLE CHAPTER

The Pentateuch contains many of the prophecies concerning the future history of the Jews. One of the most remarkable chapters is the twenty-eighth chapter in Deuteronomy.

It is one of the most solemn chapters in the Pentateuch. Orthodox Hebrews read in their synagogues each year through the entire five books of Moses. When they read this chapter, the Rabbi reads in a subdued voice. And well may they read it softly and ponder over it, for here is pre-written the sad and sorrowful history of their wonderful nation. Here thousands of years ago the Spirit of God through Moses outlined the history of the scattered nation, all their suffering and tribulation, as it has been for well nigh two millenniums and as it is still. Here are arguments for the Divine, the supernatural origin of this book which no infidel has ever been able to answer; nor will there ever be found an answer.

It would take many pages to follow the different predictions and show their literal fulfillment in the nation which turned away from Jehovah and disobeyed His Word.

Apart from such general predictions as are found in verses 64-66 and fulfilled in the dispersion of Israel, there are others which are more minute. The Roman power, which was used to break the Jews, is clearly predicted by Moses, and that in a time when no such power existed. Read verses 49-50: "The Lord shall bring a nation against thee from far, from the end of the earth, as swift as the *eagle* flieth, a nation, whose language thou shalt not understand." The eagle was the standard of the Roman armies; the Jews understood many oriental languages, but were ignorant of Latin. "Which shall not regard the person of the old, nor show favor to the young." Rome killed the old people and the children. "And he shall besiege thee in all thy gates, until thy high and fenced walls come down, wherein thou trustedst, throughout all thy land" (verse 52). Fulfilled in the siege and overthrow of Jerusalem by the Roman legions. "The tender and delicate woman among you, which would not adventure to set the sole of her foot upon the ground for delicateness and tenderness, shall eat her children, for want of all things in the siege and straitness wherewith thine enemy shall distress thee in thy gates" (54-57). Fulfilled in the dreadful sieges of Jerusalem, perhaps the most terrible events in the history of blood and tears of this poor earth. Every verse, beginning with the fifteenth, to the end of this chapter has found its oft repeated fulfillment. It does not surprise us that the enemy hates this book, which bears such a testimony, and would have it classed with legends.

Of much interest is the last verse of this great prophetic chapter. "And Jehovah will bring thee into Egypt again with ships, by the way whereof I said unto thee, Thou shalt see it

no more again; and there ye shall sell yourselves unto your
enemies for bondmen and bondwomen, and no man shall buy
you." When Jerusalem was destroyed by the Romans, all
who did not die in the awful calamity were sent to the mines
of Egypt, where the slaves were constantly kept at work without being permitted to rest or sleep till they succumbed. The
whip of Egypt fell once more upon them and they suffered
the most terrible agonies. Others were sold as slaves. According to Josephus, about 100,000 were made slaves so that
the markets were glutted and the word fulfilled, "No man shall
buy you."

THEIR DISPERSION AND PRESERVATION

When Balaam beheld the camp of Israel he uttered a
prophecy which is still being fulfilled. "Lo, the people shall
dwell alone and shall not be reckoned among the nations"
(Num. 23:9). God had separated the nation and given to
them a land. And this peculiar people, living in one of the
smallest countries of the earth, has been scattered throughout
the world, has become a wanderer, without a home, without a
land. Like Cain they wander from nation to nation. Though
without a land they are still a nation. Other nations have
passed away; the Jewish nation has been preserved. They are
among all the nations and yet not reckoned among the nations.
All this is written beforehand in the Bible. "And you will I
scatter among the nations, and I will draw out the sword after
you: and your land shall be a desolation and your cities shall
be a waste" (Lev. 26:33). "And Jehovah will scatter you
among the people, and ye shall be left few in number among
the nations, whither Jehovah shall lead you away" (Deut.
4:27). "And Jehovah will scatter you among all peoples,
from the one end of the earth even unto the other end of the
earth; and there thou shalt serve other gods, which thou hast
not known, thou nor thy fathers, even wood and stone. And
among these nations shalt thou find no ease, and there shall

be no rest for the sole of thy foot; but Jehovah will give thee there a trembling heart, and failing of eyes, and pining of soul. And thy life shall hang in doubt before thee; and thou shalt fear night and day, and shalt have no assurance of thy life. In the morning thou shalt say, Would it were even! and at even thou shalt say, Would it were morning! for the fear of thy heart which thou shalt fear, and for the sight of thine eyes, which thou shalt see" (Deut. 28:64-67). "And yet for all that, when they be in the land of their enemies, I will not reject them, neither will I abhor them, to destroy them utterly, and to break My covenant with them; for I am Jehovah their God" (Lev. 26:44). In many other passages the Spirit of God predicts their miraculous preservation.

"Massacred by thousands, yet springing up again from their undying stock, the Jews appear at all times and in all regions. Their perpetuity, their national immortality, is at once the most curious problem to the political inquirer; to the religious man a subject of profound and awful admiration."* Herder called the Jews "the enigma of history". What human mind could have ever foreseen that this peculiar people, dwelling in a peculiar land, was to be scattered among all nations, suffer there as no other nation ever suffered, and yet be kept and thus marked out still as the covenant people of a God, whose gifts and callings are without repentance. Here indeed is an argument for the Word of God which no infidel can answer. Jehovah has predicted the history of His earthly people. "Though I make a full end of all nations whither I have scattered thee, yet will I not make a full end of thee" (Jer. 30:11).

THE LAND AND THE CITY

Palestine, the God-given home of Israel, the land which once flowed with milk and honey, has become barren and desolate. Jerusalem, once a great city, the hallowed city of

---

*Milman: "History of the Jews."

David, is trodden down by the Gentiles. All this is more than once predicted in the Word of Prophecy. "I will make thee a wilderness, and cities which are not inhabited. And I will prepare destroyers against thee, every one with his weapons; and they shall cut down thy choice cedars, and cast them into the fire. And many nations shall pass by this city, and they shall say every man to his neighbor, Wherefore has the Lord done thus unto this great city? Then they shall answer, Because they have forsaken the covenant of the Lord their God, and worshipped other gods and served them" (Jer. 22:7-9). "And the generation to come, your children that shall rise up after you, and the foreigner that shall come from a far land shall say, when they shall see the plagues of that land   .   .   . even all the nations shall say, Wherefore hath Jehovah done thus unto this land, what meaneth the heat of this great anger?" (Deut. 29:22-25.)

Thus it has come to pass. Their land is being visited by Gentiles from all over the world who behold the desolations. Many other passages could be added to the above—passages which prophesied the very condition of the promised land and the city of Jerusalem which are found there now, and which have existed for nearly two thousand years.

The national rejection of Israel and the fulfillment of the threatened curses have come to pass, and the land in its barren condition witnesses to it. Even the duration of all this is indicated in the prophetic Word. There is a striking passage in Hosea. "I will go and return to My place, till they acknowledge their offence and seek My face; in their affliction they will seek Me early. Come, let us return unto the Lord; for He hath torn, and He will heal us; He hath smitten and He will bind us up. After two days will He revive us; in the third day He will raise us up, and we shall live in His sight" (Hos. 5:15—6:2). According to this prophecy Jehovah is to be in their midst and is to return to His place. It refers to the manifestation of the Lord Jesus Christ among His people.

They rejected Him; He returned to His place. They are to acknowledge their offence.

Elsewhere in the Word predictions are found which speak of a future national repentance of Israel when the remnant of that nation will confess the blood-guiltiness which is upon them. According to this word in Hosea, they are going to have affliction, and when that great affliction comes they will seek His face, and confess their sins, and express their trust in Jehovah. They acknowledge that for two days they were torn and smitten by the judgments of the Lord, afflicted, as predicted by their own prophets. A third day is coming when all will be changed. These days are prophetic days. Several ancient Jewish expositors mention the fact that these days stand each for a thousand years. The two days of affliction and dispersion would therefore stand for two thousand years, and they are almost expired. The third day would mean the day of the Lord, the thousand years of the kingdom to come.

Nor must we forget that our Lord Jesus Christ, too, predicted the great dispersion of the nation, the fall of Jerusalem, and that Gentiles were to rule over that city, till the times of the Gentiles are fulfilled. (Luke 21:10-24.)

NO GOVERNMENT, NO SACRIFICE, NO HOLY PLACE

"For the children of Israel shall abide many days without a king, and without a prince, and without a sacrifice, and without an image, and without an ephod, and without teraphim" (Hos. 3:4). No further comment is needed on this striking prediction. Their political and religious condition for 1900 years corresponds to every word given through Hosea the prophet.

PROPHECIES ABOUT OTHER NATIONS

Besides the many predictions concerning the people Israel, the prophets have much to say about the nations with whom Israel came in touch and whose history is bound up with the history of the chosen people of God. Babylonia, Assyria, Egypt, Ammon, Moab, Tyre, Sidon, Idumea, and others are mentioned in the Prophetic Word. Their ultimate fate was predicted by Jehovah long before their downfall and overthrow occurred. The Prophet Ezekiel was entrusted with many of the solemn messages announcing the judgment of these nations. The reader will find these predictions in chapters 25-37. The predictions concerning Ammon, Moab, Edom and the Philistines are recorded in the twenty-fifth chapter. Tyrus and its fall is the subject of chapters 26 to 28: 19. A prophecy about Sidon is found in the concluding verses of the twenty-eighth chapter. The prophecies concerning the judgment and degradation of Egypt are given at greater length in chapters 29 and 30. Isaiah, Jeremiah, Daniel, Amos, Obadiah, Micah, Nahum and Habakkuk, all contain prophecies concerning different nations foretelling what should happen to them. A mass of evidence can be produced to show that all these predictions came true. Many of them seemed to fail, but after centuries had passed, their literal fulfillment, even to the minutest detail, had become history.

We must confine ourselves to a very few of these predictions and their fulfillment. The siege and capture of the powerful and extremely wealthy city of Tyrus by Nebuchadnezzar, king of Babylon, is predicted in Ezek. 26: 7-11. It came literally to pass. One of the proofs is to be found in a contract tablet in the British Museum dated at Tyrus in the fortieth year of the king. The overthrow predicted by Ezekiel had come to pass. The walls were broken down and the city was ruined. The noise of the song ceased and the sound of the harps was no more heard. But not all that Ezekiel predicted had been fulfilled by the Babylonian conqueror. The Divine prediction states, "They shall lay thy stones and thy timber and thy dust in the midst of the water" (verse 12). Nebuchadnezzar had not done this. History acquaints us with the fact that the Tyrians, before the destruction of the city had come, had removed their treasures to an island about half a mile from the shore. About 250 years later Alexander came against the island city. The ruins of Tyre which Nebuchadnezzar had left standing were used by Alexander. He constructed out of them with great ingenuity and perseverance a dam from the mainland to the rock city in the sea. Thus literally it was fulfilled, "They shall lay thy stones and thy timber and thy dust in the midst of the water." The sentence pronounced upon that proud city, for so long the powerful mistress of the sea, "Thou shalt be built no more," has been fully carried out.

Of still greater interest are the prophecies which foretell the doom of Egypt. Ezekiel and Nahum mention the Egyptian city No. (Ezek. 30:14-16; Nah. 3:8.) No is Thebes and was the ancient capital of Egypt. The Egyptian name is No-Amon. It had a hundred gates, as we learn from Homer, and was a city of marvelous beauty. It was surrounded by walls twenty-four feet thick, and had a circumference of one mile and three quarters. The Lord announced through Ezekiel that this great city should be rent asunder and that its vast population should be cut off. Five hundred years later Ptolemy Laltyrus, the grandfather of Cleopatra, after besieging the city several years razed to the ground the previously ruined city. Every word given through Ezekiel had come true. One could fill many pages showing the literal fulfillment of Ezekiel's great predictions relating to Egypt. The decline and degradation predicted has come true. The rivers and canals of Egypt have dried up. The land has become desolate. The immense fisheries which yielded such a great income to the rulers of Egypt are no longer in existence. Ezek. 30:7 has found a literal fulfillment. Egypt is a land of ruins and wasted cities. The instruments whom God used in accomplishing this were strangers (Ezek. 30:12) like Cambyses, Amroo, Ochus and others. "There shall be no more a prince of the land of Egypt" (Ezek. 30:13). This too has been literally fulfilled. Ochus subdued rebellious Egypt 350 B. C., and since that time no native prince has ruled in Egypt. It is also written that Egypt should become the basest of the kingdoms, "Neither shall it exalt itself any more above the nations; for I will diminish them that they shall no more rule over the nations." This degradation has fully come to pass. Who would ever have thought that this magnificent country with its vast resources, its wonderful commerce, its great prosperity, its luxuries, the land of marvelous structures, could ever experience such a downfall! Another significant fact is that in spite of the great humiliation and degradation through which Egypt has passed for so many centuries, it is not to experience a total extinction. In this respect her fate differs from that of other nations, "They shall be there a base kingdom" (Ezek. 29: 14); this is the condition of Egypt today. And other prophets announce the same fact. One of the earliest prophets is Joel. He prophesied between 860 and 850 B. C. He predicted at that early date, "Egypt shall be a desolation." Isaiah also foretells the awful judgment of this great land of ancient culture. In the light of unfulfilled prophecy we discover the reason why God has not permitted the complete extinction of Egypt. Egypt is yet to be lifted out of the dust and is to receive a place of blessing only second to that of Israel (Isa. 19: 22-25). This will be fulfilled when our Lord comes again.

And what more could we say of Idumea, Babylonia, Assyria and other lands. Moab and Ammon, the enemies of Israel, once flourishing nations, have passed away and the numerous judgment predictions have come true. (See Jer. 48-49.) Edom is gone. "O thou that dwellest in the clefts of the rock, that holdest the height of the hill, though thou shouldest make thy nest as high as the eagle, I will bring thee down from thence, saith Jehovah" (Jer. 49: 16). "Thou shalt be desolate, O Mount Seir, and all Idumea, even all of it" (Ezek. 35: 15). It was an atheist who was first used to report that during a journey of eight days he had found in the territory of Idumea the ruins of thirty cities.

Babylonia and Assyria, once the granaries of Asia, the garden spots of that continent, enjoying a great civilization, are now in desolation and mostly unproductive deserts. The predictions of Isaiah and Jeremiah have been fulfilled. The judgments predicted to come upon Babylon were also fulfilled long ago.*

THE BOOK OF DANIEL

The Book of Daniel, however, supplies the most startling evidences of fulfilled prophecy. No other book has been so much attacked as this great book. For about two thousand years wicked men, heathen philosophers, and infidels have tried to break down its authority. It has proven to be the anvil upon which the critics' hammers have been broken to pieces. The Book of Daniel has survived all attacks. It has been denied that Daniel wrote the book during the Babylonian captivity. The critics claim that it was written during the time of the Maccabees. Kuenen, Wellhausen, Canon Farrar, Driver and others but repeat the statements of the assailant of Christianity of the third century, the heathen Porphyry, who contended that the Book of Daniel was a forgery. Such is the company in which the higher critics are found. The Book of Daniel has been completely vindicated. The prophet wrote the book and its magnificent prophecies in Babylon. All doubt as to that has been forever removed, and men who still repeat the infidel oppositions against the book, oppositions of a past

---

*"How utterly improbable it must have sounded to the contemporaries of Isaiah and Jeremiah, that the great Babylon, this oldest metropolis of the world, founded by Nimrod, planned to be a city on the Euphrates much larger than Paris of today, surrounded by walls four hundred feet high, on the top of which four chariots, each drawn by four horses, could be driven side by side; in the center a large, magnificent park an hour's walk in circumference, watered by machinery; in it the king's twelve palaces, surrounding the great temple of the sun-god with its six hundred-foot tower and its gigantic golden statue—should be converted into a heap of ruins in the midst of a desert! Who today would have any faith in a similar prophecy against Berlin or London or Paris or New York?" (Prof. Bettex.)

generation, must be branded as ignorant, or considered the willful enemies of the Bible.

NEBUCHADNEZZAR'S GREAT DREAM

The great dream of Nebuchadnezzar is recorded in the second chapter of the Book of Daniel. Nebuchadnezzar who had been constituted by Jehovah a great monarch over the earth (Jer. 27:5-9) desired to know the future. All his astrologers and soothsayers, his magicians and mediums, could not do that. Their predictions left him still in doubt (Dan. 2:29). God gave him then a dream which contained a most remarkable revelation. The great man-image the king beheld is the symbol of the great world empires which were to follow the Babylonian empire. The image had a head of gold; the chest and arms were of silver; the trunk and the thighs were of brass; the two legs of iron, and the two feet were composed of iron mixed with clay. The Lord made known through the prophet the meaning of this dream.

Nebuchadnezzar and the empire over which he ruled is symbolized by the golden head. An inferior kingdom was to come after the Babylonian Empire; its symbol is silver. This kingdom was to be followed by a third kingdom of brass to bear rule over all the earth. The fourth kingdom was to be strong as iron and was to subdue all things. Exactly three great world powers came after the Babylonian Empire, the Medo-Persian, the Graeco-Macedonian and the Roman. Interesting it is to learn, from the different metals of which the image was composed, the process of deterioration which was to characterize the successive monarchies. The fourth empire, the Roman world power, is seen in its historic division, indicated by the two legs. The empire consisted of two parts, the East and West Roman sections. Then the division of the Empire into kingdoms in which iron (monarchical form of government) and the clay (the rule of the people) should be present is also predicted. How all this has come to pass is too well known to need any further demonstration. These empires have come and gone and the territory of the old Roman Empire presents today the very condition as predicted in Nebuchadnezzar's dream. Monarchies and republics are in existence upon that territory. The final division into ten kingdoms has not yet been accomplished. The unfulfilled portion of this dream we do not follow here. The reader may find this explained in the author's exposition of Daniel.

DANIEL'S GREAT VISION OF THE WORLD POWERS

In the seventh chapter Daniel relates his first great vision. The four beasts he saw rising out of the sea, the type of nations, are symbolical of the same world powers. The lion with eagle's wings is Babylonia. Jeremiah also pictured Nebuchadnezzar as a lion. "The lion has come up from his thicket and the destroyer of the Gentiles is on his way" (Jer. 4:7). Ezekiel speaks of him as a great eagle. (Ezek. 17:3.) The Medo-Persian Empire is seen as a bear raised up on one side and having three ribs in its mouth. The one side appeared stronger because this second world empire had Persia for its stronger element. The three ribs the bear holds as prey predict the conquests of that empire. Medo-Persia conquered exactly three great provinces, Susiana, Lydia and Asia Minor. The leopard with four wings and four heads is the picture of the Graeco-Macedonian Empire. The four wings denote its swiftness and rapid advance so abundantly fulfilled in the conquests of Alexander the Great. The four heads of the leopard predict the partition of this empire into the kingdoms of Syria, Egypt, Macedonia and Asia Minor. The fourth beast, the great nondescript, with its ten horns, and the little horn, still to come, is the Roman Empire. These are wonderful things. Be it remembered that the prophet received the vision when the Babylonian Empire still existed. Here also the character of these empires typified by ferocious beasts is revealed. The great nations of Christendom which occupy the ground of the Roman Empire testify unconsciously to the truth of this great prophecy. The emblems of these nations are not doves, little lambs or other harmless creatures. They have chosen the lion, the bear, the unicorn, the eagle and the double-headed eagle.

ALEXANDER THE GREAT PREDICTED

In the eighth chapter a new prophecy is revealed through Daniel. Once more the Medo-Persian Empire is seen, this time under the figure of a ram with two horns, one higher than the other, and the higher one came up last. It foretells the composition of that empire. It was composed of the Medes and the Persians; the Persians came in last and were the strongest. It conquered in three directions. This corresponds to the bear with the three ribs in the previous chapter.

The he-goat which Daniel sees coming from the west with a great rush is the type of the leopard empire, the Graeco-Macedonian. The same swiftness as revealed in the leopard with four wings is seen here again. The notable horn upon the he-goat, symbolizing the Macedonian Empire, is Alexander the Great. Josephus tells us that Alexander was greatly moved when the Jewish high priest Jaddua acquainted him with the meaning of this prophecy written over two hundred years before. And how was it fulfilled, what is predicted in Dan. 8:5-8? 334 B. C. the notable horn, Alexander, in goat-like fashion, leaped across the Hellespont and fought successful battles, then pushed on to the banks of the Indus and the Nile and from there to Shushan. The great battles of the Granicus (334 B. C.), Issus (333 B. C.), and Arbella (331 B. C.) were fought, and with irresistible force he stamped the power of Persia and its king, Darius Codomannus, to the ground. He conquered rapidly Syria, Phoenicia, Cyprus, Pyre, Gaza, Egypt, Babylonia, Persia. In 329 he conquered Bactria, crossed the Oxus and Jaxaitis and defeated the Scythians. And thus he stamped upon the ram after having broken its horns. But when the he-goat had waxed very great, the great horn was broken. This predicted the early and sudden death of Alexander the Great. He died after a reign of 12 years and eight months, after a career of drunkenness and debauchery in 323 B. C. He died when he was but 32 years old. Then four notable ones sprang up in the place of the broken horn. This too has been fulfilled, for the empire of Alexander was divided into four parts. Four of the great generals of Alexander made the division, namely, Cassander, Lysimachus, Seleucus and Ptolemy. The four great divisions were Syria, Egypt, Macedonia, and Asia Minor.

ANTIOCHUS EPIPHANES

In verses 19 to 24 of the eighth chapter of Daniel the coming of a wicked leader, to spring out of one of the divisions of the Macedonian Empire and the vile work he was to do, is predicted. He was to work great havoc in the pleasant land, that is, Israel's land.

History does not leave us in doubt about the identity of this wicked king. He is the eighth king of the Seleucid dynasty, who took the Syrian throne and is known by the name of Antiochus Epiphanes, and bore also the name of Epimanes, i. e., "the Madman." He was the tyrant and oppressor of the Jews. His wicked deeds of oppression, blasphemy and sacrilege are fully described in the Book of the Maccabees. Long before he ever appeared Daniel saw him and his wicked work in his vision.

And all this has been fulfilled in Antiochus Epiphanes. When he had conquered Jerusalem he sacrificed a sow upon the altar of burnt offerings and sprinkled its broth over the entire building. He corrupted the youths of Jerusalem by introducing lewd practices; the feast of tabernacles he changed into the feast of Bacchus. He auctioned off the high-priesthood. All kinds of infamies were perpetrated by him and the most awful obscenity permitted and encouraged. All true worship was forbidden, and idol worship introduced, especially that of Jupiter Olympus. The whole city and land was devastated and some 100,000 pious Jews were massacred. Such has been the remarkable fulfillment of this prophecy.

Even the duration of this time of trouble was revealed; and 2,300 days are mentioned. These 2,300 days cover about the period of time during which Antiochus Epiphanes did his wicked deeds. The chronology of these 2,300 days is interesting. Judas Maccabaeus cleansed (lit. justified) the sanctuary from the abomination about December 25, 165 B. C. Antiochus died a miserable death two years later. Going back 2,300 days from the time Judas the Maccabean cleansed the defiled temple, brings us to 171 B. C. when we find the record of Antiochus' interference with the Jews. Menelaus had bribed Antiochus to make him high priest, robbed the temple and instituted the murder of the high priest Onias III. The most wicked deeds in the defilement of the temple were perpetrated by the leading general of Antiochus, Apollonius, in the year 168 B. C. We believe these 2,300 days are therefore literal days and have found their literal fulfillment in the dreadful days of this wicked king from the North. There is no other meaning attached to these days and the foolish speculations that these days are years, etc., lack Scriptural foundation altogether.

THE GREATEST OF ALL

The greatest prophecy in the Book of Daniel is contained in the ninth chapter, the prophecy concerning the 70 weeks, transmitted from heaven through Gabriel. (Dan. 9:24-27.) To many readers of the Book of Daniel it is not quite clear what the expression "seventy weeks" means, and when it is stated that each week represents a period of seven years, many Christians do not know why such is the case. A brief word of explanation may therefore be in order. The literal translation of the term "seventy weeks" is "seventy sevens." Now this word "sevens" translated "weeks" may mean "days" and it may mean "years." What then is meant here, seventy times seven days or seventy times seven years? It is evident that the "sevens" mean year weeks, seven years to each prophetic week. Daniel was occupied in reading the books and in prayer with the seventy years of the Babylonian captivity. And now Gabriel is going to reveal to him something which will take place in "seventy sevens," which means seventy times seven years. The proof that such is the case is furnished by the fulfillment of the prophecy itself.

First we notice in the prophecy that these 70 year-weeks are divided in three parts. Seven times seven (49 years) are to go by till the commanded rebuilding and restoration of Jerusalem should be accomplished. In the twentieth year of Artaxerxes the command was given to rebuild Jerusalem. It was in the year 445 B. C., exactly 49 years after the wall of Jerusalem and the city had been rebuilt. Then 62 weeks are given as the time when Messiah should be cut off and have nothing. This gives us 434 years (62 times 7). Here is a prediction concerning the death of Christ. Has it been fulfilled? Chronology shows that exactly 483 years after Artaxerxes gave the command to restore Jerusalem (445 B. C.), 434 years after the city had been restored, the death of our Lord Jesus Christ took place.

To be more exact, on the day on which our Lord Jesus Christ entered Jerusalem for the last time, the number of years announced by Gabriel expired and the Lord was crucified that week. The proof of it is perfect.

But there is more to be said. As a result of the cutting off of Messiah something else is prophesied. "And the people of the prince that shall come shall destroy the city and the sanctuary." The prince that is to come (and is yet to come) is the little horn of Dan. 7. He arises out of the Roman Empire. The people of the prince that shall come are therefore the Roman people. They have fulfilled this prophecy by destroying the temple and the city.

THE WARS OF THE PTOLEMIES AND SELEUCIDAE

The greater part of the eleventh chapter in Daniel has been historically fulfilled. It is an interesting study. So accurate are the predictions that the enemies of the Bible have tried their very best to show that Daniel did not write these prophecies several hundred years before they occurred. But they have failed in their miserable attempts. We place the startling evidence before our readers.

PROPHECY GIVEN B. C. 534

"And now will I shew thee the truth. Behold, there shall stand up yet three kings in Persia; and the fourth shall be far richer than they all: and by his strength through his riches he shall stir up all against the realm of Grecia." (Verse 2)

"And a mighty king shall stand up, that shall rule with great dominion, and do according to his will." (Verse 3.)

"And when he shall stand up, his kingdom shall be broken, and shall be divided toward the four winds of heaven; and not to his posterity, nor according to his dominion which he ruled: for his kingdom shall be plucked up even for others besides those." (Verse 4.)

"And the king of the South shall be strong, and one of his

FULFILLMENT

See Ezra 4. 5-24. The three kings were: Ahasuerus, Artaxerxes and Darius, known in history as Cambyses, Pseudo Smerdis, and Darius Hystaspis (not Darius the Mede). The fourth one was Xerxes, who, as history tells us, was immensely rich. The invasion of Greece took place in 480 B. C.

The successors of Xerxes are not mentioned. The mighty king in this verse is the notable horn seen by Daniel on the he-goat in chapter 8, Alexander the Great, 335 B. C.

B. C. 323. Alexander died young. The notable horn was broken. His kingdom was divided into four parts (four winds) after the battle of Ipsus 301 B. C. His posterity did not receive the kingdom, but his four generals, Ptolemy, Lysimachus, Seleucus Nicator and Cassander. Not one of these divisions reached to the glory of Alexander's dominion.

Asia and Greece are not followed but Syria and Egypt become

princes; and he shall be strong above him, and have dominion; his dominion shall be a great dominion." (Verse 5.)

prominent, because the King of the North from Syria, and the King of the South, Egypt, were to come in touch with the Jews. The holy land became involved with both. The King of the South was Ptolemy Lagus. One of his princes was Seleucus Nicator. He established a great dominion, which extended to the Indus.

"And in the end of years they shall join themselves together; for the king's daughter of the South shall come to the King of the North to make an agreement; but she shall not retain the power of the arm; neither shall he stand, nor his arm: but she shall be given up, and they that brought her, and he that begat her, and he that strengthened her in these times." (Verse 6.)

Here is another gap. This verse takes us to 250 B. C. The two who make an alliance are the Kings of the North (Syrian division of the Grecian Empire) and of the South (Egypt). This alliance was effected by the marriage of the daughter of the King of the South, the Egyptian Princess Berenice, daughter of Ptolemy II., to Antiochus Theos, the King of the North. The agreement was that Antiochus had to divorce his wife and make any child of Berenice his heir in the kingdom. The agreement ended in calamity. When Ptolemy died Antiochus Theos in 247 called back his former wife. Berenice and her young son were poisoned and the first wife's son, Callinicus, was put on the throne as Seleucus II.

"But out of a branch of her roots shall one stand up in his estate, which shall come with an army, and shall enter into the fortress of the King of the North, and shall deal against them, and shall prevail." (Verse 7.)

The one out of her roots (Berenice, who had been murdered) was her own brother, Ptolemy Euergetes, who avenged her death. He conquered Syria. He dealt against Seleucus II, King of the North, and slew the wife of Antiochus Theos, who had Berenice poisoned. He seized the fortress, the port of Antioch.

"And shall also carry captives into Egypt their gods, with their princes, and with their precious vessels of silver and gold; and he shall continue more years than the King of the North." (Verse 8.)

Ptolemy Euergetes did exactly as predicted. He returned with 4,000 talents of gold and 40,000 talents of silver and 2,500 idols and idolatrous vessels. Many of these Cambyses had taken to Persia.

"So the King of the South shall come into his kingdom, and shall return into his own land." (Verse 9.)

(*Literal translation*): "and the same [King of the North] shall come into the realm of the King of the South, but shall return into his own land."

In 240 B. C. Seleucus Callinicus the King of the North invaded Egypt. He had to return defeated. His fleet perished in a storm.

"But his sons shall be stirred up, and shall assemble a multitude of great forces; and one shall certainly come, and overflow, and pass through: then shall he return, and be stirred up, even to his fortress." (Verse 10.)

The sons of Seleucus Callinicus were Seleucus III and Antiochus the Great. Seleucus (Ceraunos) III began war against Egyptian Provinces in Asia Minor. He was unsuccessful. The other son Antioch invaded Egypt and passed through because Ptolemy Philopater did not oppose him. In 218 B. C. Antiochus continued his warfare and took the fortress Gaza.

"And the King of the South shall be moved with choler, and shall come forth and fight with him, even with the King of the North: and he shall set forth a great multitude but the multitude shall be given into his hand." (Verse 11.)

In 217 B. C. Ptolemy aroused himself and fought Antiochus the Great with an immense army. He defeated Antiochus. The multitude was given into the hands of Ptolemy Philopater.

"And when he hath taken away the multitude, his heart shall be lifted up; and he shall cast down many ten thousands: but he shall not be strengthened by it." (Verse 12.)

(*Literal:* "And the multitude shall rise up and his courage increase.")

"For the King of the North shall return, and shall set forth a multitude greater than the former, and shall certainly come after certain years with a great army and with much riches." (Verse 13.)

"And in those times there shall many stand up against the King of the South: also the robbers of thy people shall exalt themselves to establish the vision; but they shall fall." (Verse 14.)

"So the King of the North shall come, and cast up a mount, and take the most fenced cities: and the arms of the South shall not withstand, neither his chosen people, neither shall there be any strength to withstand." (Verse 15.)

"But he that cometh against him shall do according to his own will, and none shall stand before him: and he shall stand in the

The people of Egypt rose up and the weakling Ptolemy became courageous. His victory is again referred to. It was won at Raphia. He might have pressed his victory. But he did not make use of it but gave himself up to a licentious life. Thus "he was not strengthened by it."

About 14 years later, 203 B. C., Antiochus assembled a great army, greater than the army which was defeated at Raphia, and turned against Egypt. Ptolemy Philopater had died and left an infant son Ptolemy Epiphanes.

Antiochus had for his ally Philip, King of Macedon. Also in Egypt many rebels stood up. And then there were, as we read in Josephus, wicked Jews, who helped Antiochus. These "robbers of thy people" established the vision. They helped along the very things which had been predicted, as to trials for them.

All this was fulfilled in the severe struggles, which followed.

The invasion of the glorious land by Antiochus followed. He subjected the whole land unto himself. He also was well dis-

glorious land, which by his hand shall be consumed." (Verse 16.)

"He shall also set his face to enter with the strength of his whole kingdom, and an agreement shall be made with him; thus shall he do: and he shall give him the daughter of women, corrupting her: but she shall not stand on his side, neither be for him." (Verse 17.)

"After this shall he turn his face unto the isles, and shall take many: but a prince [literally: Captain] for his own behalf shall cause the reproach offered by him to cease; without his own reproach he shall cause it to turn upon him." (Verse 18.)

"Then he shall turn his face toward the fort of his own land: but he shall stumble and fall, and not be found." (Verse 19.)

"Then shall stand up in his estate a raiser of taxes in the glory of the kingdom: but within few days he shall be destroyed, neither in anger, nor in battle." (Verse 20.)

posed towards the Jews because they sided with Antiochus the Great against Ptolemy Epiphanes.

This brings us to the years 198-195 B. C. Antiochus aimed to get full possession of Egypt. An agreement was made. In this treaty between Antiochus and Ptolemy Epiphanes, Cleopatra, daughter of Antiochus was espoused to Ptolemy. Why is Cleopatra called "daughter of women?" Because she was very young and was under the care of her mother and grandmother. The treaty failed.

A few years later Antiochus conquered isles on the coast of Asia Minor.

The captain predicted is Scipio Asiaticus. Antiochus had reproached the Romans by his acts and he was defeated. This defeat took place at Magnesia 190 B. C.

Antiochus returns to his own land. He came to a miserable end trying to plunder the temple of Belus in Elymais.

This is Seleucus Philopater B. C. 187-176. He was known as a raiser of taxes. He had an evil reputation with the Jews because he was such an exactor among them. His tax-collector Heliodorus poisoned him and so he was slain "neither in anger, nor in battle."

PROPHECY GIVEN B. C. 534

FULFILLMENT

"And in his estate shall stand up a vile person, to whom they shall not give the honor of the kingdom: but he shall come in peaceably, and obtain the kingdom by flatteries." (Verse 21.)

This vile person is none other than Antiochus Epiphanes. He had no claim on royal dignities, being only a younger son of Antiochus the Great. He seized royal honors by trickery and with flatteries. He is the little horn of chapter 8.

"And with the arms of a flood shall they be overflown from before him, and shall be broken; yea, also the prince of the covenant." (Verse 22.)

He was successful in defeating his enemies. The prince of the covenant may mean his nephew Ptolemy Philometor. He also vanquished Philometor's generals.

"And after the league made with him he shall work deceitfully: for he shall come up, and shall become strong with a small people." (Verse 23.)

He feigned friendship to young Ptolemy but worked deceitfully. To allay suspicion he came against Egypt with a small force but took Egypt as far as Memphis.

"He shall enter peaceably even upon the fattest places of the province; and he shall do that which his fathers have not done, nor his father's father; he shall scatter among them the prey, and spoil, and riches: yea, and he shall forecast his devices against the strongholds, even for a time." (Verse 24.)

He took possession of the fertile places in Egypt under the pretense of peace. He took Pelusium and laid seige to the fortified places Naucratis and Alexandria.

"And he shall stir up his power and his courage against the King of the South with a great army; and the King of the South shall be stirred up to battle with a very great and mighty army; but he shall not stand: for they shall forecast devices against him." (Verse 25.)

This King of the South is Ptolemy Physcon, who was made king after Philometor had fallen into the hands of Antiochus. He had a great army but did not succeed, because treason had broken out in his own camp.

"Yea, they that feed of the portion of his meat shall destroy him, and his army shall overflow: and many shall fall down slain." (Verse 26.)

Additional actions of Antiochus and warfare, in which he was successful, followed.

"And both these kings' hearts shall be to do mischief, and they shall speak lies at one table; but it shall not prosper: for yet the end shall be at the time appointed." (Verse 27.)

The two kings are Antiochus Epiphanes and his associate Philometor. They made an alliance against Ptolemy Euergetes II, also called Physcon. But they spoke lies against each other and did not succeed in their plans.

"Then shall he return into his land with great riches; and his heart shall be against the holy covenant; and he shall do exploits, and return to his own land." (Verse 28.)

In 168 B. C. he returned from his expedition and had great riches. Then he marched through Judea and did his awful deeds. A report had come to his ears that the Jewish people had reported him dead. In the first and second book of the Maccabees we read of his atrocities. Then he retired to Antioch.

"At the time appointed he shall return, and come toward the South; but it shall not be as the former, or as the latter." (Verse 29.)

He made still another attempt against the South. However, he had not the former success.

"For the ships of Chittim shall come against him; therefore he shall be grieved, and return, and have indignation against the holy covenant: so shall he do; he shall even return, and have intelligence with them that forsake the holy covenant." (Verse 30.)

The ships of Chittim are the Roman fleet. When within a few miles of Alexandria he heard that ships had arrived. He went to salute them. They delivered to him the letters of the senate, in which he was commanded, on pain of the displeasure of the Roman people, to put an end to the war against his nephews. Antiochus said, "he would go and consult his friends;" on which Popilius, one of the legates, took his staff, and instantly drew a circle round Antiochus on the sand, where he stood; and commanded him not to pass that circle, till he had given a definite answer. As a grieved and defeated man he returned and then he fell upon Judea once more to commit additional wickedness. Apostate Jews sided with him.

"And arms shall stand on his part and they shall pollute the sanctuary of strength, and shall take away the daily sacrifice, and they shall place the abomination that maketh desolate." (Verse 31.)

This brings us to the climax of the horrors under Antiochus Epiphanes. The previous record of it is contained in chapter 8. He sent Apollonius with over 20,000 men to destroy Jerusalem. Multitudes were slain, and women and children led away as captives. He issued a command that all people must conform to the idolatry of Greece. A wicked Grecian was sent to enforce the word of Antiochus. All sacrifices ceased and the God-given ceremonials of Judaism came to an end. The temple was polluted by the sacrifices of swine's flesh. The temple was dedicated to Jupiter Olympius. Thus the prediction was fulfilled.

"And such as do wickedly against the covenant shall he corrupt by flatteries: but the people that do know their God shall be strong, and do exploits.

"And they that understand among the people shall instruct

These verses describe the condition among the Jewish people. There were two classes. Those who did wickedly against the covenant, the apostate, and those who knew God, a faithful remnant. The apostates sided with many: yet they shall fall by the sword, and by flame, by captivity, and by spoil, many days.

"Now when they shall fall, they shall be holpen with a little help: but many shall cleave to them with flatteries." (Verses 32-34.)

the enemy, and the people who knew God were strong. This has reference to the noble Maccabees. There was also suffering and persecution.

MANY MORE FULFILLED PROPHECIES

Many other fulfilled prophecies might be quoted. In the last chapter of Daniel an interesting prediction is made concerning the time of the end. "Many shall run to and fro, and knowledge shall be increased." Sir Isaac Newton, the discoverer of the law of gravitation, wrote on Daniel and expressed his belief that some day people would travel at the rate of fifty miles an hour. The French infidel Voltaire many years later laughed at Newton's statement and held it up to ridicule. The time of the end is here and the prophecy of Dan. 12:4 has come true.

In the New Testament are also written prophecies which are now in process of fulfillment. 1 Tim. 4:1, 2; 2 Tim. 3:1-5; 4:1-3; 2 Pet. 2; Jude's Epistle, and other Scriptures predict the present day apostasy.

UNFULFILLED PROPHECY

As stated before, there are many unfulfilled prophecies in the Bible. The literal fulfillment of prophecies in the past vouches for the literal fulfillment of every prophecy in the Word of God. Some of them were uttered several thousand years ago. The world still waits for their fulfillment. May we remember that God does not need to be in a hurry. He knows indeed the end from the beginning. He takes His time in accomplishing His eternal purposes. And may we, His people, who know and love His Word, not neglect prophecy, for the Prophetic Word is the lamp which shineth in a dark place.

CHAPTER V

THE COMING OF CHRIST

BY PROFESSOR CHARLES R. ERDMAN, D. D.,
PRINCETON THEOLOGICAL SEMINARY, PRINCETON, NEW JERSEY

The return of Christ is *a fundamental doctrine* of the Christian faith. It is embodied in hymns of hope; it forms the climax of the creeds; it is the sublime motive for evangelistic and missionary activity; and daily it is voiced in the inspired prayer: "Even so: Come, Lord Jesus."

It is peculiarly *a Scriptural doctrine.* It is not, on the one hand, a dream of ignorant fanatics, nor, on the other, a creation of speculative theologians; but it is a truth divinely revealed, and recorded in the Bible with marked clearness, emphasis and prominence.

Like the other great truths of revelation it is *a controverted doctrine.* The essential fact is held universally by all who admit the authority of Scripture; but as to certain incidental, although important, elements of the teaching, there is difference of opinion among even the most careful and reverent students. Any consideration of the theme demands, therefore, modesty, humility and abundant charity. According to the familiar view outlined in this paper, the Bible describes the "second coming of Christ" as *personal, glorious, imminent.*

I. HIS COMING WILL BE PERSONAL

By *personal* is meant all that may be suggested by the words *visible, bodily, local;* and all that may be contrasted with that which is spiritual, providential, figurative. Of course, *the spiritual presence of Christ* is a blessed reality; one of the most comforting and inspiring of truths is the teaching that Christ does come to each believer, by His Holy Spirit, and dwells within, and empowers for service and suffering and growth in grace; but this is to be held in harmony with the other blessed truth that Christ will some day literally appear again in bodily form, and "we shall see Him" and shall then "be like Him," when "we see Him as He is."

Nor yet did that special manifestation of the Holy Spirit at *Pentecost* fulfill the promise of Christ's return. Subsequent to Pentecost, Peter urged the Jews to repent in order that Jesus, whom for a time "the heavens had received," might be "sent back again;" he wrote his epistles of comfort based upon the hope of a returning Lord, while Paul and the other inspired Apostles, long after Pentecost, emphasized the coming of Christ as the highest incentive for life and service.

According to the interpretation of others, Christ is said "to come" in various *providential events of history*, as notably in the destruction of Jerusalem. This tragedy of history is supposed by many to fulfill the prophecies spoken by Christ in His great discourse on the Mount of Olives, recorded in Matthew 24, and Mark 13, and Luke 21. When one combines these predictions, it becomes evident that the capture of the holy city by Titus was a real but only a partial fulfillment of the words of Christ. As in the case of so many Old Testament prophecies, the nearer event furnished the colors in which were depicted scenes and occurrences which belonged to a distant future, and in this case to "the end of the age." When Jerusalem fell, the people of God were not delivered nor the enemies of God punished, nor did "the sign of the Son of Man" appear in the heavens, as was predicted of the time when He comes again; and long after the fall of the city, John wrote in Gospel and in Apocalypse of the coming of the King.

Nor is the coming of Christ to be confused with *death*. It is true that this dark messenger ushers us into an experience which is, for the believer, one of great blessedness; "to depart is to be with Christ, which is very far better," "to be absent from the body" is "to be at home with the Lord;" but death is for us inseparable from pain and loss and sorrow and tears and anguish; and even those who are now with their Lord, in heavenly joy, are waiting for their bodies of glory and for the rewards and reunions which will be theirs at the appearing of Christ.

More marvelous than the scenes at Pentecost, more startling than the fall of Jerusalem, more blessed than the indwelling of the Spirit or the departure to be with the Lord, will be the literal, visible, bodily, return of Christ. No event may seem less probable to unaided human reason; no event is more certain in the light of inspired Scripture. "This same Jesus which is taken up from you into heaven shall so come *in like manner* as ye have seen Him go into heaven." "Behold, He cometh with clouds; and *every eye shall see Him*" (Acts 1:11; Rev. 1:7).

II. HIS COMING, GLORIOUS

This coming of Christ is to be *glorious*, not only in its attendant circumstances, but also in its effects upon the Church and the world. Our Lord predicted that He would return "in His own glory, and the glory of His Father, and of the holy angels" (Luke 9:26). He will then be revealed in His Divine majesty. Once during His earthly ministry, on the mount of transfiguration, there was given to His followers a glimpse of the royal splendor He had for a time laid aside, and in which He will again appear.

As on the great day of atonement the high priest put off his usual robes "for glory and for beauty" and appeared in spotless white. when he offered the sacrifices for sin and went into the holy place to intercede for the waiting people, so our Great High Priest laid aside the robes of His imperial majesty when stooping from heaven He assumed His garb of sinless flesh, and offered Himself as the perfect sacrifice and entered into the holy places not made with hands to appear in the presence of God for us; but as the high priest again assumed his garments of scarlet and blue and purple and gold when he came forth to complete his work in the presence of the people, so Christ, when He returns to bless, and to receive the homage of the world, will be manifest in His Divine glory. (Heb. 9: 24-28.) As He appeared to Isaiah in his vision, to the disciples on the holy mount, to Saul on his way to Damascus, to John on Patmos, so will the Son of Man appear when, as He promised, He is seen "sitting at the right hand of Power, and coming on the clouds of heaven" (Matt. 26: 64). Nothing could be more natural than such a triumphant return of the risen, ascended Lord. What a pathetic picture Christ would present in the history of the race, if, after all His claims and promises, the world should see Him, last of all, hanging on a cross as a malefactor, or laid lifeless in a tomb! "He was despised and rejected of men;" but He is to return again "with power and great glory," attended by thousands of the heavenly host. As the Epistle to the Hebrews strikingly says: "When He again bringeth in the first born into the inhabited earth He saith, And let all the angels of God worship Him" (Heb. 1: 6).

> "Thou art coming, O my Saviour,
> Thou art coming, O my King,
> In Thy beauty all resplendent;
> In Thy glory all transcendent;
> Well may we rejoice and sing:
> Coming! in the opening East
> Herald brightness slowly swells;
> Coming! O my glorious Priest,
> Hear we not Thy golden bells."

Then Christ will *reign in glory* over all the world. It is true that now "all power" has been given to Him "in heaven and on earth," but that power has not been fully manifest; "we see not yet all things put under Him." He has "sat down on the right hand of God," but He is "henceforth expecting till His enemies be made the footstool of His feet." He is now reigning, seated on His Father's throne; but this world is still in reality a revolted province, and Christ is yet to sit upon His own throne; then "before Him every knee will bow, and every tongue confess that He is Lord" (Heb. 10:12, 13; Phil. 2:10, 11).

These expressions need not be interpreted with such crass literalness as to suggest that Christ will rule visibly in some one earthly locality, "establishing in Jerusalem an oriental court;" but they at least mean that the coming of Christ will be followed by the universal reign of Christ. "When the Son of Man shall come in His glory, and all the angels with Him, then shall He sit on *the throne of His glory*" (Matt. 25:31). He will determine who may enter and who must be excluded from His kingdom. He will then say: "Come ye blessed of My Father, inherit the kingdom prepared for you from the foundation of the world." Then will be fulfilled His prediction: "Not every one that saith unto Me, Lord, Lord, shall enter into the kingdom of heaven, but he that doeth the will of My Father who is in heaven. Many *will say to Me* in that day, Lord, Lord, . . . and then *will I* profess unto them, I never knew you, depart from Me, ye that work iniquity" (Matt. 7:21-23). He will be the supreme Judge, but He will also be manifest as the universal Ruler in His perfected kingdom. Then the voices will be heard proclaiming: "The kingdom of the world is become the kingdom of our Lord, and of His Christ; and He shall reign forever and ever" (Rev. 11:15).

In this glory of Christ His followers are to share. *The resurrection of the dead* will take place when He returns: "For as in Adam all die, so also in Christ shall all be made alive. But each in his own order: Christ the first fruits; then they that are Christ's at His coming." The *body* of the believer is thus to be raised in *glory*. "It is sown in corruption; it is raised in incorruption: it is sown in dishonor; it is raised in glory." As to how the spirits now with Christ are to be united with their resurrection bodies, the Bible is absolutely silent; but we know that this will be at the coming of the Lord. (1 Cor. 15: 22, 23, 42, 43.)

Then, too, the bodies of *living believers* will be glorified, and made deathless and immortal like the body of their Divine Lord. "For our citizenship is in heaven; whence also we wait for a Saviour, the Lord Jesus Christ: who shall fashion anew the body of our humiliation, that it may be conformed to the body of His glory" (Phil. 3: 20, 21). Sometimes it is carelessly said that "nothing is so sure as death"; one thing is more sure; it is this: some Christians will never die. One generation of believers will be living when Christ returns, and they will be translated, without the experience of death. What "is mortal will be swallowed up of life." They never will be unclothed," but "clothed upon" with the glory of immortality. "Behold, I tell you a mystery: We shall not all sleep, but we shall all be changed, in a moment, in the twinkling of an eye, at the last trump; for the trumpet shall sound, and the dead shall be raised incorruptible, and we shall be changed" (1 Cor. 15: 51, 52; 2 Cor. 5: 4).

Then, also, will be the blessed *reunion in glory* of the risen and the transfigured followers of Christ. "For this we say unto you by the word of the Lord, that we that are alive, that are left unto the coming of the Lord, shall in no wise precede them that are fallen asleep. For the Lord Himself shall descend from heaven, with a shout, with the voice of the archangel, and with the trump of God: and the dead in Christ shall rise first; then we that are alive, that are left, shall together with them be caught up in the clouds to meet the Lord in the air: and so shall we ever be with the Lord" (1 Thess. 4: 13-18).

> "Some from earth, from glory some,
> Severed only *'Till He Come.'*"

The time of the return of the Lord will be, furthermore, the time of *the reward* of His servants. The Son of Man is likened to a nobleman who has gone "into a far country to receive for himself a kingdom, and to return." He has entrusted various talents to his servants with the command to use them wisely, until his return. When he has "come back again, having received the kingdom," *then* he "maketh a reckoning with them." It is popularly said, and in a sense it is true, that when our loved ones go to be with Christ "they have gone to their reward"; but more strictly speaking, the full reward of the blessed awaits the coming of Christ. Whatever may be meant by being "set over many things," or having "authority over ten cities," the complete recompense of the faithful is "at the resurrection of the just." (Matt. 25: 14-23; Luke 19: 11-27; Luke 14: 14.)

That the real coronation day of the Christian is not at death but at "the appearing of Christ" was strikingly suggested by Paul when, realizing that he was to die before the Lord returned, he gave to Timothy his triumphant farewell: "I have fought the good fight, I have finished the course, I have kept the faith: henceforth there is laid up for me the crown of righteousness, which the Lord the righteous Judge shall give to me *at that day*: and not to me only, but also to all them that have loved *His appearing*" (2 Tim. 4:7, 8). So Peter encourages pastors to be faithful, by the familiar promise: "And when the chief Shepherd *shall be manifested*, ye shall receive the crown of glory that fadeth not away" (1 Peter 5: 1-4). In large measure this reward will consist in being changed into a moral likeness to Christ. This is far more marvelous than the transfiguration of our bodies, but no less real. "Beloved, now are we the children of God, and it is not yet made manifest what we shall be. We know that if He shall be manifested, we shall be like Him; for we shall see Him even as He is" (1 John 3: 1-3). The reward which awaits the followers of Christ further includes the fulfillment of the blessed prophecies which declare the saints are *to reign* with Christ. "Know ye not that the saints shall judge the earth . . . Know ye not that we shall judge angels?" "If we endure we shall also reign with Him." "I appoint unto you a kingdom . . . and ye shall sit on thrones judging the twelve tribes of Israel." (1 Cor. 6: 2, 3; 2 Tim. 2: 12; Luke 22: 30.) Whatever may be denoted by promises so full of wonder and mystery, they do not mean that "the saints are to rule on earth *in the flesh*." Believers will previously have been "raised in glory," transfigured, translated. As co-regents with their Lord they may be privileged to perform blessed ministries for the world, but they nevertheless will belong to His immortal and heavenly kingdom. "They are like the angels of God . . . being the children of the resurrection" (Luke 20: 35, 36).

Such a rule of Christ and His people must secure unparalleled blessedness for the world. "The end of the world" does not mean, in prophecy, the end of the earth and the destruction of its inhabitants; but the end of "the present age," which is to be followed by *an age of glory*. The "present evil age" is predicted to close amid scenes of fiery judgment upon the enemies of God, and with portents and convulsions which will affect the very earth itself; but the results will be what is figuratively described as the "new heavens and the new earth wherein dwelleth righteousness." Nature itself will become more beautiful and joyous. "The whole creation which is groaning and travailing in pain together until now will be delivered from the bondage of corruption unto the liberty of the glory of the children of God" (Rom. 8: 21). In spite of the sin and failures of man, we are not to look for the destruction of this globe, but for an era when the true full life of humanity will be realized, when all shall know the Lord from the least unto the greatest, when all art and science and social institutions shall be Christian, when "nation shall not lift up sword against nation, neither shall they learn war any more"

(Isa. 2:1-4). Such an age, of which poets have sung and philosophers have dreamed, such an era as psalmists, and prophets, and apostles have promised, will dawn at the coming of the King. Inspired by such a hope the waiting Church has learned to sing:

> "Come, Lord, and tarry not;
> Bring the long looked for day;
> O, why these years of waiting here,
> These ages of delay?

> "Come, and make all things new;
> Build up this ruined earth;
> Restore our faded Paradise,
> Creation's second birth.

> "Come, and begin Thy reign
> Of everlasting peace;
> Come, take the kingdom to Thyself,
> Great King of righteousness."

III. IMMINENT

The Bible further describes the coming of Christ as *imminent*. It is an event which may occur in any lifetime. Whatever difficulties the fact involves, there is no doubt that all the inspired writers and their fellow Christians believed that Christ might return in their generation. This has been the normal attitude of the Church ever since. Paul describes believers as men "who have turned to God from idols" and who "wait for His Son from heaven." Christians are further described as "those that wait for Him," and as "those that love His appearing." They are everywhere in the New Testament exhorted to "watch," and to be ready for the return of their Lord. His coming is their constant encouragement and inspiration and hope. (1 Thess. 4:10; 2 Peter 4:8; Matt. 24:42; Mark 13:35, 37; Luke 21:36; Phil. 4:5.)

However, "imminent" does *not* mean *"immediate."* Confusion of these ideas has led some writers to assert that "Paul and the early Christians were mistaken in their views as to the Lord's return." But, when Paul used such a phrase as *"we that are alive and remain unto the coming of the Lord,"* he meant simply to identify himself with his fellow Christians, and to suggest that, if he lived until Christ came, their blessed experience would also be his. He could not have said, *"ye that are alive and remain;"* that would have indicated that Paul was to die first. This he did not then know. He believed that the Lord *might* return in his life time; he never asserted that He *would*.

"Imminence" as related to our Lord's return indicates *uncertainty* as to time, but *possibility* of nearness. "Take ye heed, watch, for ye know not when the time is" (Mark 13:33). Such statements rebuke those who have brought the doctrine into disrepute by announcing dates for "the end of the world," and by setting times for the coming of Christ. So, too, they suggest caution to those who assert that the age is *now* drawing to its close; it *may* be, but of this there is no certainty. These Scriptural exhortations to watch seem to contradict, also, those who teach that a "Millennium," a thousand years or a protracted period of righteousness, *must* intervene between the present time and the advent of Christ.

Those who hold this last view are commonly called "Post-Millennialists" to distinguish them from "Pre-Millennialists," who hold that the return of Christ will precede and usher in such an age of universal blessedness.

The great objection to the Pre-Millennial position is the apparent prediction of 2 Peter 3, that at the coming of Christ, in "the day of the Lord," the earth will be destroyed; there could then be *no place* for a millennium. The difficulty in the Post-Millennial theory is the repeated description of this present age as one of mingled good and evil, in which iniquity, as well as righteousness, continues to develop uninterruptedly;

there is thus *no time* for a millennium before the Lord returns. As to the passage from Peter, it is obviously no more subversive of one of these theories than of the other. No one can possibly review the picture, which the Apostle draws in his two epistles, of the apostasy and skepticism and godlessness already prevailing and surely deepening as "the day of the Lord" draws near, and find any place for a previous millennium before "that day." The predictions of fiery judgments and consequent "new heavens and new earth" must be read in connection with Isaiah 65 and 66, from which Peter is quoting. It will then be seen that these expressions are in-so-far figurative that the earth still continues with its life, its nations, its progress, after these judgments are over. Terrific convulsions, and governmental, social and cosmic changes, only introduce a new and better age. So, too, "the day of the Lord" is a familiar phrase, and as we read Zech. 14 we see that while, in that day, the Lord comes amidst appalling portents, His coming and the day itself are followed by a scene of great blessedness on this same earth; the Nile is still flowing in its course and the nations are going up to Jerusalem to worship. (Note also that in 2 Pet. 3: 10 the most ancient manuscripts do not read "burned up" but "discovered.")

There are other positive statements of Scripture which intimate that *the millennium* follows the coming of Christ.

According to Daniel, it is *after* the Son of Man comes with the clouds of heaven that He is given "dominion and glory and a kingdom, that all peoples, nations and languages should serve Him, . . . and the kingdom and the dominion and the greatness of the kingdom *under the whole heaven*," are "given to the people of the saints of the Most High; . . . and all dominions shall serve and obey Him" (Dan. 7: 13, 14, 27). According to the Psalms, the appearing of the Lord, in flaming fire upon His adversaries, *prepares the way* for the establishment of His glorious kingdom, as "He comes to rule the world with righteousness and the peoples with equity" (Psa. 96, 97,

98, etc.). According to Paul (2 Thess. 1 and 2) the advent described by Daniel is not to an earth which is enjoying millennial peace, but it is "in flaming fire" to destroy an existing "Man of Sin" whose career is the culmination of the lawlessness already manifest and to continue until the personal coming of Christ. According to our Lord Himself His return is to bring "the regeneration," not the destruction of the world (Matt. 19: 28; Luke 22: 28-30). But this rule of blessedness is preceded by judgments that come "as a snare on all the earth" (Luke 21: 29-36). According to Peter, "seasons of refreshing" and "the restitution of all things," not annihilation of the globe, will come with the return of Christ (Acts 3: 19-21). According to John, the coming of Christ (Rev. 19) *precedes* the millennium. (Rev. 20.)

However great the divergence of views among students of prophecy may seem to be, and in spite of the many varieties of opinion among the representatives of the two schools which have been mentioned in passing, the *points* of *agreement* are far *more important*. The main difference is as to the order, rather than as to the reality of events.

The great body of believers are united in expecting both an age of glory and a personal return of Christ. As to many related events they differ; but as to the *one great precedent condition* of that coming age or that promised return of the Lord there is absolute harmony of conviction: *the Gospel must first be preached to all nations* (Matt. 24: 14). The Church must continue to "make disciples of all the nations . . . even unto the end of the age" (Matt. 28: 19, 20).

This is therefore a time, not for unkindly criticism of fellow Christians, but for friendly conference; not for disputing over divergent views, but for united action; not for dogmatic assertion of prophetic programs, but for the humble acknowledgment that "we know in part;" not for idle dreaming, but for the immediate task of evangelizing a lost world.

For such effort, no one truth is more inspiring, than that of the return of Christ. None other can make us sit more lightly by the things of time, none other is more familiar as a Scriptural motive to purity, holiness, patience, vigilance, love. Strengthened by this blessed hope let us press forward with passionate zeal to the task that awaits us:

> "Till o'er our ransomed nature
> The Lamb for sinners slain,
> Redeemer, King, Creator,
> In bliss returns to reign!"

CHAPTER VI

IS ROMANISM CHRISTIANITY?

BY T. W. MEDHURST,

GLASGOW, SCOTLAND

I am aware that, if I undertake to prove that *Romanism is not Christianity*, I must expect to be called "bigoted, harsh, uncharitable." Nevertheless I am not daunted; for I believe that on a right understanding of this subject depends the salvation of millions.

One reason why Popery has of late gained so much power in Great Britain and Ireland, and is gaining power still, is that many Protestants look on it now as a form of true Christianity; and think that, on that account, notwithstanding great errors, it ought to be treated very tenderly. Many suppose that at the time of the Reformation, it was reformed, and that it is now much nearer the truth than it was before that time. It is still, however, the same; and, if examined, will be found to be so different from, and so hostile to, real Christianity, that it is not, in fact, Christianity at all.

Christianity, as revealed in the Sacred Writings, is salvation by Christ. It sets Him before us as at once a perfect man, the everlasting God, the God-man Mediator; who, by appointment of the Father, became a Substitute for all who were given Him. It teaches that by Him God's justice was magnified, and His mercy made manifest; that, for all who trust in Him, He fulfilled the law, and brought in *a complete righteousness;* and that by this alone they can be justified before God. It teaches that His death was a perfect sacrifice, and made full satisfaction and atonement for their sins, so that God lays no sin to their charge, but gives them a free and full pardon; that He has ascended to the right hand of God, and has sent down the Holy Spirit to be His only Vicar and Representative on earth; that He is the only Mediator between the righteous God and sinful man; that it is by the Holy Spirit alone that we are convinced of sin, and led to trust in Jesus; that all who trust in Him, and obey Him with the obedience of faith and love, are saved, and, being saved, are made "kings and priests unto God," and have "eternal life" in Him.

This is Christianity, the Christianity which the Apostles preached. But side by side with the Apostles, Satan went forth also, and preached what Paul calls *"another* gospel." Paul did not mean that it was *called* "another gospel;" but that as Satan "beguiled Eve through his subtlety" (2 Cor. 11:3), so some, while professing to teach the Gospel, were turning men away "from the simplicity that is in Christ;" and by doing so, did, in fact, teach "another gospel." Paul, speaking of those who were thus deceived, said, "I marvel that ye are so soon removed from Him that called you into the grace of Christ unto *another gospel* which is *not another;* but there be some that trouble you, and would pervert the Gospel of Christ." He means that there can be but *one Gospel,* though something else may be called the gospel; and he says of those who had thus perverted "the Gospel of Christ": "If any one preach any other gospel unto you . . . let him be accursed" (Gal. 1:6-9). He calls those who did so "false apostles, deceitful workers, transforming themselves into the apostles of Christ;" and he adds, "no marvel; for Satan himself is ·transformed into an angel of light. Therefore, it is no great thing if his ministers also be transformed as the ministers of righteousness; whose end shall be according to their works" (2 Cor. 11:13-15).

Let us consider well the meaning of these passages of Scripture. Paul says that there cannot be another Gospel; the conclusion, therefore, is evident, that these teachers were not teachers of Christianity, but of *a Satanic delusion.*

I submit that the teaching of Rome is at least as different from that of the Sacred Writings as that which Paul calls "another gospel;" and that, therefore, his words authorize us to say that Romanism is not Christianity.

FIRST, Christianity consists of what Christ has taught, and commanded in Scripture. But Romanism does not even profess to be founded on Scripture only: it claims a right to depart from what is contained in it—a right to add 'to Scripture what is handed down *by tradition;* and both to depart from and add to Scripture by making *new decrees.* It forbids the cup to the people, for instance, in what it calls "the mass," and yet admits that it was not forbidden to them at "the beginning of the Christian religion" (Council of Trent, Session 21, chap. 2). It says that councils and the pope have been empowered by the Holy Spirit to make decrees by which, in reality, the doctrines delivered by Christ are *entirely annulled.* To show how extensively this has been done, let the reader endeavor to trace the full effect of what Rome teaches as to baptismal regeneration, transubstantiation, justification by means of sacraments and deeds done by us, the invocation of saints—things which are entirely opposed to the teaching of Christ.

The canons of the Council of Trent, which sat at intervals from 1545 to 1563, may be called the Bible of Romanism. They were translated into English, as late as 1848, by a Roman Catholic priest, under the sanction of Dr. Wiseman. The Council tells us that one end for which it was called was "the extirpation of heresies." What, then, according to it, is *the standard of truth?* It tells us that Rome receives *The Sacred Scriptures* and *"The Unwritten Traditions* . . . preserved in continuous succession in the Catholic Church, with *equal affection of piety and reverence"* (Session 4); also that "no one may dare *to interpret* the Sacred Scriptures" in a manner contrary to that "Church;

whose it is to judge respecting the true sense and inter-pretation of the Sacred Scriptures;" nor may any one inter-pret them "in a manner contrary to the unanimous consent of *the fathers"* (Session 4).

Christ commands us to "prove all things" (1 Thess. 5:21); to "search the Scriptures" (John 5:39); to ascertain for our-selves, as the Bereans did, whether what we hear agrees with what we read in Scripture (Acts 17:11). He commands us to "hold fast the form of sound words," uttered by Himself and His Apostles (2 Tim. 1:13); to "contend earnestly for the faith *delivered once for all* to the saints" (Jude 3). But Rome says, "Let no one dare to do so"—let all *"Christian princes . . . cause* [*men*] *to observe"* our decrees (Session 16), nor *"permit"* them *to be "violated by heretics"* (Session 25). The Romanist must not dare to have an opinion of his own; his mind must exist in the state of utter prostration and bondage; he must not attempt to understand the Scripture himself. And if others attempt it—if they dare to receive the teaching and do the will of Christ, instead of receiving fictions and obeying commands of men, which wholly subvert and destroy the truth and will of Jesus, Rome commands the civil ruler to restrain them; and, by the use of fines, imprisonment, and death, to compel them, if possible, to renounce what God requires them to maintain and follow, even unto death.

The Bible, the whole Bible, nothing but the Bible, is the standard and the rule of Christianity. To know its meaning for ourselves, to receive its teaching, to rely on its promises, to trust in its Redeemer, to obey Him from delight of love, and to refuse to follow other teaching, is Christianity itself. But Romanism denies all this; and therefore, Romanism is not Christianity.

SECONDLY: Christ commanded us to show *"meekness"* towards those *who oppose us* (2 Tim. 2:25). He says, *"Love your enemies, bless those who curse you, do good*

*to those who hate you, and pray for those who use you
despitefully and persecute you"* (Matt. 5:44).

But Romanism teaches men *to hate,* and, if they are able,
to persecute to the death all those who will not receive it.
Its deeds have been diabolical and murderous.   It is
"drunken with the blood of the saints." It has inscribed on
the page of history warnings which appeal to the reason
and the feelings of all generations.   Such a warning is
what is told of the 24th of August, 1572. On that day the
Protestants of Paris were devoted to slaughter by members
of the Papal Church. For the one offence of being Protestants,
thousands were slain.   The streets of Paris ran with blood;
everywhere cries and groans, were mingled with the clangor
of bells, the clash of arms, and the oaths of murderers. The
king, Charles IX, stood, it is said, at a window, and, every
now and then, fired on the fugitives. Every form of guilt,
cruelty, and suffering, made that fearful night hideous and
appalling. Never, in any city, which has professedly been
brought under the influence of Christianity, was there such
a revelling in blood and crime. You may say, "Why do you
recall the atrocities of a time so remote?" I answer, Because
this deed received the sanction of the Church of Rome as a
meritorious demonstration of fidelity to Romish precepts and
doctrines. When the tidings of this wholesale murder were
received in Rome, the cannon of St. Angelo were fired,
the city was illuminated and Pope Gregory XIII and his
cardinals went in procession to all the churches, and offered
thanksgivings at the shrine of every saint. The Cardinal
of Lorraine, in a letter to Charles IX, full of admiration and
applause of the bloody deed, said, "That which you have
achieved was so infinitely above my hopes, that I should have
never dared to contemplate it; nevertheless, I have always
believed that the deeds of your Majesty would augment the
glory of God, and tend to immortalize your name."

Some say that Rome has ceased to persecute. But this is not the fact; either as to her acts, or rules of action. *She asserts that she is unchanged, unchangeable; that she is infallible, and cannot alter,* except so far as necessity, or plans for the future, may require; and facts are often occurring which prove that persecution is still approved by her. Rome has little power now; her persecuting spirit is kept in abeyance for a time; but it is still there. When it is free from restraint, it knows no way of dealing with difference of opinion but by the rack, the stake, the thumbscrew, the iron boot, the assassin's dagger, or a wholesale massacre. Let all who value their liberty, all who love the truth as it is in Jesus have no fellowship with such deeds of darkness, nor with those who work them. Let us show that we have no sympathy with such a cruel spirit; and that we love the names and memory of the noble army of martyrs of the Reformation; of those who sealed their faith with their blood; of those who died to release their country and their posterity from the bondage of Rome.

I agree with Dr. Samuel Waldegrave, when he says that, "The Convocation of the English clergy did wisely, when, in the days of Elizabeth, they enacted that every parish church in the land should be furnished with a copy of Foxe's Book of Martyrs;" and that it would be well if a copy of it were "in every house, yea, in every hand;" for "Rome is laboring, with redoubled effort, for the subjugation of Britain," and "the people have forgotten that she is a siren who enchants but to destroy."

THIRDLY: As to *the sacrifice of Christ,* Christianity teaches that He was *"offered once for all,* to bear the sins of many" (Heb. 9:28); that those who are sanctified by His sacrifice are so "by the offering of the body of Jesus Christ *once for all"* (10:10); that "by *one offering* He has *perfected forever* those who are sanctified," or made holy

(10:14): these passages declare that the sacrifice of Christ was offered *once for all, never to be repeated.* But Rome declares that Christ is sacrificed anew, every time that the Lord's supper, which she calls "the mass," is celebrated; and that those who administer it are *sacrificing priests.*

The Council of Trent (Session 22) says, "Forasmuch as in this Divine sacrifice, which is celebrated in the mass, that same Christ is contained, and immolated in an unbloody manner, who once offered Himself in a bloody manner, on the altar of the cross, the holy synod teaches that *this sacrifice is truly propitiatory,* and that, *by means therof,* this is effected—that we obtain mercy and find grace in seasonable aid, if we draw nigh unto God, contrite and penitent, with a sincere heart and upright faith, with fear and reverence. For the Lord, *appeased by the oblation thereof,* and granting the grace and gift of penitence, forgives even heinous crimes and sins. For *the victim is one and the same,* the same now offering by the ministry of *priests,* who then offered Himself on the cross, the manner alone of offering being different." The synod commands the use of lights, incense, and the traditional vestments; also that the priests "mix water with the wine."

In chapter 9, canon 1, the synod says, "If any one say that in the mass *a true and proper sacrifice is not offered* to God; or, that *to be offered,* is nothing else but that Christ is given us to eat; let him be anathema."

In canon 3, it decreed that, "If any one say that the sacrifice of the mass is only a sacrifice of praise and thanksgiving; or that it is a *bare commemoration of the sacrifice consummated on the cross, but not a propitiatory sacrifice;* or, that it profits him only who receives; and that it ought not to be offered for *the living and the dead for sins, pains, satisfactions,* and other necessities; let him be anathema."

The Christ of Romanism is one who is sacrificed again and again for the remission of the sins both of the living and the dead; for those alive, and for those in purgatory. *Is this the Christ of Christianity?*

In canon 1 of its 13th Session, the synod says, "If any one deny that, in the sacrament of the most holy Eucharist, are contained truly, really and substantially *the body and blood, together with the soul and divinity of our Lord Jesus Christ,* and consequently the whole Christ, but say that He is only therein as in a sign, or in figure, or virtue; let him be anathema."

The Christ of the Bible, and of Christianity, is in heaven "at the right hand of God," where "He ever lives to make intercession for those who come to God through Him" (Rom. 8:34; Col. 3:1; Heb. 7:25); nor will He come in bodily form to earth again until He comes the second time, without sin, unto salvation, to be admired in all those who believe (Heb. 9:28; 2 Thess. 1:10). But the Christ of Romanism is upon the altars of Rome; He is said to be brought there by the magic spell of her priests, and to be there in the form and shape of a *wafer.* What a fearful blasphemy! The priest pronounces certain words, gives the solemn consecration, and then elevates the wafer. *Taste* it—it is wafer; *touch* it—it is wafer; *look* at it—it is wafer; *smell* it—it is wafer; *analyze* it—it is wafer; but the priest affirms, the Council of Trent affirms, Romanism affirms, the poor victims of delusion affirm, as they bow down before it, *"This is our Christ—our God!"* Here is the climax of this superstition—it exhibits for the person of Christ a morsel of bread: Is that morsel of bread the Christ of the Bible? Is that system which declares it to be so, Christianity?

FOURTHLY: Christianity is in direct opposition to Romanism as to *the mode of a sinner's justification before God.*

What say the Scriptures? "By deeds of law shall no flesh living be justified before God" (Rom. 3:20). "Therefore we conclude that a man is justified by faith, without deeds of law" (3:28). "Even David describes the blessedness of the man to whom God imputes righteousness without works" (Rom. 4:6). Israel, "being ignorant of the righteousness of God, and seeking to establish their own righteousness, have not submitted themselves to the righteousness of God. For Christ is the end of the law for righteousness to every one who believes," or has faith (10: 3, 4).

"God was in Christ, . . . not imputing their trespasses unto them" (2 Cor. 5:19). "God has made Him to be sin for us, who knew no sin; that we might be made the righteousness of God in Him" (5:21). "Therefore, being justified by faith, we have peace with God through our Lord Jesus Christ" (Rom. 5:1). The doctrine thus taught by Christianity is that all men are sinners; that without justification there is no hope for any sinner; that we are justified by the imputation of Christ's righteousness alone; and that His righteousness is received through faith.

Now, *what says Romanism?* It says that the righteousness by which men are justified is that which the Holy Spirit, by the grace of God, through Christ, makes them *work out for themselves;* that it is received by means of "the sacrament of baptism . . . without which no one was ever justified;" that it is received *"in ourselves,"* when we are renewed by the Holy Spirit; that it is a righteousness "imparted," "infused," "implanted," and not imputed (Session 6, chapter 7). Among the declarations of the Council are these: "If any one say that justifying faith is nothing else but confidence in the Divine mercy which remits sin for Christ's sake; or, that this confidence alone is that whereby we are justified; let him be anathema" (Session 6, canon 12). "If any one say that . . . good works are merely the fruits and signs of justification obtained, but not *a cause of the increase thereof;* let him be anathema" (canon 24). "If any one say . . . that he who is *justified by good works,* which are done by him through the grace of God and the merit of Jesus Christ, whose living member he is, does not truly *deserve* increase of grace, *eternal life*," etc. . . . "let him be anathema" (canon 32). Thus Romanism anathematizes the preaching of true Christianity!

I will mention but one more proof that Romanism is not Christianity, though there are many others which might be given.

FIFTHLY: Christianity says "there is *one Mediator between God and men, the man Christ Jesus*" (1 Tim. 2:5), who is at the right hand of the Father (Eph. 1:20), where He "ever lives to make intercession" for us (Heb. 7:25). Christianity says that there is but *one Mediator;* that we cannot draw near to God except through Jesus.

What says Romanism? I quote from "a book of devotion for every day in the month of May," published by Papal authority. "Great is the need you have of Mary in order to be saved! Are you innocent? Still your innocence is, however, under great danger. How many, more innocent than you, have fallen into sin, and been damned? Are you penitent? Still your perseverance is very uncertain. Are you sinners? Oh, what need you have of Mary to convert you! Ah, if there were no Mary, perhaps you would be lost! However, by the devotion of this month, you may obtain her patronage, and your own salvation. Is it possible that a mother so tender can help hearing a Son so devout? For a rosary, for a fast, she has sometimes conferred signal graces upon the greatest of sinners. Think, then, what she will do for you for a whole month dedicated to her service!"

Here you see that Mary is everything; that Jesus Christ is nothing. Romanism teaches also that it is right to ask the intercession of all departed saints (Session 25). How dreadful is it that sinners are thus kept back from Jesus, and are prevented from reaching God through Him.

Popery is emphatically *anti-Christian:* it is the adversary of Christ in all the offices which He sustains. It is the enemy of His *prophetic* office; for it chains up that Bible which He

inspired. It is the enemy of His *priestly* office; for, by the
mass it denies the efficacy of that sacrifice which He offered
once for all on Calvary. It is the enemy of His *kingly* office;
for it tears the crown from His head to set it on that of the
Pope.

Can that be *truly called* Christianity, then, which is the
reverse of it? Can that be *fitly treated* as Christianity which
hates it, denounces it, and tries to destroy it? Can that be
Christianity which forbids liberty of conscience, and the right
of private judgment? Which commands the Bible to be
burned? Which teaches the worship of saints and angels?
Which makes the Virgin Mary command God? Which calls
her the Mother of God, and the Queen of Heaven? Which
sets aside the mediation of Christ, and puts others in His
place? Which makes salvation depend on confession to man,
and this is a confessional so filthy that Satan himself might
well be ashamed of it? Can that be Christianity which condemns the way of salvation through faith, as a damnable
heresy? Can that be Christianity which, by the bulls of its
Popes, and decrees of its councils, requires both princes and
people to persecute Christians? Which actually swears its
bishops and archbishops to persecute them with all their might?
Can that be Christianity which has set up, and still maintains,
the Inquisition? That which has been so cruel, so blood-
thirsty, that the number slain by it of the servants of Christ,
in about 1,200 years, is estimated at fifty millions, giving an
average of 40,000 a year for that long period? No, it cannot
be! With a voice of thunder, let Protestants answer, "No!"

To aid such a system is to fight against God. He demands
that we "resist the devil" (James 4:7), and have no fellowship
with "works of darkness" (Eph. 5:11). *"No peace with
Rome,"* must be on our lips, and be in our lives. *"No peace
with Rome,"* whether wearing her scarlet undisguised, or using
the cloak of a Protestant name.

The voice from heaven (Rev. 18:4): *"Come out of her, My people,* that ye be not partakers of her sins, and that ye receive not of her plagues," is proof that there may be true Christians in the Roman body; but it is proof also that even while *in* it, they are not *of* it; and that they will strive to escape from it, so as not to share in its sins.

We are informed by God that this system is *the work of Satan;* that his ministers are "transformed as the ministers of righteousness, whose end shall be according to their works" (2 Cor. 11:15); that it is he who turns men away "from the simplicity which is in Christ" (11:3); that it is he who is the author of that "mystery of iniquity" which was at work even while the Apostles were still living, and which was to be further revealed, and to remain, till it should be consumed by Christ, and "destroyed by the brightness of His coming;" a system which is "according to *the working of Satan,* with all power, and signs, and lying wonders, and with all deceivableness of unrighteousness in them that perish; because they received not the love of the truth that they might be saved" (2 Thess. 2:7-10).

May those who love God, and yet have some connection with this system, listen to the command, *"Come out of her, My people."* May we in no degree partake of her sins: may we renounce, with a holy loathing, all her symbols; throw off, with righteous indignation, all allegiance to her corruptions. May we have nothing of Romanism in our *doctrines,* but contend earnestly for the pure faith of the Gospel of Jesus. May we have nothing of Romanism in our *discipline.* May we be subject, in all matters of religious faith and practice, to *the Word of God,* and to that alone. May we have nothing of Romanism in our *services,* in our *buildings,* in our *forms,* in our *attire.* Because Israel burned incense to the brazen serpent which Moses had made, Hezekiah broke it in pieces. (2 Kings 18:4.) For the like reason, let us cease to use, on person or building, that form of the cross which the Romanist treats with superstitious regard. *"Come out of her."*

Ye who seek salvation, go to Jesus. Him has God exalted to be a Prince and a Saviour. He is able to save to the uttermost those who come to God by Him. *The Father* is ready with out-stretched arms to clasp the penitent prodigal in His embrace. *The Son* is ready to give a free, full, complete forgiveness to every redeemed sinner, and to justify all who come unto God by Him. *The Holy Spirit* is ready to sanctify, renew, instruct, and help all who call upon Him. *The assembly* of saved sinners on earth is ready to welcome you to partake of its fellowship and of its joys. *Angels* are ready with harps attuned, and fingers upon the chords, to give you a triumphant welcome, and to rejoice over you with joy. Come just as you are; come at once. *"Him that cometh to Me,"* says Christ, *"I will in no wise cast out"* (John 6:37).

CHAPTER VII

ROME, THE ANTAGONIST OF THE NATION

BY REV. J. M. FOSTER, BOSTON, MASSACHUSETTS

The Roman Catholic Church, both in Scriptures and in Christian history, figures as a politico-ecclesiastical system, the essential and deadly foe of civil and religious liberty, the hoary-headed antagonist of both Church and State. John Milton said: "Popery is a double thing to deal with, and claims a two-fold power, ecclesiastical and political, both usurped, and one supporting the other." Let us consider a few undeniable facts.

I. *ROME IS THE NATION'S ANTAGONIST BE-CAUSE IT IS A CORRUPT AND CORRUPTING SYS-TEM OF FALSEHOOD AND IDOLATRY THAT POL-LUTES OUR LAND.*

Cardinal Manning said: "The Catholic Church is either the masterpiece of Satan or the kingdom of the Son of God" ("Lectures on the Four-fold Sovereignty of God," London, 1871, page 171). Unquestionably, it is not the latter. Cardinal Newman declared: "Either the Church of Rome is the house of God or the house of Satan; there is no middle ground between them" (Essays 11, page 116). We solemnly affirm that she is not the former. The Church of Rome is Satan's counterfeit of the true Church of Christ. The heathen sacrificed to devils, not to God. As Israel took their idols from the nations about them, Rome Papal took her idolatry from Rome Pagan. When the "barbarian hordes" from the North over-ran the Roman Empire and dismembered it, the Bishop of Rome sent missionaries among them, proposing a union of Christianity and paganism. The pagan temples and priests and rites were incorporated with the Christian Church, and Rome became "baptized heathenism." "They feared the Lord and served graven images." The Bishop of Rome naturally had great influence among them. At his suggestion the lost unity of the Western Empire was restored in recognizing him as the official ecclesiastical head. The Greek Emperor at Constantinople, Phocas, desired to strengthen his authority in the west and invoked the aid of the Roman bishop. Boniface III saw his opportunity and made a deal. If the Byzantium Emperor would acknowledge him as universal bishop, he would accede. Phocas recognized Boniface III in 606 A. D. The pagans worshipped the Caesars. Roman Catholics pay Divine honors to the pope. They ascribe to him the names, titles, attributes, words and works of God. The name of God and His works have been ascribed to the pope by their theologians, canonists, councils and the popes themselves. By the authority of canon law the pontiff is styled the Almighty's vicegerent. This is treason. The second commandment forbids worshipping of God by images, and yet Rome Papal has introduced the image worship of Pagan Rome, only changing the names. The Virgin Mary is substituted for Venus. The image of Christ takes the place of Jupiter. The idols of the pagan temples were not so numerous' as the idols of the Romish cathedrals today. Pope Pius IV called the Council of Trent, which issued its creed in 1564. This creed of Pius IV, together with the decree of the immaculate conception of the Virgin Mary, promulgated in 1854, and that of the pope's infallibility, issued in 1870, mark the doctrinal status of Rome today. Let us note a few facts in regard to this.

1. *Rome restricts the use of the Bible.* The fourth rule of the congregation of the "Index of Prohibited Books", approved by Pius IV and still in force, runs as follows: "Since it is manifest by experience that if the Holy Bible in the vulgar tongue be suffered to be read everywhere without dis-

tinction, more evil than good arises, let the judgment of the bishop or inquisitor be abided by in this respect, so that, after consulting with the parish priest or the confessor, they may grant permission to read translations of the Scriptures, made by Catholic writers, to those whom they understand to be able to receive no harm, but an increase of faith and piety from such reading (which faculty let them have in writing). But whosoever shall presume to read these Bibles, or have them in possession without such faculty, shall not be capable of receiving absolution of their sins, unless they have first given up their Bibles to the ordinary." This prohibition has been followed up by later declarations. Pope Leo XII, in an Encyclical dated May 3, 1824, addressed the Latin bishops thus: "We also, venerable brothers, in conformity with our apostolic duty, exhort you to turn away your flocks from these *poisonous pastures* [i. e., vernacular Bibles]. Reprove, entreat, be instant in season and out of season, that the faithful committed to you (adhering strictly to the rules of the 'Congregation of the Index') be persuaded that if the Sacred Scriptures be everywhere indiscriminately published, more evil than advantage will arise thence, because of the rashness of men." And the way of the laity to the reading of the Holy Scriptures is further blocked by the second article in the creed of Pius IV: "I do admit the Holy Scriptures in the same sense that Holy Mother Church hath held and doth hold, whose business it is to judge the true sense and interpretation of them. Nor will I ever receive or interpret them except according to the *unanimous consent* of the Fathers." As the "Holy Mother Church" publishes no commentaries on the Holy Scriptures, nor "authorized interpretation" of Holy Writ; and as "the unanimous consent of the Fathers" is impossible, they having commented freely, each according to his ability, the way of the laity to the Word of God is closed. The difference between Protestantism and Romanism is, the Bible is an open book to the one and a sealed book to the other. The Reformed Churches have translated the whole Bible into 517 languages and dialects—all the great trunk languages spoken by three-fourths of the world's inhabitants —and published 300,000,000 copies. The Roman Church keeps the Bible locked up in the Latin tongue. It is true the Douay Bible was published, the New Testament in 1582 at Rheims, and the Old Testament at Douay in 1609. This is Rome's English Bible. But the people are forbidden to read it. A distinguished French Romanist, Henri Lasserre, struck with the fact that the children of the church knew "the Divine Book only in fragments, without logical or chronological order," brought out a translation of the four Gospels, for which he obtained the sanction of the Archbishop of Paris and of the Pope. The result was an immediate sale of 100,000 copies, so eager were the French Romanists for this novel work. But the Index shortly interfered. The Pope's express sanction was withdrawn, the printing and the sale peremptorily stopped, under the pretext that some passages were translated inaccurately. The fragments in Latin were preferred as *safer* than the whole in a language everyone could understand. Rome has made only two translations, and those not spontaneously, but because the inquirers *insisted* upon their possession. These two are for Uganda and for Japan. The large number of Protestants compelled the Roman missionaries to accede to the demands of their own inquirers and converts that they should possess the wonderful Book which their fellow-countrymen were reading.

2. *Rome accepts the Apocrypha of the Old Testament.* The Apocrypha came this way. The larger part of the Jews never returned from the Babylonian captivity, but were dispersed in many countries. They had the Old Testament Hebrew Scriptures. They also had other writings, produced after Malachi, but not of equal authority. About B. C. 280, Ptolomy, the King of Egypt, invited Hebrew rabbi to come to Egypt and translate the Hebrew Scriptures into Greek. The

other Jewish writings were translated also, and used by the Alexandrian Jews of the dispersion, although they did not hold them as part of the Old Testament. In course of time the Latin language superseded the Greek in the West, and in their ignorance of Hebrew, Latin translations were made, not from the original Hebrew, but from the Greek version, and the Apocrypha was translated with it. Most of the Christian fathers had no knowledge of Hebrew, and read the Scriptures in Greek and Latin. They distinguished the Bible from the Apocryphal writings. So did Jerome, in his Latin Vulgate, 404 A. D., translated from Hebrew and Chaldee. So did Philo and Melito, A. D. 160, and the Jewish Talmud of the fifth century, and the great Roman Cardinal Cajetan (1518) and the learned Roman Catholic Archbishop Ximenes, to whom we owe the famous Complutensian Polyglot (1517), and Josephus (who lived about the time of Christ). Augustine differed from Jerome as to the authority of the Apocrypha, but Augustine did not know Hebrew and his testimony is valueless. But not one of the thirty bishops in the Council of Trent could read Hebrew, and only a few knew the Greek. And yet that utterly incompetent Council decreed the Apocrypha to be a part of God's Holy Word, and to be accepted under pain of anathema.

3. *Rome accepts tradition as of equal authority with the Scriptures.* The Council of Trent (Session IV): "Seeing clearly that this (saving) truth and (moral) discipline are contained in the written books and the written traditions received by the Apostles from the mouth of Christ Himself or from the Apostles themselves, the Holy Ghost dictating, have come down even unto us, transmitted, as it were, from hand to hand;" and again: "Every sort of doctrine which is to be delivered to the faithful is contained in the Word of God, which is divided into Scripture and tradition." But such stupendous assertions require clear evidence. Where is "tradition" found? Has Rome recorded and registered it?

Where is the digest and proof of it for the faithful to examine? How is it tested? How is it shown to be necessary? Abbe Migne made a compilation of the decrees of councils and writings of the ancients in 220 thick volumes, and called it "The Catholic Tradition". To this, many other works must be added. Are these mountains of chaff to be dug through before Christ is found? This is Satan's way of lies.

4. *Rome has seven sacraments.* Here is the decree of the Council of Trent: "If anyone saith the sacraments of the new law were not all instituted by Jesus Christ our Lord, or that they are more or less than seven, to-wit: baptism, confirmation, the Eucharist, penance, extreme unction, orders, and matrimony; or even that any one of these seven is not truly and properly a sacrament; let him be anathema" (Session VII; canon 1). The definition of a sacrament given by the Council was: "A visible sign of invisible grace, instituted for our sanctification." But the Scriptures teach that "A sacrament is an holy ordinance instituted by Christ, wherein by sensible signs, Christ and the benefits of the new covenant are represented, sealed and applied to believers." According to this there are only two sacraments of the New Testament: baptism and the Lord's Supper. The other five, penance, confirmation, extreme unction, orders, and matrimony, are not sacraments. Here the Church of Rome usurps the prerogatives of the Lord Jesus Christ, the sole and only Head of His body the Church.

5. *Rome teaches transubstantiation.* The Council of Trent (Session XII, chapter 4): "By the consecration of the bread and wine a conversion is made of the whole substance of the bread into the substance of the body of Christ our Lord, and of the whole substance of the wine into the substance of His blood, which conversion is by the Holy Catholic Church suitably and properly called transubstantiation." To this add Article V of the creed of Pius IV: "In the most holy sacrament of the Eucharist there are truly, really and

substantially the body and blood, together with the soul and divinity, of our Lord Jesus Christ." This doctrine, as the English Archbishop recently described it, "depends upon the acceptance of a metaphysical definition expressed in terms of mediaeval philosophy." The philosophy is that of Aristotle, who attempts to draw a distinction between "substance" and "accidents"—substance being the inner reality in which the qualities or accidents, the taste, smell, form, color, etc., inhere. But this contradicts the testimony of our senses. It is unreasonable and entirely unscriptural.

6. *Rome sacrifices the mass.* By sacrifice they mean "an act of external worship in which God is honored as the principle and end of man and all things, by the oblation of a visible creature, by submitting it to an appropriate transformation by a duly qualified minister" (Cath. Dic., page 813). This is its comment upon the Eucharistic sacrifices: "All that is included in the idea of sacrifice is found in the Eucharist. There is the oblation of a sensible thing, viz., of the body and blood of Christ under the appearance of bread and wine." "There is the mystical destruction of Christ the victim, for Christ presents Himself on the altar as in a state of death, through the mystical separation between His body and blood." "In this sacrifice of thanksgiving we offer God the most excellent gift He has bestowed upon us, viz., the 'Son in whom He is well pleased.'" Is not this awful presumption? Their Eucharistic sacrifice they hold to be "one with that of the cross; on the cross and altar we have the same victim and the same priest." Pope Pius V said: "Protestants have no sacrifice because the Reformation abolished the mass." But the old answer of Bishop Jewel is as true as ever: "Indeed the mass is abolished through the gracious working of God. . . . They did tell us that in their mass they were able to offer Christ, the Son of God, unto God His Father for our sins. Oh, blasphemous speech, and most injurious to the glorious work of our redemption! Such kind of sacrifice we have not. Christ

Himself is our High Priest . . . by whom we are sanctified, even by the offering of Christ once made, who took away our sins and fastened them upon the cross. . . . This is our sacrifice, this is our propitiation and sacrifice for the whole world. How, then, saith Pope Pius, we have no sacrifice?"

7. *Rome denies the cup to the laity.* The Council of Trent pronounces two anathemas as to this. One will suffice. "If anyone saith that the Holy Catholic Church was not induced by just cause and reasons to communicate under the species of bread only, laymen, and also clerics, when not consecrating, let him be anathema" (Session XXI; canon 1, 20). This is unscriptural. Our Lord instituted the feast in the use of both bread and wine. Down to the fifteenth century both elements were used. Denying the cup to the laity was the culmination of many previous errors, such as confounding the sign and the thing signified, the propitiating sacrifice of the mass, the priesthood of ministers and the stupendous miracle of converting bread and wine into the real flesh and blood of Christ.

8. *Rome traffics in masses.* The priests claim to remove souls from purgatory for a certain number of masses, each having a certain price. Not long ago Queen Christina of Spain left money for 5,000 masses to be said for herself and 5,000 for her husband. As no priest could offer the mass more than once a day, they had to be let out to country priests. More recently, the Abbe Brugidon endeavored to raise money toward building a church in Rome by receiving payment for masses to be said when the church was completed. There is much doubt as to whether the church will ever be built, but 260,000 masses have been already paid for. A number beyond the power of the Abbe ever to accomplish. Such stupendous frauds will shock the moral sense of the Christian world and awaken the Church to a recognition of the mystery of iniquity in the Church of Rome.

II. *ROME IS THE NATION'S ANTAGONIST BE-CAUSE IT IS A POLITICAL SYSTEM OF FOREIGN DESPOTISM.*

Rome Pagan persecuted the Christians. Rome Pagan became Rome Christian under Constantine and ceased persecuting. Rome nominally Christian became Rome Papal and persecuted more severely than before. The pope controlled the kingdoms of Europe for twelve centuries. How did he gain this power? After the pope became universal bishop he longed to be free from the Byzantine yoke and wield civil power himself. His opportunity came at last to realize his ambition. Here it is. Clovis the Great entered Gaul and destroyed the Roman army in the battle of Soissons in 486. He then established the French monarchy and became the first of the dynasty of Merovingian kings. The Merovingian dynasty continued two hundred and fifty years, when it was superseded by the Carlovingian dynasty. The change came thus: Childeric III was the last of the Merovingian kings, a weak, incapable prince. Charles Martel was "the Mayor of the Palace," which placed him next to, but not on, the throne. The Saracens invaded France and threatened European civilization. Charles Martel conquered them in a seven days' battle between Tours and Poitiers in 732, and saved Europe from the scourge of Mohammedanism. The government of France was henceforth practically in his hands. His son and successor, Pepin, wished to remove Childeric III and establish himself on the throne of France, but he must have a legal permit. He appealed to the pope at Rome for such authority. The pope's opportunity had come. He offered to do as Pepin desired, providing Pepin would free the Holy See from the domination of Byzantium. So Pepin led his army across the Alps and conquered the provinces, entered Rome, made Stephen III a free Prince. The pope became the king of kings in 755. He girded on two swords, one on each side, emblems of temporal and spiritual power. And the pope crowned Pepin King of France. Now, the pope desired to revive the old Roman Empire. In 800 Charlemagne, the son and successor of Pepin, was invited to Rome and crowned by Pope Leo III as "Emperor of the Romans." In return for this Charlemagne decreed that one-tenth of all incomes must be given to the church on the severest pains of forfeiture. But the pope must have grounds for such assumptions of power. And so the "false decretals" of Isadore, which are now universally considered to have been bold and unblushing forgeries, were promulgated between 847 and 853. And about 858 the "Donation of Constantine," which is now acknowledged by Romanists to be spurious, was made to do service. These were requisitioned by Pope Nicholas I. The system grew as Innocent III placed the iron crown upon the head of Otho I in 962, as the "King of the Holy Roman Empire of the Germans"; as Hildebrand enforced celibacy upon his English clergy in 1073; as Adrian IV granted Ireland to King Henry II in 1156; and as Boniface VIII issued his famous Bull, Unum Sanctum, in 1303, which was quoted by Pope Pius IX in his Encyclical of 1864, and is good canon law today. Here are its contents: "1. It is necessary to salvation that every man should submit to the pope. 2. This is a necessary consequence of the dogma of papal supremacy. 3. It condemns the assertion by the state of any power over church property. 4. The temporal power of Christian princes does not exempt them from obedience to the head of the church. 5. The material sword is drawn for the church, the spiritual by the church. 6. The material sword must co-operate with the spiritual and assist it. 7. The secular power should be guided by the spiritual as the higher. 8. The spiritual has the pre-eminence over the material. 9. The temporal power is subordinate to the ecclesiastical as to the higher. 10. The temporal power, if it is not good, is judged by the spiritual. 11. To the ecclesiastical authority [that is, to the pope and his hierarchy] the words of the prophet Jeremiah apply: 'Lo, I have set thee this day over the nations and over the kingdoms, to root up and pull down and to waste and to destroy; and to build and to plant.' 12. When the temporal power goes astray it is judged by the spiritual. 13. For obtaining eternal happiness, each one is required to submit to the pope. 14. The supremacy of the pope even in temporal things is to be enforced. 15. The pope recognizes human authorities in their proper place, till they lift their will against God."

The Holy Roman Empire reached its climax in 1164 when Hadrian IV trod on the neck of Frederick of Barbarossa, and went out of commission in 1806, when Napoleon Bonaparte compelled Joseph II to abdicate. When Victor Immanuel II entered Rome in 1870 and made the Quirinal the capital of United Italy, the pope called himself "the Prisoner of the Vatican" and issued one of the most shocking excommunications against the conqueror: "By the authority of the Almighty God, the Father, Son and Holy Ghost; and of the holy canons and of the undefiled Virgin Mary, mother and nurse of our Saviour, and of the celestial virtues, angels, archangels, thrones, dominions, powers, cherubim and seraphim; and of all the holy patriarchs and prophets, and of the apostles and evangelists, and of the holy innocents, who, in the sight of the Holy Lamb, are found worthy to sing the new song; and of the holy martyrs and holy confessors, and of the holy virgins and of the saints, together with all the holy and elect of God; we excommunicate and anathematize him, and from the threshold of the holy church of God Almighty we sequester him, that he may be tormented in eternal excruciating sufferings, together with Dathan and Abiram and those who say to the Lord God, 'Depart from us, we desire none of Thy ways!' And as fire is quenched by water, so let the light of him be put out forever more. May Father, Son and Holy Ghost curse him. May he be damned wherever he may be; whether in the house or in the field, whether in the highway or in the byway, whether in the wood or water, and whether in the church. May the Virgin Mary, St. Michael, St. John, St. Peter, St. Paul, the choir of the holy virgins, curse him. May he be cursed in living and dying, in eating and drinking, in fasting and thirsting, in slumbering and sleeping, in watching and walking, in standing or sitting, in lying down or walking, and in blood-letting. May he be cursed in his brain; may he be cursed in all his faculties; may he be cursed inwardly and outwardly; may he be cursed in his hair; may he be cursed in the crown of his head; in his temples, in his forehead and his ears; in his eyebrows, in his cheeks, in his jaw-bones, in his nostrils; in his foreteeth and his grinders; in his lips and in his throat; in his shoulders and in his wrists; in his arms, his hands and his fingers. May he be damned in his mouth, in his breast, in his heart and in all the viscera of his body. May he be damned in his veins and in his groin and in his thighs, in his hips; in his knees; in his legs, feet and toe-nails. May he be cursed in all the joints and articulations of his body. From the top of his head to the sole of his foot may there be no soundness in him. May the Son of the living God, with all the glory of His majesty, curse him; and may heaven with all the powers that move therein rise up against him, curse him, and damn him! Amen. So let it be. Amen."

But while the pope was pouring out the vials of his wrath, the Prussian army was sweeping the French at Sedan and Napoleon III surrendered and the German Empire became a firm union. The pope ex-communicated the German prelates who refused to accept the dogma of the pope's infallibility. They refused to vacate their parishes and the Ultramontanes attempted to force them out. The Germans interfered and the iron Chancellor, Bismarck, declared in the Parliament, "We are not going to Canossa, either physically or spiritually," and on July 4, 1872, the German Reichstag passed a law expelling the Jesuits from the Empire. France has later followed in separating Church and State and banishing the monastic orders. Spain has followed the same example and Portugal is doing likewise. But Great Britain and the United States persist in flirting with the great whore of the Tiber. The coronation oath of King George V was modified and "Home Rule" is voted to Ireland to please the Vatican. In the United States they have 11,000,000 and control 1,500,000 votes of the city governments of Boston, New York, Chicago and others and have ninety-five per cent of the municipal offices filled by Rome. The press of the country is censored by Roman Jesuits. The government at Washington went to Canossa when the President sent Judge Taft to Rome to consult the pope about the friars in the Philippines, the only difference being, Henry IV went in a coarse sackcloth and barefoot in the snow, standing at the gate three days, while Taft went in a swallow-tailed coat and white vest and shoes on his feet, and was received at once. But he bargained to pay the pope $7,500,000 for claims not worth $1,000,000 in the Islands; then $406,000 for damages to church property in quelling a rebellion provoked and fostered by the friars themselves. The solid Roman vote is a menace in our national elections. The Roman hierarchy owns $300,000,000 in America. They have a parochial school system and clamorously demand a share in the public school fund. Their policy is the refinement of duplicity. They join the Jews, infidels and skeptics in driving the Bible from our public schools, on the ground that the State is only a secular corporation and has no right to teach morals and religion. Then they turn with hypocritical distress and exclaim: "The public schools are godless, their education is dangerous because secular and an education without morals and religion is incomplete and vicious: we have built and equipped our parochial schools that our children may have an education in which morals and religion have their proper place and due share of attention; therefore we demand as a matter of fairness that the public school funds be shared with us to lighten this burden which we are forced to carry." But the answer which the organic people should return is: "This is a Christian State; the public school system is its agency for building up a Christian citizenship; morals and religion, so far as they are essential for discharging the functions of Christian citizenship, shall be taught in our public schools; and the school funds shall not be divided." While Cardinal Gibbons can have President Taft and his cabinet, the Judges of the Supreme Court, Senators and Representatives attending mass in the Roman Catholic Cathedral at Washington, the great political parties bidding for the solid Roman vote in national elections, and our national policy in the Philippines dictated by the Vatican, Rome may reasonably expect to capture our public schools through the Philippine educational policy. But our blessed Lord is upon the throne and His cause shall prevail.

PUBLISHERS' NOTICE

Particular attention is hereby called to the following points:

1. All English-speaking Protestant pastors, evangelists, missionaries, theological professors, theological students, Y. M. C. A. secretaries, Y. W. C. A. secretaries, Sunday School superintendents, religious lay workers, and editors of religious publications throughout the earth, who so desire, are entitled to a free copy of each volume of "THE FUNDAMENTALS." Any person, belonging to one of these classes, who has not received the earlier volumes, may obtain them upon application to the undersigned. *State plainly* which volumes are wanted, and *state also the line of Christian work engaged in* and the denominational affiliation. After an order is sent in, allow at least two weeks (and more if from a distance) for filling it.

2. Changes of address should be promptly reported. *Write plainly* both the old and the new addresses *in full.*

3. In case any person receives two or more copies of any one volume, *kindly notify us.* These books are too valuable and the demand for them too great to permit waste through duplication. However, where extra copies have been received, they need not be returned, but may be loaned or otherwise placed in circulation.

4. To meet the demand on the part of the laity each volume is being furnished postpaid at a cost of fifteen cents per copy, eight copies for one dollar, or one hundred copies for ten dollars. (In Great Britain, 8d; 4s 2d; and £2 1s 1d, respectively.) These prices will be applied to the cost of issuing future volumes.

5. Do not send currency or personal checks. *Remit by post office money order, or by bank draft* on Chicago, New York, or London, making the same payable to the Testimony Publishing Company.

6. Foreign correspondents should be careful to prepay card and letter postage *in full.* Otherwise we are compelled to pay *double* the amount of the deficiency.

7. Pay no attention to the post card request in the "Foreword" of Volume IX. The blank card referred to therein no longer accompanies that volume.

8. Please bear in mind that we publish nothing except "THE FUNDA-MENTALS," and do not issue any catalogue.

In conclusion, we would emphasize once more the *great importance* of writing plainly and briefly, and always giving *full address*—street (or rural route) number, post office, state, and (if outside of the United States) country.

Much time and delay will be saved by carefully reading and complying with the foregoing directions.

TESTIMONY PUBLISHING COMPANY,

808 North La Salle Street
Chicago, Ill., U. S. A.

The Fundamentals

A Testimony to the Truth

Volume XII

Compliments of
Two Christian Laymen

TESTIMONY PUBLISHING COMPANY
(Not Inc.)
808 North La Salle Street
Chicago, Ill., U. S. A.

(See change of address in Publishers' Notice, page 6.)

"To the Law and to the Testimony"
Isaiah 8:20

A STATEMENT BY THE
TWO LAYMEN

Rev. A. C. Dixon, D. D., in the fall of 1909, while pastor of the Moody Church in Chicago, organized the Testimony Publishing Company. He also edited the first five volumes of "THE FUNDAMENTALS," but upon being called to London early in the summer of 1911 to become pastor of the Metropolitan Tabernacle, founded by the late Charles H. Spurgeon, he found it necessary to give up the editorial work on the books.

The next five books were taken in hand by the late Louis Meyer, a Christian Jew, who worked so strenuously in the securing and editing of matter for "THE FUNDAMENTALS" that his health failed. He departed to be with Christ July 11, 1913, in Monrovia, California. His widow and children are now residing in Pasadena, California.

Rev. R. A. Torrey, D. D., Dean of the Bible Institute of Los Angeles, edited Volumes XI and XII, two articles, however, in Volume XI having been approved by Dr. Meyer and passed on to Dr. Torrey when he took up the work.

The following are the names of the original Committee to whom was committed full supervision of the movement: Rev. A. C. Dixon, D. D., Rev. R. A. Torrey, D. D., Rev. Louis Meyer, D. D. (deceased 1913), Mr. Henry P. Crowell, Mr. Thomas S. Smith, Mr. D. W. Potter, Rev. Elmore Harris, D. D. (deceased 1911).

The following names were added later to the foregoing: Prof. Joseph Kyle, D. D., LL. D., Prof. Charles R. Erdman, D. D., Mr. Delavan L. Pierson, Rev. L. W. Munhall, D. D., Rev. T. C. Horton, Rev. H. C. Mabie, D. D., Rev. John Balcom Shaw, D. D.

To these men for their always efficient and painstaking service, rendered practically without any material remuneration whatever, are due the heartfelt thanks, not only of the

Two Laymen, but of the thousands who have received the books. Every member of the Committee without exception has been faithful to his trust.

Mr. Giles Kellogg has been the Los Angeles trustee of the Testimony funds, and Mr. J. S. McGlashan the Chicago trustee. The Walton and Spencer Company of Chicago have been the printers. The faithful services rendered by all of these thoroughly merit this word of appreciation.

Mr. Thomas E. Stephens, editor of the "Moody Church Herald," has been the Business Manager from the beginning, and the Moody Church and Moody Bible Institute have contributed in many ways to the success of the work.

The original plan was for twelve volumes to be issued one every two or three months, but owing to the difficulty of realizing on securities that had been put up for this work, the intervals between the later volumes have been greatly prolonged, but with the present volume the original plan is complete.

It may be of interest to state that over 2,500,000 copies of the twelve volumes have been published and circulated, and that the call for back volumes has been so insistent as to make necessary the reprinting of over a quarter of a million additional copies of the earlier issues, thus bringing the total output up to nearly 3,000,000 copies.

Approximately one-third of these 3,000,000 copies have gone to countries outside of the United States. About one-half of the latter have been sent to various parts of Great Britain, and the rest to other foreign countries. The great majority of Protestant missionary workers of the world have received them. The present mailing list comprises about 100,-000 addresses of Christian workers, all of whom have asked for "THE FUNDAMENTALS."

Since the movement began, some 200,000 letters have been received, including many requests for the continuance of this testimony in some form. In compliance with these requests it

4

is planned to undertake its continuance through "The King's Business," which is published by the Bible Institute of Los Angeles, and of which Dr. Torrey will be the editor-in-chief. Dr. Torrey was for many years the Superintendent of the Moody Bible Institute of Chicago, until he left that work to undertake his world-wide work as an evangelist. He is now Dean of the Bible Institute of Los Angeles.

The Testimony Publishing Company, from the very inception of its work of publishing "THE FUNDAMENTALS," has been absolutely free from commercialism, and the continuance of this testimony through "The King's Business" is also to be kept absolutely free from commercialism. Any profits arising from subscriptions to the magazine are to be used for free Scripture and tract distribution and missionary work.

It is purposed for "The King's Business" not merely to give the best articles that can be secured along the line of testimony of the twelve volumes of "THE FUNDAMENTALS," but also to make helps on the International Sunday School lessons a special feature of the magazine. We assume that in doing this a need will be supplied which will greatly increase the effectiveness of Sunday School teaching. In conclusion we would state that arrangements have been made to send the April number of "The King's Business" to all the readers of "THE FUNDAMENTALS."

PUBLISHERS' NOTICE

Particular attention is hereby called to the following points:

1. All English-speaking Protestant pastors, evangelists, missionaries, theological professors, theological students, Y. M. C. A. secretaries, Y. W. C. A. secretaries, Sunday School superintendents, religious lay workers, and editors of religious publications throughout the earth, who so desire, are entitled to a free copy of each volume of "THE FUNDAMENTALS." Any person, belonging to one of these classes, who has not received the earlier volumes, may obtain such as may not be out of print upon application to the undersigned. *State plainly* which volumes are wanted, and *state also the line of Christian work engaged in* and the denominational affiliation. After an order is sent in, allow at least two weeks (and more if from a distance) for filling it.

2. Changes of address should be promptly reported. *Write plainly* both the old and the new addresses *in full.*

3. In case any person receives two or more copies of any one volume, *kindly notify us.* These books are too valuable and the demand for them too great to permit waste through duplication. However, where extra copies have been received, they need not be returned, but may be loaned or otherwise placed in circulation.

4. To meet the demand on the part of the laity each volume is being furnished postpaid at a cost of fifteen cents per copy, eight copies for one dollar, or one hundred copies for ten dollars. (In Great Britain, 8d; 4s 2d; and £2 1s 1d, respectively.)

5. Do not send currency or personal checks. *Remit by post office money order, or by bank draft* on Chicago, New York, or London, making the same payable to the Testimony Publishing Company.

6. Foreign correspondents should be careful to prepay card and letter postage *in full.* Otherwise we are compelled to pay *double* the amount of the deficiency.

7. Pay no attention to the post card request in the "Foreword" of Volume IX. The blank card referred to therein no longer accompanies that volume.

In conclusion, we would emphasize once more the *great importance* of writing plainly and briefly, and always giving *full address*—street (or rural route) number, post office, state, and (if outside of the United States) country.

Much time and delay will be saved by carefully reading and complying with the foregoing directions.

TESTIMONY PUBLISHING COMPANY,
808 North La Salle Street
Chicago, Ill, U. S. A.

☞*After May 1, 1915, the address of the Testimony Publishing Company will be 536-558 South Hope Street, Los Angeles, California.*

6

FOREWORD TO VOLUME XII

It was the original plan of the Two Laymen who gave the money for the work that there should be twelve volumes of "THE FUNDAMENTALS." The present volume, therefore, completes the plan as originally mapped out.

Such a wide desire has been manifested that this testimony be continued in some way after the issue of the present volume that the Two Laymen, yielding to these pleas, have decided upon a plan for the continuance of the testimony, which they themselves have stated on the preceding pages of the present book.

We have been greatly cheered by the letters that have poured in upon us from ministers, missionaries, editors, Sunday School Superintendents and others since the publication of Volume XI. Of course, there has been some criticism, but in very few instances has this criticism been of an unkindly character.

The present volume will be sent to about one hundred thousand English-speaking Protestant pastors, evangelists, missionaries, theological professors, theological students, Y. M. C. A. secretaries, Y. W. C. A. secretaries, Sunday School superintendents, religious editors and lay workers throughout the earth. May we ask the prayers of every reader that it may be as abundantly blessed as its predecessors have been unto the strengthening of the faith of Christians, unto the defence of the truth against the various forms of error so prevalent at the present day, and, above all, in stirring up Christians everywhere to more active effort and more earnest prayer for the conversion of a great number of the unsaved.

By a vote of the Committee having the publication in charge, it was decided that this closing volume should be largely devoted to evangelism at home and abroad. Every one invited to write on some phase of this work has accepted our invitation with the exception of Dr. Andrew Murray. He seemed to be the logical person to write the article on "The Place of Prayer in Evangelism." He wrote us expressing his earnest desire to do this work, but declining to do it because of his increasing age and the multiplicity of duties that were pressing upon him.

There is a large circle of prayer of men and women in all parts of the earth who know God, who are upholding before Him the work of "THE FUNDAMENTALS." We earnestly request other men and women who believe in prayer and who know how to pray to join this circle of prayer, that in answer to believing and united prayer the truth may have new power and that a world-wide revival of religion may result.

All editorial correspondence in connection with "The Fundamentals" should be addressed to the Executive Secretary of The Fundamentals, 1945 La France Avenue, South Pasadena, California. As this is the closing volume of the series, of course no other manuscripts should be submitted by anybody. If any one has submitted a manuscript which has not been returned, we shall be glad to return it, if stamps are sent for that purpose and if it is in our hands.

All business correspondence should be addressed to The Testimony Publishing Company, 808 North La Salle Street, Chicago, Ill., U. S. A. (After May 1, 1915, to 536-558 South Hope Street, Los Angeles, Calif.)

CONTENTS

THE FUNDAMENTALS

VOLUME XII

CHAPTER I

THE DOCTRINES THAT MUST BE EMPHASIZED IN SUCCESSFUL EVANGELISM

BY EVANGELIST L. W. MUNHALL, M. A., D. D.,
GERMANTOWN, PHILADELPHIA, PENNSYLVANIA

First of all, What constitutes Successful Evangelism? Some will answer, "Great audiences, eloquent preaching and soul-stirring music." But I reply, "We may have all these and not have real evangelism; as we may have successful evangelism without them."

Others will answer, "Any movement that will add large numbers to the membership of the churches." I reply, "We may have successful evangelism and not many be added to the churches; and, we may have large numbers added to the churches' membership without successful evangelism."

Yet others will answer, "A work or effort that will bring into the church people who will be steadfast." I reply, "We may have members added to the church who will hold out, and the work, evangelistically, be unsuccessful; and we may have a highly successful evangelistic work and the accessions to the churches from it not hold out for any great length of time." Let us briefly consider three points:

First, No matter how great the multitude, eloquent the preaching and soul-stirring the singing, if the God-ordained conditions are not fully met, failure is inevitable. While these things are of value they are dispensable. Great successes have been achieved without them.

Second, I have known not a few evangelistic campaigns to be successful, as such, in a marked degree, and one or more churches identified with it, professedly, received but a few members, or none, from the movement. They united in the movement from wrong motives. They were not prepared for the work; were formal, worldly and unspiritual; were without faith. Putting nothing of value into the work, they got nothing out of it. Or the work was not properly followed up.

Also, I have known not a few widely advertised and thoroughly organized evangelistic campaigns, in which mere sentiment was far more conspicuous than the Holy Spirit, and the lachrymals more frequently appealed to than the intellect and conscience; and large numbers were added to the membership of the co-operating churches, who knew nothing whatever of the regenerating work of the Holy Ghost.

Third, I have known not a few persons who have been faithful members of the church for many years and never been born again—"had a name to live and were dead." There are many churches full of life, and apparently great successes, because of humanitarian, educational and socialistic matters in which they are engaged, and entertainments that they give from time to time; and some of the members who give most time and money to these things, and take most pride in them, are spiritually dead.

Also, I have known persons, who were, without doubt, saved and sincere, to unite with the church as a result of an evangelistic campaign, to run well for a season and then fall away; and the falling away was unjustly charged to the campaign. The real cause of it may have been one or more of the following reasons: *First,* The atmosphere of the church was not congenial, being unspiritual and cold. This is of vital importance to "babes in Christ." *Second,* In not a few instances the pastors, instead of "feeding the church of God," with "the sincere milk of the word, that ye may grow thereby," were like those mentioned in the twenty-third chapter of Jeremiah;

or have turned their pulpits into lecture platforms, and the members going for bread received a stone; and in many cases were off after false teachers who promised them what they needed, and what they should have received at home. *Third,* The positively bad example set by a large majority of the members of most churches, in that they conspicuously fail to meet their solemn obligations to God and the church.

And there are yet other reasons for the falling away of the weak and inexperienced.

But again it is asked, "What constitutes successful evangelism?" I answer, "Preaching the Gospel according to Divine conditions and directions." In the great commission, as given by Matthew, Jesus said, "Teach all nations." Make disciples, is what the word "teach" here means. Mark puts it in these words, "Preach the Gospel to every creature." Luke states it thus, "Repentance and remission of sins should be preached in His name among all nations." And in Acts 1:8, Jesus said, "But ye shall receive power, after that the Holy Ghost is come upon you: and ye shall be witnesses unto Me both in Jerusalem, and in all Judea, and in Samaria, and unto the uttermost part of the earth."

THE CONDITIONS

What are the conditions? *First, Discipleship.* Jesus commissioned only such. One must know, experimentally, the power and joy of the Gospel before he is competent to tell it out.

Second, Power. The disciples were told to "Tarry ye in the city of Jerusalem until ye be endued with power from on high." Since the apostles and disciples of our Lord, who waited personally upon His wonderful ministry and witnessed His marvelous doings, were not qualified for testimony and service without power from on high, we, most surely, must have Divine help. "Without Me ye can do nothing."

Third, Faith,—since the Almighty One has said, "For as

the rain cometh down, and the snow from heaven, and re-
turneth not thither, but watereth the earth, and maketh it
bring forth and bud, that it may give seed to the sower and
bread to the eater: so shall My word be that goeth forth out
of My mouth: it shall not return unto Me void, but it shall
accomplish that which I please, and it shall prosper in the
thing whereto I sent it," the proclaimer need have no mis-
giving as to the result, knowing full well that "He is faithful
that promised."

THE DIRECTIONS

What are the directions? *First, "Go into all the world"*
and tell it "to every creature." The field is the wide world;
and the good news is for every soul of man.

Second, It is to be "preached." The God-sent preacher is
a *kērux*—a herald. He has no message of his own. It is
the King's message he is to proclaim. According to the
heraldic law, if the herald substituted so much as a word of
his own for the king's, he was beheaded. If this law was
enforced in these days a lot of preachers would lose their
heads, indeed many have lost their heads, judging by the kind
of messages they are delivering.

Third, The preacher is to be brave, a witness—*martus*—
martyr. All the apostles, like our Lord, went to martyrdom
for faithfully proclaiming *the* Word of God. The Master said,
"If they have persecuted Me, they will also persecute you."
And, "Woe unto you, when all men shall speak well of you,
for so did their fathers to the false prophets." Paul said,
"If I yet pleased men, I should not be the servant of Christ."
The mind of the natural man is enmity against God; therefore the unsaved demand of the preacher, "Prophesy not unto
us right things, speak unto us smooth things, prophesy de-
ceits;" and a premium is placed upon finesse by many in authority in the church. Because of this, it requires as sublime
courage in these days to speak faithfully the Word of God as

was shown by Micaiah, when he stood before Ahab, Jehosaphat and the four hundred lying prophets; or Simon Peter when he said to the threatening, wrathful rulers of Israel, "We cannot but speak the things which we have seen and heard." There never was so much need of fearlessness on the part of the servant of God as in these days; brave true men, who will not receive honors of men, or seek their own, are absolutely necessary to successful evangelism.

THE MESSAGE

Now then, as to the message itself: Timothy was commanded to "Do the work of an evangelist;" and, in doing it, to "Preach the Word * * * with all long-suffering and doctrine." Doctrinal preaching is therefore necessary to evangelistic success. But what doctrines? I answer, *First, Sin— its universality, nature and consequences.*

(a) Universality. "As by one man sin entered into the world, and death by sin; and so death passed upon all men, for that all have sinned, * * * by one man's offence death reigned by one, * * * by the offence of one, judgment came upon all men to condemnation, * * * by one man's disobedience many were made sinners," etc. (Romans 5:12-21. See also Psa. 51:5; 58:3; Ecc. 7:20; Rom. 3:10; 1 John 1:8, 10, etc.)

(b) Nature. There are numerous words in the Bible rendered sin; and these words mean iniquity, offence, trespass, failure, error, go astray, to cause to sin, and miss the mark. In 1 John 3:4 we are told that "Sin is the transgression of the law." The word rendered transgression is *anomia,* and means lawlessness. Failure to conform to the law is as certainly sin as to violate the commandments of God. Unbelief is sin. (John 16:9; 3:18.)

In Genesis 6:5 we are told, "God saw that the wickedness of man was great in the earth, and that every imagination of the thoughts of his heart was only evil continually," and in Gen. 8:21, "The imagination of man's heart is evil from his youth." The word rendered imagination in these passages signifies also the desires and purposes of the individual. Therefore guilt lies in the desires and purposes as certainly as in the act. The common law requires that one shall have committed an overt act of violation before he can be adjudged guilty. But according to the Divine law one is guilty even though he never committed an overt act, since guilt lies in the desires and purposes of the heart. "Whosoever hateth his brother is a murderer" (1 John 3:15). "Whosoever looketh on a woman to lust after her hath committed adultery with her already in his heart" (Matt. 5:28). "The Lord seeth not as man seeth; for man looketh on the outward appearance, but the Lord looketh on the heart" (1 Sam. 16:7). Because of the "lust of the flesh, and the lust of the eyes, and the pride of life," every mouth is stopped and the whole world is guilty before God. (Rom. 3:19.)

The Almighty and Sovereign Creator is infinite in holiness. Therefore His "law is holy, and the commandment holy, and just, and good." Sin is ruinous, heinous and damning: the most awful thing in the universe.

(c) Consequences. Sin separates and estranges the sinner from God; and he becomes an enemy of God by wicked works (Rom. 8:7), has no peace (Isa. 57:21), no rest (Isa. 57:20), is polluted (Eph. 4:17-19), condemned (John 3:18), and without hope (Eph. 2:12). Oh, the curse and ruin of sin!

If unrepenting and unbelieving, the future has for him, *first,* inexorable and awful judgment. (See Matt. 25:30-46; Heb. 9:27; Jude 14, 15; Rev. 20:11-13; 22:11-15.) *Second,* the wrath of God. (See Ezra 8:22; Psa. 21:9; John 3:36; Rom. 1:18; 2:5; 4:15; 5:9; 12:19; 13:4; Eph. 2:3; 5:6; Col. 3:6; 1 Thess. 1:10; Rev. 6:16, 17; 14:10; 16:19; 19:15, etc.) And *third,* eternal torments. (See Psa. 11:6; Isa. 33:14; Dan. 12:2; Matt. 3:12; 22:11-13; 23:33; 25:41,

46; Mark 9:43, 48; Luke 12:5; 16:22-31; John 5:28, 29; 2 Thess. 1:7-9; Heb. 10:28, 29; 2 Peter 3:5-12; Rev. 19:20; 20:14, 15; 21:8, etc.)

The preacher who ignores these three awful and inexorable truths preaches an emasculated gospel, be he never so faithful in proclaiming other truth. He who preaches the love of God to the exclusion of God's justice and wrath proclaims but idle sentiment. No one will ever truly desire salvation unless he first realizes that there is something to be saved from. "By faith Noah, being warned of God of things not seen as yet, moved with fear, prepared an ark to the saving of his house" (Heb. 11:7); all of which symbolizes the sinner's condition, need, motive and hope. In no way can the love of God be so clearly, beautifully and convincingly set forth as in the fact that God makes plain to the sinner his condition and peril, and then shows him the way of escape, having, in His great mercy, Himself provided it at infinite cost. Now, at this point the Gospel comes in as indeed good news, showing God's love for the sinner.

The supreme motive for the atoning work of our Lord was His infinite love for us. The supreme object had in view was to save us from eternal ruin. "For God so loved the world, that He gave His only begotten Son, that whosoever believeth in Him should not perish, but have everlasting life" (John 3:16). Our Lord, while among men, had far more to say about the doom of the finally impenitent than about love and heaven. Is it not wise and safe to follow His example who said, "The word which ye hear is not Mine, but the Father's which sent Me." How can any minister reasonably expect to have evangelistic success if he fails to imitate the Master in this particular?

"When I say unto the wicked, O wicked man, thou shalt surely die; if thou dost not speak to warn the wicked from his way, that wicked man shall die in his iniquity; but his blood will I require at thy hand" (Ezek. 33:8).

Second, Redemption through Jesus' blood. "The Lord laid on Him the iniquity of us all" (Isa. 53:6) "The Son of Man came * * * to give His life a ransom for many" (Mark 10:45). "For Christ also hath once suffered for sins, the just for the unjust, that He might bring us to God, being put to death in the flesh, but quickened by the Spirit" (1 Peter 3:18). "For He hath made Him to be sin for us, who knew no sin; that we might be made the righteousness of God in Him" (2 Cor. 5:21). "For Christ is the end of the law for righteousness to every one that believeth" (Rom. 10:4). "Christ hath redeemed us from the curse of the law, being made a curse for us; for it is written, Cursed is every one that hangeth on a tree" (Gal. 3:13). "And ye are not your own. For ye are bought with a price" (1 Cor. 6:20. See also Lev. 17:11; Heb. 9:22; Matt. 20:28; 26:28; John 3:14, 16; Rom. 3:24-26; 5:9; 1 Cor. 1:30; 10:16; 2 Cor. 5:14-21; Eph. 1:7; 2:13-17; Col. 1:14, 19-22; 1 Tim. 2:6; Heb. 9:12-14, 24-26; 10:19; 13:12; 1 Peter 1:2, 18, 19; 2:24; 1 John 1:7; Rev. 1:5; 5:9; 12:11). On no other ground than the cross can the sinner be justified and reconciled to God. If the atoning work of our Lord was not vicarious, then the sacrifices, ordinances, types and symbols of the old economy are meaningless and of no value. The moral influence theory of Bushnell is all right for the saint; but the atonement is of no value to the sinner if it is not substitutional.

More than thirty years ago, in Denver, Colorado, I met an aged Congregational minister, who was a pastor in Hartford, Connecticut, during Dr. Horace Bushnell's pastorate in the same city. He told me this: "I spent an hour with Dr. Bushnell the day before he died. He then said to me, 'Doctor, I greatly fear some things I have said and written about the atonement may prove to be misleading and do irreparable harm.' He was lying upon his back with his hands clasped over his breast. He lay there with closed eyes, in silence, for some moments, his face indicating great anxiety. Directly, opening his eyes and raising his hands he said, 'O Lord Jesus,

Thou knowest that I hope for mercy alone through Thy shed blood.' "

Third, Resurrection. "If Christ be not risen, then is our preaching vain and your faith is also vain. * * * Ye are yet in your sins;" and "they also which are fallen asleep in Christ are perished. If in this life only we have hope in Christ, we are of all men most miserable. But now is Christ risen from the dead, and become the firstfruits of them that are sleeping" (1 Cor. 15:14-20). Jesus was "declared to be the Son of God with power * * * by the resurrection from the dead" (Rom. 1:4). Therefore the apostles and disciples went everywhere preaching "Jesus and the resurrection." (See Acts 2:24-32; 3:15; 4:2, 10, 33; 5:30; 17:18, 32; 23:6; 24:15, 21; 1 Cor. 15:3-8; 1 Peter 1:3-5.) "He was delivered for our offences, and was raised again for our justification" (Rom. 4:25). "By the resurrection of Jesus Christ, who is gone into heaven, and is on the right hand of God; angels and authorities, and powers being made subject unto Him" (1 Peter 3:22). "Wherefore He is able also to save them to the uttermost that come unto God by Him, seeing He ever liveth to make intercession for them" (Heb. 7:25).

Fourth, Justification. "Being justified freely by His grace through the redemption that is in Christ Jesus: Whom God hath set forth to be a propitiation through faith in His blood, to declare His righteousness for the remission of sins that are past, through the forbearance of God; to declare, I say, at this time His righteousness: that He might be just, and the justifier of him which believeth in Jesus" (Rom. 3:24, 25, 26). "And you, that were sometime alienated and enemies in your mind by wicked works, yet now hath He reconciled in the body of His flesh through death, to present you holy and unblameable and unreproveable in His sight" (Col. 1:21, 22). "Who shall lay anything to the charge of God's elect? It is God that justifieth" (Rom. 8:33), for "There is therefore now no condemnation to them which are in Christ Jesus; for the law of the spirit of life in Christ Jesus hath made me free from the law of sin and death" (Rom. 8: 1, 2). Believers are "not under the law, but under grace" (Rom. 6: 14) and can rejoicingly say, judicially, of course, "As He is, so are we in this world" (1 John 4: 17).

Fifth, Regeneration. The unchristian man is spiritually dead (Rom. 5: 12), and must be "born again," or "he cannot see the kingdom of God" (John 3: 3).

Richard Watson defined regeneration as "That mighty change in man wrought by the Holy Spirit, by which the dominion which sin has over him in his natural state, and which he deplores and struggles against in his present state, is broken and abolished; so that with full choice of will and the energy of right affections, he serves God freely, and runs in the way of His commandments."

He who receives Jesus as Saviour and Lord, is made a "partaker of the Divine nature" (John 1: 12, 13; 2 Peter 1: 4): "He is a new creature [creation]: old things are passed away, behold, all things are become new" (2 Cor. 5: 17).

THE METHOD

The following is the method: The words of the Gospel "are spirit, and they are life" (John 6: 63). If the repenting sinner receives them into his heart and life to believe and obey them (James 1: 21); the Holy Spirit operating through them accomplishes the new birth (James 1: 18), and he will be "born again, not of corruptible seed, but of incorruptible, by the Word of God, which liveth and abideth forever" (1 Peter 1: 23). Saved, "By the washing of regeneration and renewing of the Holy Ghost; which He shed on us abundantly through Jesus Christ our Saviour; that being justified by His grace, we should be made heirs according to the hope of eternal life" (Titus 3: 4-7. See also John 1: 12, 13; Gal. 6: 15; Eph. 2: 1-3; Col. 2: 13, etc.)

Sixth, Repentance. Repentance means a change of mind; and this change of mind is brought about by the Holy Spirit, through the knowledge of the sinner's condition, needs and peril, by which the sinner is convicted "of sin, and of righteousness, and of judgment" (John 16:8), and is induced to yield himself wholly, immediately and irrevocably to God. (See Matt. 9:13; Mark 6:12; Luke 13:2-5; 24:47; Acts 2:38; 3:19; 17:30; 26:20; Rom. 2:4; 2 Cor. 7:9, 10; 2 Tim. 2:25; 2 Peter 3:9.)

Seventh, Conversion. Conversion means to turn about or upon. When the unsaved sinner is convinced of sin and resolves to turn from his transgressions and commit his ways unto the Lord, he has repented; and when he acts upon that resolve, and yields himself to God in absolute self-surrender, he is converted. (See Psa. 19:7; 51:13; Matt. 18:3; Acts 3:19; James 5:19, 20.)

Eighth, Faith. Until the sinner changes his mind with regard to his relation to God, and resolves with all his heart to do it, his faith is a vain thing, he is yet in his sins; but, when he sincerely repents and turns to God, and believes the record God has given of His Son, his faith is of the heart and unto righteousness. (Rom. 10:9, 10. See also Heb. 11:6; Rom. 10:17; Gal. 5:22; Eph. 2:8; Gal. 3:6-12; 2:16-20; Rom. 4:13-16; 3:21-28; Acts 16:30, 31; John 6:47.)

Ninth, Obedience. Faith is a vital principle. "If it hath not works, is dead, being alone" (James 2:17, 18). Two things are required of the believer, immediately upon his profession of faith in Jesus as Saviour and Lord, namely, verbal confession and water baptism. "With the heart man believeth unto righteousness; and with the mouth confession is made unto salvation" (Rom. 10:10. See also Psa. 107:2; Matt. 10:32, 33; Rom. 10:9; 1 John 4:15, etc.) "He that believeth and is baptized shall be saved" (Mark 16:16). The believer is not saved because he is baptized; but, baptized because he is saved. We are saved through faith alone, but not the faith that is alone, because "Faith without works is dead, being alone." Water baptism is a divinely ordained ordinance whereby the believer witnesses to the world that he died with Christ, and is risen together with Him," an habitation of God through the Spirit. (See Matt. 28:19, 20; Acts 2:38, 41; 8:12, 13, 16, 36, 38; 9:18; 10:47, 48; 16:15, 33; 19:5; 22:15, 16; Rom. 6:3, 4; Col. 2:12; 1 Peter 3:21; 1 John 2:3; 3:22.)

Tenth, Assurance. Salvation from spiritual death by the new birth, and from the guilt of sin in justification, immediately follows "repentance toward God, and faith toward our Lord Jesus Christ." "For by grace have ye been saved through faith" (Eph. 2:8). "These things have I written unto you, that ye may know that ye have eternal life, even unto you that believe on the name of the Son of God" (1 John 5:13). It is here stated that certain things are in God's Word by which the believer is to know he has eternal life. Here are some of them: "He that heareth My Word, and believeth on Him that sent Me, *hath* eternal life, and cometh not into judgment, but *hath* passed out of death into life" (John 5:24). "He that hath the Son *hath* the life." "Whosoever believeth that Jesus is the Christ *is* begotten of God" (1 John 5:12, 13. For confirmation see 1 John 2:3; 3:14, 24; 4:20, 21; etc.).

"And by Him every one that believeth *is* justified" (Acts 13:39)—an accomplished work. So the Bible uniformly teaches. Believing these words of assurance, one finds peace and joy. It is the business of the preacher to make this matter plain to converts, that they may be surely and safely anchored; and "that their hearts may be comforted, they being knit together in love, and unto all riches of the full assurance of understanding, that they may know the mystery of God, even Christ, in whom are all the treasures of knowledge hidden" (Col. 2:2, 3).

There are some other doctrines, of a persuading character, such as Love, Heaven, Hope, Rewards, that may be emphasized to advantage in an evangelistic campaign; but, those I have enumerated will most surely be owned of God in the salvation of souls, if proclaimed as they should be.

In going about among the churches as I do, I find three things increasingly true. First, Ministers and people in large numbers are awakening to the fact that the so-called "new theology" and up-to-date methods are utterly barren of spiritual results. Prof. A. H. Sayce once said, "Higher criticism saves no souls." Second, Because of this indisputable fact, very many are turning again to the doctrines of the historic faith, for it is seen that they are still workable and produce results as in former times. Third, Great numbers of ministers are seeing that their ministry is a failure unless it results in the salvation of souls. They really feel as did the late Henry Ward Beecher. While conducting an evangelistic campaign in Brooklyn Tabernacle I one day met Mr. Beecher. As he held my right hand in both of his, he said: "I hear you are having a great blessing in your meetings with Dr. Talmage. I very much wish we could have you for a campaign in Plymouth Church." He trembled as he held my hand. He then said, "But I fear my people would not stand for it." Then, after hesitating for a few minutes he added, "I would like to see an old-time Holy Ghost revival in Plymouth Church before I go hence." He then broke down and cried as if his heart would break. Three weeks later, to a day, his body was laid in the grave.

Life and opportunity are ours. Men are dying, and the whole world lieth in the wicked one, lost in the ruin of sin. Redemption is an accomplished fact, and salvation is possible for all. We have been chosen to tell out the message of life and hope; and are assured of glorious success if faithful; if unfaithful we had better never been born.

CHAPTER II

PASTORAL AND PERSONAL EVANGELISM, OR WINNING MEN TO CHRIST ONE BY ONE

BY REV. JOHN TIMOTHY STONE. D. D.,

CHICAGO, ILLINOIS,

EX-MODERATOR GENERAL ASSEMBLY PRESBYTERIAN CHURCH,

U. S. A.

The story of evangelism is the specific history of the Cross of Christ. Great movements and revivals have made up much of its general history, but slowly and quietly through the years and centuries the Evangel has won, as men and women have led their fellow human beings to repentance and have by precept and example followed in the footsteps of their Lord.

Jesus Christ won most of His followers and chose His Apostles one by one. He called men to Himself, and they heard and heeded His call. The multitudes sought Him and heard Him gladly, but He sought individuals, and those individuals sought others and brought them to Him. John the Baptist said: "Behold the Lamb of God," and Andrew his disciple heard and followed. Andrew found his own brother Simon and brought him to Jesus. Jesus the next day found Philip and bade him follow Him; Philip found Nathaniel and answered his questionings by the Saviour's previous reply, "Come and see." The Master called Matthew from his unworthy work, and so the other Apostles. Saul of Tarsus was arrested by the Divine individual call as he pursued his intense and terrorizing campaign against the early Christians. His "Who art Thou, Lord?" was followed by his complete surrender as he asked, "What wilt Thou have me to do?"

All through those first decades of the early Church, and on through the ages, individual work for individuals has progressed and accomplished results. How largely the Gospels, the Acts and the Epistles verify this fact! Even the marvelous work of Philip in Samaria was not the immediate plan of God, but the Spirit sent him past Jerusalem, down into the desert at Gaza, that he might win the Ethiopian eunuch to Christ, and through him no doubt countless hosts of Africa. The missionary journeys and efforts of Paul were filled with personal service. His letters are filled with personal messages. Some of his most important letters, such as Philemon, the Timothys and Titus, are addressed and written to individuals. His winning of Onesimus in Rome, and the letter to Philemon which resulted, is one of the most effective and beautiful experiences recorded in all the Word of God.

God has used men mightily in reaching vast multitudes of people, even from the days of His own ministry and the days of Peter and his associates at Pentecost. Even at this time, two hundred years after his unparalleled ministry, we are reminded of George Whitefield, who preached at times to fully thirty thousand people in the open air, and won his thousands and tens of thousands. We recall the vast multitudes who were reached by our own Moody and Sankey; we note the vast audiences who flocked to hear Mr. Spurgeon, week after week, year after year. The strong evangelists of our own generation verify before our very eyes God's honor placed on those to whom He gives such signal power. But our thought goes back to the great universal method our Lord Himself instituted, of reaching the individual by his fellow man.

The Almighty could have so arranged His Divine plan that He Himself, without human help, might arrest and enlist followers as He did with Saul of Tarsus, but this was not His plan. By man He would reach men. Human mediums of power must do His wondrous work. Man must go, in the power of His Spirit "into all the world, to preach the Gospel to every creature." And His promise was sure and permanent: "Lo, I am with you alway."

GOD'S HOLY SPIRIT

The first requisite in winning men to Christ must be the presence and power of the Holy Spirit. "It is expedient that I go away from you, for if I go not away, the Holy Spirit will not come." With His presence "greater works" than the works of Christ "shall ye do." "Ye shall *receive power* when the Holy Spirit is come upon you, *and ye shall be witnesses.*" To live in the power of God's Holy Spirit, and to know that He is present and will lead, is in itself an assurance of a joyful and successful service. The Spirit will constantly "call to our remembrance the things of Christ," and hence we may not be anxious as to the words we are to speak, for He will direct us and speak for and through us.

So many times we are fearful and embarrassed, but this will not be the case if we are under the influence momentarily of God's Spirit. "He will guide us into all truth." "He will not speak of Himself," but will glorify Christ. That which we say in weakness He will use with power, and "His word will not return unto Him void, but will accomplish that whereunto it was sent." We may always take for granted His preparation, for He does not send but calls us. His word is not "Go," but "Come." Thus we will always be on the alert for opportunities to speak the things He would have us, and our words and thoughts will be those which He suggests and honors. We will be nourished constantly by His Word within, and equipped with His sword for sustained protection and aggressive attack. If His Word abides in us, we will never be weak in body, nor unprepared and weaponless. His Spirit will also give us courage and endurance, and the fearless one who has stability and patience need not fear the unexpected nor the aggressive opponent. The Spirit of God also prepares the one whom we must approach, and is working in his heart as well as with our words.

Prayer is also a real factor in our lives, and we live in His presence by the true conversational method of association.

As God speaks to us through His Word, so we talk with Him in prayer, and the place and surroundings are of little relative importance, as we are always with Him and He with us. The word we speak and the act we perform is the expression of Himself, and the impression is bound to be His as well, for our association with Him takes others into His presence as they communicate and associate with us. We may pray before and after and as we speak with others, and do it so naturally and impulsively that we may actually live in the atmosphere of prayer without hypocrisy and without pretense. And prayer will become more and more a power in our work as we approach individuals from the very presence of the unseen but not unknown God. Assurance and confidence result, and we are agreeably surprised with ourselves to find that our happiness does not depend so much upon the evidence of our success as upon the consciousness of our faithfulness.

We will also seek to win others to Christ that they too may be used by His Spirit and associated with Him, rather than simply to obtain salvation; not what we can do *for* them, but what God's Spirit can and will do *with* them.

The Spirit of God will also lead us to gain from others the experiences and methods through which they have gone to learn to do this work for Him; hence conferences and testimony will take on new life and gain keener interest. We will overlook littleness, and the greatness of God is seen in His confidence placed in those who win others to Him. Criticism will give place to appreciation and suggestion to expressions of gratitude. We will see in others what God sees, and fail to see what we have seen before by way of fault and error. We will also learn to take the difficult things to God in prayer instead of taking them to men in controversy, and will be surprised to find how many easily adjust themselves for us.

God's Spirit will also prompt us to spend longer seasons alone and seriously think upon life's greatest issues and values. Prayer will be less general and more specific and individual.

Souls will mean more, and things less. Lives will become more
attractive and fascinating, and books, papers and stories will
only control interest when related to lives which can be influenced for and by Him.

The last verse of "In the Secret of His Presence" asks the
real question:

"Would you like to know the secret of the sweetness of the
    Lord?

Go and hide beneath His shadow; this shall then be your re-
    ward.

And whene'er you leave the silence of that happy resting place,

You must feel and bear the image of the Master in your face."

This will be the result, and others will be won by you as
they see in your very face the reflection of Christ, because His
Spirit dwells within you.

THE BIBLE

A second most necessary element in winning men to the
Master is a knowledge and appropriate use of God's Word.
We must be workmen who need not to be ashamed, who can
rightly divide the Word of Truth. The use of the Bible is
the greatest advancing weapon for Christ. The worker who
knows his Bible will constantly read it for strength and apply
it in dealing with the unconverted. He will not argue with
men, nor talk *about* God's Word, but he will explain *with* it,
and repeatedly refer to it. An open Bible before and with
an inquirer almost always means conversion and spiritual
growth to follow. When dealing with your subject, ask if he
has ever considered what the Bible says on the point under
discussion. For instance, a man tells you he does not take
much stock in what you have been saying about the necessity
of the Cross; it seems somewhat foolish to him. Do not be
angry, but reply pleasantly that you do not blame him a bit, in
fact, Paul himself writes, in his first letter to the Corinthians,

that men will feel exactly that way. Tell him you appreciate his frankness, and meanwhile pull your Testament from your pocket or take it from the table, and turn to the passage in First Corinthians, one, eighteen; or better still, hand him another copy of the Bible open to the place, and read from your own copy: "For the preaching of the Cross is to them that perish foolishness, but unto us which are saved it is the power of God." Then, before he is angered or troubled about that word "perish," ask him to notice in the same connection the twenty-first verse, just below: "For after that in the wisdom of God the world by wisdom knew not God, it pleased God *by the foolishness* of preaching to save them that believe." These passages will at least arrest his attention, and unconsciously interest him somewhat in reading the Bible himself.

I well remember a somewhat like experience to this suggested, which happened in my parish calling years ago. I was talking in the office of a man who was a confessed unbeliever, when he made some such criticism of a former sermon he had heard. I followed the course outlined, and after reading the verses, he remarked upon their application, and told me he would "look into the Pauline writings." He became later a fairly regular attendant in church, and sometimes came to our Bible class.

From such a chapter as that, I would take a man into the second chapter, which attracts one from the very first sentence, "I came not with excellency of speech or of wisdom, declaring unto you the testimony of God, for I was determined not to know anything among you but Jesus Christ and Him crucified." Then read the fifth verse: "That your faith should not stand in the wisdom of men, but in the power of God." Then the ninth verse, with its wonderful vision: "Eye hath not seen, nor ear heard, neither hath entered into the heart of man the things which God hath prepared for them that love Him." This verse will prove a vista to many to scenes beyond.

Ask a man who doubts God's love for him if he has ever carefully considered that his salvation does not so much rest upon his confidence in his own belief as in God's confidence in *him*. Tell him that faith grows by use and action. Ask him to pray, "Lord, I believe; help Thou my unbelief." Turn to Hebrews, eleven one, and read it from the Revised Version, which is far stronger in this verse: "Faith is the assurance of things hoped for, the conviction of things not seen." Then go on with this great "Faith chapter." Stop and dwell upon some of the references, if it will add to the interest. Remember to have an open Bible before your companion as you read. Reading to a man will not help a listener and reading with you will. Let the eye help the ear, and make it personal by letting him follow you as you read. Perhaps sometimes ask him to read an occasional verse that needs emphasis, and then you comment on it, asking him to read on.

If a man does not understand how God can love him, do not discuss it, but turn to First Corinthians, the thirteenth chapter, and read it slowly and thoughtfully. Always begin that chapter with the last verse of the twelfth: "And yet show I unto you a more excellent way." Change the word "charity" to "love." When you get to the fourth verse, intersperse a remark such as this: "Have you ever read anything more wonderful than this: 'Love suffereth long and is kind, love envieth not, love vaunteth not itself, is not puffed up, doth not behave itself unseemly, seeketh not her own, is not easily provoked, thinketh no evil.'" Why, each verse of this wonderful chapter will grow more and more impressive as one reads on. Then read through the first verse of chapter fourteen, which gives us the admonition, "Follow after love and desire spiritual gifts." Ask a man if such attainment as this isn't worth while. Turn before he answers to John three, sixteen: "For God so loved the world that He gave His only begotten Son, that whosoever believeth in Him should not perish, but have everlasting life." "For God came not into the world to condemn the world, but that the world through Him might be saved."

In other words win a man by the love of God. Before he can question again, ask him to turn, or better, take his Bible and turn for him, to Luke the fifteenth chapter, and beginning with the eleventh verse, read together the parable of the Prodigal Son. Then quickly and easily turn to First John, the third chapter: "Behold what manner of love the Father hath bestowed upon us, that we should be called the sons of God. Therefore the world knoweth us not, because it knew Him not." Read on a way in that chapter, and then turn over to the fifth chapter and read there. Then turn to Revelation three, twenty, and read: "Behold, I stand at the door and knock; if any man hear My voice and open the door, I will come in to him and he to Me, and he shall go in and out and find pasture."

Tell him in connection with this verse the story of Holman Hunt, the great artist who painted, "The Light of the World." Describe the picture till he recalls it, of Christ standing before the latticed door, knocking, holding a lantern in the other hand, the distant love in the Master's eye showing that the interest of His thought was within the cottage. Tell him how Holman Hunt, after the picture had been painted, called in a friendly artist to criticise the picture. His friend, after scrutinizing the picture, said, "But you have no latch on the door." "No," replied the great painter, referring to this verse, "the latch of this door is on the inside. 'Behold, I stand at the door and knock. If any man hear My voice and *open* the door.'"

Show how Christ respects the human life by knocking and not forcing His entrance, and how if the individual opens He will come in and abide.

If you have one burdened with a sense of his own guilt and sin, turn to Isaiah one, eighteen: "Come now and let us reason together, saith the Lord. Though your sins be as scarlet, they shall be as white as snow; though they be red like crimson, they shall be as wool." Then turn to Romans seven and eight and read with him from verse fourteen. I have personally known more men reached by these chapters than by any others. They are a sort of photograph or mirror to most men of their own very lives. Just note that fifteenth verse: "For what I do, I allow not; for what I would, that do I not, but what I hate, that do I." Then verse seventeen: "Now then it is no more I that do it, but sin that dwelleth in me." Read on, verse after verse, until you get to that powerful verse, the eleventh of the eighth chapter. Then you will have to stop. "But if the Spirit of Him that raised up Jesus from the dead dwell in you, He that raised up Christ from the dead shall also quicken your mortal bodies by His Spirit that dwelleth in you."

This verse will inspire most men who need it. It lifts a man out of himself. There is actual life power in its truth. The thrill and longing is liable to come especially after a man has realized what sin is doing in and for him. I have known many a man look up at that verse and ask if it could be possible for him to attain such a thing. Of course it can. That eleventh verse, led up to aright by that which precedes it, will arouse almost any heart. Then take a man right over to chapter twelve: "I beseech you, therefore, brethren." Tell your man how the first eleven chapters of Romans are the theory of Paul's great theme of "Justification by Faith," and that now in the twelfth we have the practical, hence the "therefore." "I beseech you, therefore, brethren, by the mercies of God, that ye present your bodies a living sacrifice, holy, acceptable unto God, which is your reasonable service, and be not conformed to this world, but be ye transformed by the renewing of your mind, that ye may prove what is that good and acceptable and perfect will of God."

Tell a man the glory of sacrifice, and what it means to live that kind of a life, subject to God's will. Turn over then to Ephesians three, the fourteenth verse, and read Paul's great prayer with him, telling him you want him to know how a man who felt those truths of Romans could pray for other men. Then read all that prayer, Ephesians three fourteen, through verse twenty-one. Re-read verses twenty and twenty-one. This verse will lead us to our knees, and that means victory. Let us consider in this connection the subject of

PRAYER

We do not estimate the place and power prayer has in winning others to Christ, prayer for others in intercession, and prayer with others as we take them individually into the very presence of God.

First, prayer for them. No matter what your method or lack of method may be, take those for whom you are working up to God in prayer. Pray for them by name; pray that you may approach them aright and appeal to them with Divine wisdom. Pray that you may be able to put yourself in their place, and be patient as well as wise with them. Pray that you may turn to the right Scripture, and use the appropriate illustrations, to help them. Pray that you may lead them to Jesus instead of talking with them about Him. Pray that they may be responsive and willing. Pray that their sins may not hinder them from giving their best selves to the consideration of this all-important subject. Pray that they may see in you that vital interest and real sincerity which will actually arouse them. Pray that their companions and surroundings may not prove a barrier or hindrance to them. Pray that you may converse with them on the essentials and not spend the time on unimportant and relative matters.

Pray that you may not be timid or careless, but fearless, clear and exact. Pray that human sympathy and love may influence you to show your heart and soul to touch and melt their hearts. Pray that just the favorable opening may come to you, and that you may be ready to use it. Pray most of all for the Holy Spirit's power with you.

Then secondly, pray *with* the individual. After Scripture has had its chance, and decision should be reached, get your friend on his knees, and ask him to decide after you have poured out your heart to God for and with him. I have known more men who have yielded on their knees than anywhere else. At just the right time, when genuinely prompted by loving impulse and sincere motive, your hand placed upon his shoulder may help him make the decision. To let one know you love him for Christ's sake breaks many a heart. When thus praying, no matter how cold your heart may have been, you will feel three are present rather than two, and the third is the Saviour of men.

When you pray with the one for whom you are working, be most specific and plain in your petition. Then ask him to pray for himself. If he cannot, frame his prayer for him, and ask him to repeat. Bring him then and there to a decision if possible, and seal the occasion with prayer again. Pray frequently between questions, if led. Remember the destiny of a human soul is in the balance. Pour out your soul to God and labor with Christ for that soul. When nothing one could say, quote or argue would help or convince, I have seen men yield on their knees and rise to their feet happy and confident in Christ. Sometimes a subtle and unconfessed sin is lurking in the mind or heart, and that keeps from decision. On one's knees in prayer, this is liable to be yielded, and the life freed from the fetters of concealed guilt.

Sometimes an unforgiving spirit is the cause of delay. There is no place so sure to overcome bitterness or hatred as the place of prayer. Leading the human life into the place of prayer will bring Divine power into the work, and conquers where you might fail.

Another form of prayer *for* the individual may be used by putting down upon a list or card the names of those for whom you are praying. We have in our own church a small card which is distributed occasionally at the prayer service and at other spiritual gatherings, which is entitled "Prayer List." On it there are spaces for names, and a blank line for the name of the signer and the date. A small footnote states that a copy of the card may be mailed to the pastor, although it is not required or urged. The list is for the individual Christian, a definite prayer for a definite soul. Many of these cards are handed in to me, and we thus unite in prayer for these souls. It is a real method of binding pastor and people in prayer for individuals.

A prayer list which includes all your friends is a most inspiring and useful method. One whom you see each day will be next in alphabetical order to a missionary in central India or in Japan. Home problems will come sometimes next to far-distant hopes, and the whole world comes to your very room through the power of prayer. As the years go by, so many whose names are there before you give themselves to God, and so many causes for gratitude come. In days past, I tore up a card when the heart yielded to God, but now we leave the card just the same, for one needs prayer surely after conversion fully as much as before, that growth and grace may abound. Prayer for individuals also makes one alert when opportunities open to speak to them, and directs aright conversation at such times. It also frees us from mind-wandering and perplexity in prayer. We grow specific and very definite, and learn to ask for those things which we really want. Friendship and companionship mean more when we realize that we are meeting each other through Christ at the throne of grace, and individuals are conscious of greater power than human speech when they know that you are praying for them.

Recently, when a man yielded to Christ, he replied, when told by his friend he had long prayed for him: "Well, I knew something was influencing me, for I have felt unhappy and dissatisfied until now, and it was not natural for me to be troubled about myself."

Prayer is, then, a most effective and powerful agency in winning others.

We ought also to pray more in our *public utterances* for the immediate and direct result of our preaching; that souls may be converted; that hearts may be arrested in sin and turned to God. Dr. Maltbie Babcock used to pray for a verdict then and there, that souls might yield during that very service. When a congregation feels that a preacher actually expects results, they begin to expect and pray for them too. If the soul hungers for souls, then public as well as private prayer will claim them.

METHOD AND MEANS

We must now take up the subject of method and means. The method is, after all, secondary, and if it becomes too set and orderly, it will be self-destructive, for as soon as one sees your method, the heart and mind are steeled against it, and there is little or no interest. When God's Spirit leads, we are responsive to all kinds of openings and ways. Instead of studying approach we simply advance as the plan opens before us, and we find ourselves doing in an unexpected way the very work we have always hoped to do. A revival of God's Spirit means the disregard of former ways and means, and an initiation of new and untried channels. We regard and value less the method, and seek only for the result.

It is wise and right for us, however, to consider methods and means. Christ Himself began His work with reaching individuals and training them to work for others. When Dr. Bruce wrote "The Training of the Twelve," he gave us the scholarly development of this truth. The Founder of our faith gave Himself largely to twelve men, and one of these was not worthy and another extremely vacillating. With them He walked, to them He revealed Himself in conversation, precept, parable and miracle. They grew like Him and followed His teaching. Five hundred millions of souls today honor Him as His followers, but He did not gain this vast multitude of myriad tongues and tribes by organizing a great band, but by the selection and training of twelve men. True, the multitudes sought Him, as they had followed John the Baptist, but He did not seek the multitudes. Great throngs followed many of those early disciples and preachers, even up through the latter centuries, and many were mightily used in preaching to great throngs of men, but Christ's method still remains—He sought individuals. What if He had never talked with that poor Samaritan woman at the well-side; we would never then have had those wondrous words in the fourth chapter of John: "Whoso drinketh of this water shall thirst again; but whoso drinketh of the water that I shall give him shall never thirst; but the water that I shall give him shall be in him a well of water springing up into everlasting life." What if these words had never occurred in the Gospels?— and they would not if Christ had not passed through Samaria and taken pity on that poor sinful woman and talked with her. What if He had never spent time with Nicodemus when he sought the Master by night? What rich and significant words those He uttered then on regeneration: "Ye must be born again. The wind bloweth where it listeth, and thou hearest the sound thereof, but canst not tell whence it cometh or whither it goeth; so is every one who is born of the Spirit." Suppose Christ had never overtaken the two disciples as they walked to Emmaus after His crucifixion, and we had never known those words of His and that experience they had as their hearts burned within them. He turned and saw the two disciples of John who had heard John the Baptist say, "Behold the Lamb of God." Andrew went from Christ to find his brother Peter, and brought him to Jesus. The next day Jesus Himself found Philip and told him, "Follow Me." Philip found Nathaniel. All through His work on earth, Christ saw and found individuals. Zacchæus was called out of a tree, Matthew from a money-changer's seat, but these men became winners and leaders of other men. Saul of Tarsus was not let alone because he was a persecutor, but was arrested on a highway with a personal word and question. His reply was: "Who art Thou?" and "What wilt Thou have me to do?" Paul, although a great preacher, worked too with individuals, in no more beautiful way ever illustrated than in the touching love he showed for Onesimus, the Phrygian runaway slave, whom he sent back to his master and Paul's friend at Colossae, Philemon.

The greatest advantage which the large meeting has is so interesting individuals in the truth that they will inquire from individuals who are ready to help them, as to the application of the truth they hear. A valuable series of meetings is only sure in interest and result as individuals invite, seek and lead others to be present, and then follow them by individual effort. The successful revivals of today must follow this method if permanent and large results are to be attained. God works through men, and individuals must reach other individuals.

One of the most efficient means some have used is that of training men and women to call upon those in their neighborhood and personally invite them to services—not a formal invitation, but a call in which they may get acquainted and feel at home with one another; one call followed up with another until a friendliness springs up and there is a response. There are many departments in church life that take this work up, such as the Home Department of our Sunday Schools, pastors' aid and visitation societies, and relative organizations; but there should be a more definite personal responsibility put upon our members as they come into our church, in reaching others, and in extending to them the definite invitation to attend God's house and give their lives to the Master. The Church of Christ universal has an immense force in herself to face the work of winning others to Christ, but we have not used that force. The foreign missionary lands have appreciated this fact in the work they are doing, and in some places the condition of winning others has been imposed upon new members before they are accepted into full communion. For instance, before a new member is received into the Korean Church, the convert must not only confess his faith in Christ, but also lead another to Christ.

What if our membership were really working for others individually, and were trained with that in view? What if we called the attention of our new members to this very obligation and expectation? Some of our churches have had no new members for several years, and some have very few. On the other hand, here is a great force of hundreds of thousands who are not working in the very line of activity which it is their privilege and duty to use. Suppose a church with one hundred members so impressed this upon fifty per cent of its membership that each one of those fifty should win one soul to Christ. It would mean that that church added fifty per cent of its membership the next year. If a church of five hundred members were to use twenty per cent of its membership, each winning one soul a year to Christ, that would be a hundred members added to that church. On the other hand, why should we not expect that many of our members should have one or more representatives at every communion? This would mean, if five or six communions were held during the year, that fifty such workers would add from two hundred fifty to three hundred to the membership of that individual church in a year.

Now, there is no question that a pastor has his definite work of preaching. He must also realize that, no matter how intense and far-reaching that work may be, his pre-eminent work should be in his pulpit; but it is also his work to shepherd his flock, and a shepherd cannot properly do that work without teaching his flock to follow him. He first must be an inviter and winner of men to Christ, and he must train his people to follow him. The great need of the Church today is a work within herself, in which her members may become individual and definite workers for the Lord Jesus Christ, and the winners of others to Him. In some of our churches, this method and means of reaching others has been carefully and thoroughly organized, so that regular organizations of young people and others go out regularly to do this work in their neighborhood, inviting others to attend the church and afterward winning them individually to Christ. We do not find that all such visitors are able immediately to become personal workers, but we do find that this work tends to lead them to desire to do that work, and in many instances leads them into efficient service. In our own church, hundreds upon hundreds have been won in this way, and we now have from fifty to sixty young people who are doing this work regularly, week after week, the result being that the influence is felt upon all our services, and hundreds are present at our services who would not be there except for this personal invitation and direct association.

We would here quote from a recent book upon this subject,* which I prepared for the work in our own church here in Chicago:

"Some five years ago, in reviewing carefully a ministry of about fifteen years, I was convinced of certain effective and many ineffective results. This practical inventory led me to consider the method, means and value of relative activities. It was very clear to me that much public work had not yielded results equal to certain private and personal service, although the latter is more easily known and tabulated. It was also evident that the work of the preacher and pastor is not concluded in bringing men to Christ, but in inspiring and training them to become the winners of others.

"In talking with colleagues in the ministry and gathering occasional evidence from varied churches, I discovered that a great weakness in the Church exists in a lack of masculine

---

*"The Invitation Committee," published by Presbyterian Board of Publication, Philadelphia, Pa. Leather, 25 cts.

spiritual leadership—the difficulty of finding strong men to fill spiritual offices and to lead in spiritual service—Boards of Trustees being more easily filled than Elders' or Deacons' Boards, men more responsive to ushering or even to taking official duty, than to taking a Sunday School superintendency or class, or attending and participating audibly in the weekly prayer service. I also found men ready to relieve one in distress or assist materially in any emergency, who seemed embarrassed and helpless when asked to assist or direct in things spiritual.

"Since this actual condition has been discovered, the effort has been made to remedy it by giving constant and faithful attention to individual Christians, not only pointing out the way of growth through exhortation and inspiration, but through instruction, example and personal direction.

"The community in which our church is placed has many thousands who are unreached and unattracted by any church. It has large numbers of youths of both sexes and many young families. Although there are many whose homes are permanent, even a larger number are transient and hence apt to scatter and drift farther from all moorings.

"No pastor nor force of professional assistants can hope successfully to reach such a field, but trained membership can, and young men and young women who are interested, instructed and directed can see in such a neighborhood a vast storehouse of raw human material which may be made into finished product for God. Better still, such latent life may become energized and utilized to win and save itself with responsive, joyful life.

"Organization has accomplished much, but the work and worker need Divine inspiration and spiritual food as well, and the Word of God, prayer and common sense combine to make the work effective and permanent. This little handbook is thus sent out to assist in meeting that need, that the hundreds of young men and young women already won may become winners of others; and primarily that the half hundred young people now working on these Invitation Committees may have a ready reference in time of immediate need.

"We have also felt that our need may be the need of others elsewhere, and cordially extend to you as well, our comradeship."

In connection with this same little volume, there are certain practical notes which we would also give to you:

"One cannot use God's Word without studying it.

"You cannot win others to Christ unless you believe in Him and keep near Him yourself.

"*He* must work *through* you. 'Apart from Me ye can do nothing.'

"Prayer must be a reality and a power to you. 'Ask, and ye shall receive.'

"Confidence in Christ's power must attend your effort. 'I can do all things in Him which strengtheneth me.'

"Common sense means putting yourself in the other man's place. Do not merely argue. Use the Word of God.

"Do not do all the talking; win the confidence of the one for whom you are working, and let him tell his story.

"Do not be in haste. Remember 'God's delays are not denials.' Work and wait. Be patient and persistent.

"Pray *with* your man as well as *for* him. Don't be afraid of falling on your knees in the presence of another.

"Get him to pray for himself.

"Learn to pray anywhere and in any posture—in an office or an automobile, in a quiet spot on the street, standing, sitting or kneeling, but always reverently.

"Get your man alone. Do not present the matter when another is present. (Exceptional cases may occur, as at times when talking with husband and wife.)

"Study your case beforehand (when possible).

"Do not approach your case with fear but with prayer and faith. 'It shall be given unto you . . . . what you shall speak.'

"Learn how by doing, and gain confidence through experience.

"Remember you are not only Christ's representative but that God's Holy Spirit is working through you. The power is His.

"Approach and do your work with a happy heart and with joy. Always show that 'the joy of Jehovah is your strength.'

"Beware of the temptation to postpone. The evil one prompts such suggestion. Many a man is never asked to give his heart to Christ because a good impulse was averted by indecision and the false plea of 'a better time to speak.'

"If you fail, do not be discouraged, but determine to get nearer to God and to gain more power through your apparent failure. Write a good letter to the one you have failed to reach or failed to find after repeated calling. Many have been won by correspondence. He knows you are interested very definitely if you write.

"Win back to service the Christian man who has lost interest, and lost touch with Christ and the Church."

Robert Speer has well said, "When we love men for what we know Christ can make them, we shall go after them for Him." We might add, "To persuade one soul to lead a better life is to leave the world better than you found it." God has certainly a very definite work for individuals to do in His Kingdom, and the Christian worker needs to realize that his duty is to set people to work and to train them in this service.

Another very effective method is by correspondence. So many times when we do not find people at home, or when we are not able to approach them as we desire, if we would sit down and write a direct and personal letter, it would have its weight and influence. Several years ago I knew a pastor who was very much discouraged with his work, who entered upon this method, and it resulted in a large accession to his church at the next communion. He has always been a different man and valued aright the power of the pen in personal correspondence. It should not be a substitute for a personal interview, but is a wonderful addition to it, and where the one is denied the other can be used.

The ways and methods for reaching others are manifold, and thank God they are as diversified as the personalities and training of those who are workers. God has new methods and ways to use constantly, but we must be alert in this great work, and reach out in faith and in earnestness.

One of the best means of reaching others is to be able to put one's self directly in the place of another, to feel his temptations, to understand his difficulties, and to be willing to meet him upon his own ground and with his own needs. If we can establish this human sympathy, we have gone a great way toward reaching others.

Another most effective way must be through the Sunday School and through the regular channels of active association. Whatever we can do to bring to others the positive need of settling this question for one's self, communicants' classes, catechetical classes, individual pastor's classes, all such methods should be used. A pastor should get into the public and private schools of the boys and girls of his own parish, to know where they live and what their work is and what their problems are, and then he should plan in some way to meet them individually. A pastor should go to the various Sunday School classes in his own Sunday School, not regularly or at stated times, but sometimes informally or by definite arrangement with the teacher, thus getting into touch with the scholars and .neeting them upon their own ground. He should also arrange special classes, to meet them and talk over their relationship to Christ. All through the church, he should have those who are so interested in individuals that they will take to him the special cases and refer them to him.

But after all, the greatest method in the world, the greatest means of all in winning others to Christ, is that of persistent, patient, faithful prayer. This, followed by action and associated with all the details of service, will be rewarded. Times of revival will spring up. Others will wish for special services and methods and will suggest them, and before we know it our churches will be alive with a newness of material, and we will find that men and women are not only crying out, "What must we do to be saved?" but "How may we win others to the Master?" We will all become "workmen who need not to be ashamed, rightly dividing the Word of Truth," and we will realize that God's Word shall not return to Him void, but "shall accomplish that whereunto it is sent."

Surely, "He that winneth souls is wise."

CHAPTER III

THE SUNDAY SCHOOL'S TRUE EVANGELISM

BY CHARLES GALLAUDET TRUMBULL,

EDITOR "THE SUNDAY SCHOOL TIMES," PHILADELPHIA,
PENNSYLVANIA

There are more than thirty million persons reported in the enrollment of the Sunday Schools of the world. But if all these persons, and all church members as well, knew what the Sunday School is really for, the enrollment would leap upward millions upon millions.

The Sunday School is often spoken of as the child of the church, or the church of tomorrow, or a branch or department of the church. It is more than any and all of these.

The true Sunday School is the Church of Jesus Christ engaged in systematic study and teaching of the Word of God for three great purposes: to bring into the body of Christ those within the membership of the Sunday School who are not yet members of the church or of Christ; to train up those who are in Christ into a full-grown knowledge and appropriation of the riches which are theirs because they are Christ's; and to send out into the world fully equipped, victorious soul-winners who shall be Christ's living epistles to those who do not yet know Him.

The whole superb work of the Sunday School centers about its text-book, the Word of God. Bible study in the Sunday School is made the means of the three-fold purpose of the Sunday School. The Sunday School is the great organized movement of the Church of God for Bible study which has for its end salvation, character building, and equipment for evangelism. Or to describe the work of the Sunday School partly in theological terms, the purpose of the Sunday School is Bible study for justification, sanctification and service.

Whoever needs to know what the Bible has to say about next-world freedom from the penalty of our sins, and this-world freedom from the power of our sin, together with the supernatural power of God as the equipment of the full grown man for service, may properly be in the Sunday School. Only those who do not need the fullest possible message of the Bible on these subjects can logically stay outside the Sunday School.

And that means that few can logically or safely stay outside the Sunday School. The true Sunday School is the whole Church of God engaged in systematic Bible study to ascertain the whole will of God as revealed in His Word for their lives. With the cradle roll at one end of the age limit for non-attending members and the home department at the other end for non-attending members, there is little reason today for any one to remain outside the membership of the Sunday School. It is not necessary to attend the Sunday services of the Sunday School in order to be a member in full and regular standing. Literally the entire church membership can with great profit be enrolled: babies, invalids, shut-ins, traveling men, mothers tied down by home duties, railroad men, telegraph or telephone operators,—the Sunday School welcomes the representatives of every walk in life. Blessed stories are told of the home department, such as of the engineer miles from his Sunday School, safeguarded in the cab of his locomotive by his nearness to his Lord, and rejoicing in his privilege of studying the same Sunday School lesson that the boys and girls in the home school are poring over. Or about the telegraph operators who, miles apart from each other, compare notes over the wire about their Sunday School lesson. Cradle roll members don't do much reading or studying for themselves; but when the enthusiastic, tactful, loving cradle roll superintendent hurries around to a home in the neighborhood and asks for the name and enrollment of the baby not yet twenty-four hours old, you may be sure that that household, especially the father and mother, are not offended at this show of interest in the little life which is all the world to them. And stony hearts that may have seemed hopelessly remote from the Gospel have been warmed and won to a wide-open acceptance of the love of Jesus Christ because the littlest member of the family first entered the Sunday School through the cradle roll.

Thus it is that, from any way we look at it, the true Sunday School is a mighty evangelistic agency. If the Sunday School isn't evangelistic, it isn't the Sunday School. It may bear the name of the Sunday School, but that does not make it one. The true Sunday School of the Church of Jesus Christ exists solely to make the whole wonderful reach and splendor of the Good News better known, both to those within and without.

A young crockery merchant in New York State who rejoiced in Christ as his Saviour had found that when he flung himself in conscious helplessness on his Lord and asked to be used for the saving of others, his Lord took him at his word. Saving souls became his great joy and interest. He wanted to do more systematic work in that line, and to know the Bible in a more systematic way. The city in which he lived numbered one hundred thousand people; but he found that there was not a men's Bible class connected with any Sunday School there numbering as many as ten members. Yet there were sixteen thousand young men in that city.

While his own home church was being decorated, the entire Sunday School just then meeting as one class in a rear room, this man-hunter noticed some young men waiting outside to walk home with their girls after school. He invited them to crawl in under the rafters of the partially finished church, and with him find a place for a Bible class that he then and there asked them to form with him. They liked the novelty of the idea, and the class was formed, the members sitting on the back of a seat while their teacher faced them, standing. Under the scaffolding, amid dirt and plaster, he taught his first men's class, praying and telling the lesson story in simple language.

From that beginning the young crockery merchant got more and more interested in bringing together young men for organized Bible study in Sunday School classes. In six months his class of eighteen had grown to one hundred and eight. In the next seventeen years, three hundred and fifty-two men were won to Christ in that one class. He gave up his crockery business to give his whole time to young men's Sunday School Bible classes. After he had brought three hundred thousand men into the Sunday School for organized effort and systematic Bible study, his ideas got large, and he went on until he actually began to talk about wanting a million—not dollars, but men. It is not as easy to get a million men enrolled in an organized Bible class movement as it is to get three hundred thousand, even if you have a whole continent to work in; and perhaps some didn't expect to see "the man who wants a million," as he liked to call himself, succeed during his life-time in his expansive wish. But he got his million; and now he signs his letters, "Yours for a million more." Marshall A. Hudson, Founder and President of the World's Baraca Bible Class Union, has shown what just one department of the true Sunday School can be and do as a mighty evangelistic agency. His work would not stay limited to men, but has reached out to a similar work for women, the Philathea movement.*

The quiet, persistent, undefeatable evangelistic work of

---

*Two little books telling of Mr. Hudson's methods, one on the Baraca work for men, the other on the Philathea work for women, may be had from the Baraca Supply Company, Syracuse, New York, at 50c each.

the Sunday School is going on all the time, in ways not as widely known as is the blessed work of the Baraca and Philathea classes, but none the less effective on that account. The writer had once been speaking at the mid-week meeting of a city church on personal soul winning, and had, among other things, urged the duty of being willing to risk mistakes in doing this work, rather than make the greatest mistake of saying nothing for Christ. After the meeting a woman came up and told him of her experience. She was a Sunday School teacher with a class of girls, and she had longed to lead to Christ one of her class. She shrank from having a face-to-face talk upon the subject with the girl, but finally determined to make the effort, and she went to see the girl at her home. She found her in; and although she had ample opportunity alone with her to speak of the purpose of her call, her courage failed her, and, talking about anything and everything but that for which she had come, she finally rose and said good-bye without having once mentioned the subject. Starting home in discouragement, the teacher had not gone far from the house when she wheeled around and went back again. She rang the bell once more. The girl came to the door herself; and this time the teacher, not trusting herself to go inside and sit down again, told her young friend as they stood together in the doorway why she had called to see her, and in a blundering, faltering way said that she wished the girl would give herself to Jesus Christ as her Saviour. Then she left the house for the second time, and went home, but not before the young girl had shown her that she was very angry with her teacher for having dared to speak so directly on that subject to her.

At the next communion service of their church the teacher was overjoyed to see that young girl among those who publicly confessed the Lord Jesus Christ as their Saviour. Hurrying over to the girl, at the close of the service, the teacher told her how glad she was that she had taken this step. And then she said to her, "Tell me, what was it that finally influenced you to do this?"

"Why, it was what you said to me that day you called," was the reply.

And a Sunday School teacher was glad that she had dared to "make a mistake" for her Lord.

There are many methods of evangelism of which the Sunday School makes blessed use. "Decision Day" when wisely observed has resulted in great blessing. On this day a direct appeal to accept Jesus Christ as Saviour is made from the platform to the school or the department as a whole, and opportunity is given for formal response in the way of signed cards or otherwise. The observance of such a day is most blessed when there has been earnest, faithful preparation for it in prayer, by teachers and officers. It seems better not to have the day announced in advance to the school, but only to teachers and officers, that they may prepare for it in prayer and in personal work.

But the all-the-time evangelism of the faithful teacher is the surest and most effective. Most effective, that is, if accompanied by all-the-time prayer. Prayer meetings of the teachers for the conversion and consecration of the pupils is a secret of the continuously evangelistic Sunday School.

What sort of teaching is done in the Sunday School in which true evangelism is conspicuous?

It is teaching that assumes that the whole Bible is the inspired Word of God; unique, authoritative, infallible. The acceptance of destructive criticism's theories and conclusions can have no place in this teaching.

The evangelistic school knows that all men (and "men" means men, women and children) are lost until saved by the blood of Jesus Christ. The teaching in such a school brings out clearly the lost condition of the entire human race by nature, and recognizes no possibility of salvation by education, character, or any other works of man. It gives full recognition to education as the duty and privilege of the Christian, but it does not substitute education for salvation.

The evangelistic Sunday School holds up the Lord Jesus Christ as the only Saviour of men, accepting the Word of the Holy Spirit that "neither is there any other name under heaven, that is given among men, wherein we must be saved." And because no man or created being can save another created being that is spiritually lost, the uncreated deity of Jesus as Saviour is recognized and declared. The new birth, accomplished by the Holy Spirit in the one who believes in Jesus Christ as Saviour, marks the passage from death unto life,— that is the Gospel of the evangelistic Sunday School.

The workers in such a Sunday School know that no human being can save a soul; they know that no human being, no matter how faithfully and truly he tells the story of salvation and offers the Gospel invitation, can win another soul to Christ or enable that soul to believe on Christ as Saviour. It is recognized that this act of acceptance and belief is not the result of human teaching or telling or persuading or inviting, but is a supernatural work of God. Therefore the evangelistic teacher depends chiefly upon prayer to succeed in the chief mission of the Sunday School. The teacher recognizes that prayer is the great secret, the great essential of effective evangelism. The evangelistic teacher prays souls into salvation before even expecting to be used to that end in teaching or personal conversation.

Not all so-called Sunday Schools are evangelistic. Not all are being supernaturally used of God in the miraculous work of bringing lives into the new birth and the new life in Christ Jesus. There are dangers that threaten the Sunday School of today probably more than in any preceding generation. These dangers not only threaten; they are disastrously and effectively at work in many schools.

The undermining work of the destructive criticism has crept into Sunday School lesson helps. Not only in so-called "independent" courses of Bible study but in helps on the International Lessons, issued by regular denominational boards, are found lesson comments that assume the error and human authorship of parts of the Bible instead of inerrant, inspired authorship. It has been a distressing thing to many to note this terrible encroachment of the Adversary as he uses the very tools of the Church of Christ to lead teachers and pupils away from the hope of eternal life. For, as has been well pointed out, the Adversary's first move is to discredit parts of the Bible, then the atonement of Jesus Christ, then the deity of Christ. And without a Saviour who is God the "evangelism" of the Sunday School is not the Good News.

Not long ago "The Sunday School Times" had occasion to investigate a certain "Completely Graded Series" of Sunday School lessons (not the International Graded Lessons) of which the publisher said: "These lessons are already in use in thousands of up-to-date Sunday Schools. The various courses of study have been prepared under the direction of men who are recognized as authorities in this country in religious education, and they therefore embody the results of the latest scholarship." Upon looking into the lesson courses themselves, such statements as the following were found:

"It is easy to see that the age that produced the Gospels would not be anxious for scientific accounts of the deeds of Jesus, but that it would expect of Him exactly the acts that are attributed to Him. It is possible therefore that some events, like the restoration of the centurion's servant, were simple coincidences; that others, like the apparent walking of Jesus on the water, were natural deeds which the darkness and confusion caused to be misunderstood; that others, like the turning of water into wine, were really parables that became in course of time changed into miracles. As nearly all the miracles not of healing had their prototypes in the Old Testament, many of them at least were attributed to Jesus because men expected such deeds from their Messiah, and finally became convinced that He must have performed them. —EDITOR."

The foregoing paragraph was from a help for the Intermediate teacher. In a similar volume for the Junior teacher there appeared the following discussion of the reasonableness of miracles:

"There are some scholars who find traces of this tendency to magnify the marvelous even in the Gospels themselves, which, with all their uniqueness, are human documents, written by flesh and blood human beings. For example, in our story of Jairus' daughter, Mark's account, as we have seen, leaves us in doubt whether the little girl was really dead, or only in a swoon, or state of coma. In Matthew's later account, however, we find that Jairus says to Jesus, 'My daughter is even now dead.' When they reach the house, flute players, hired for the funeral, are already on the scene. This increases the marvel of the story, but does not seem to add to its moral significance. It is possible that not a few of the accounts of miraculous deeds, attributed to Jesus, are the product of this same tendency. By this is meant the tendency to magnify the marvelous, as seen in apocryphal legends, arising from a 'vulgar craving for signs and wonders.'"

Junior teachers were told, in explanation of the omission of the story of Ananias and Sapphira:

"This fear is explained by the story of Ananias and Sapphira, which precedes this sentence in the complete text of Acts. This story is like a number of other ancient narratives, in that the facts are probably recorded with substantial accuracy; but the author's own interpretation of these facts seems to us, in these days, not altogether satisfactory. There is no reason for doubting the account of the deception practised on the apostles by this unscrupulous couple, Ananias and Sapphira; nor the account of Peter's rebuke; nor the statement that they both died shortly after receiving the rebuke. In that period of the world's history people would inevitably conclude that this death was a direct manifestation of the Divine wrath invoked by Peter. This interpretation, however, seems inconsistent with the Christian conception of God as a loving and patient Father. On account of the primitive ideas which it reflects, the story has been omitted from the Junior Bible."

As was editorially stated in "The Sunday School Times," which discussed this series of lessons, it is only too true that: "There are those who have not taught the whole Christ of the New Testament and the Old, but have been busy about the presenting of a different and lesser Person. They have followed and taught Jesus of Nazareth as the ideal teacher and leader, acknowledging Him as indeed the most extraordinary development among the noblest sons of God, and the Gospel story of Him as usually reliable, but they have not been presenting Jesus unreservedly as the eternal Christ in all that the Scriptures in their uttermost struggling for full expression claim that He is; as all that He was, very Life itself to the disciplined mind and the revolutionized personality of Paul; as all that He is to those who daily testify in word and deed to liberty from the crushing bondage of sin by His indwelling."

The same editorial discussed the peril of teaching a "modified Christ." It went on to say:

"It is no uncommon thing to find teachers of the Bible who are thus teaching a modified Christ. The cautionary attitude, to say the least, of a type of influential scholarship, on the trustworthiness of the Scriptures, and the encouraging of suspended opinion as to the claims of Christ, are more confusing and insidious in their results on the mind and the life than a flat denial of cherished truth by confessed unbelievers. The New Testament writers, on the one hand, are not wholly able within the range of human vocabularies to find language that will release the streams of inspired truth concerning the Lord Jesus. In their most rapt ecstasy, as in their apologetic, they cannot exalt the Christ as they would, because not He, but language, is inadequate. They simply cannot say enough of Him. But, on the other hand, there is a type of modern scholarship not without its influence upon the trained and untrained Bible teacher alike, which is careful not to say too much of Jesus. There is a restraint in its deliverances about Him, a cautious and reserved detachment, which would seem to belong as a method rather to the outside observer than to the inner disciple. Ethical and social leadership and supremacy are freely attributed to Jesus, but this type of Biblical scholarship does not seem, in dealing with Jesus, to be dealing with the same eternal Christ who was disclosed to John and Peter and Paul and others of like mind and experience. Indeed, the limitless ascriptions of John, the sweeping declarations of Peter, the passionate abandon of Paul, by no means characterize this kind of scholarship. On the contrary, its Jesus is far less than the New Testament Christ; its New Testament a record quite open to reasonable doubt. Yet the superior advantages of lesson helps embodying the results of this attitude toward Jesus and the record of his life are widely urged upon teachers and pupils in the Sunday School today."

Just here those who have the Sunday School at its highest point of evangelistic efficiency should have clearly before them the facts concerning the course of Graded Lessons issued by the American Section of the International Committee. It is a seventeen year course, of which sixteen years of study have been issued, running from the first year "Beginners, for four-year-olds, through the third year Senior, for nineteen-year-olds." The writer had occasion to discuss this course of lessons in the columns of "The Sunday School Times" just before the International Sunday School Convention held in Chicago in June of 1914, and takes the liberty of printing here a portion of what was said at that time:

"These lessons are rendering a greatly needed service in awakening the Sunday School world to the claims and rights of the child. They are showing what a supremely delicate and difficult task it is to bring to the child, in the way that child nature is entitled to, the instruction that God intends. It is to be hoped that these lessons have made it impossible for the Sunday School ever to go back to what may have been its former carelessness, indifference, and ignorance on this subject.

"There is welcome evidence that the Graded Lessons are resulting in bringing pupils to decision for Christ. Mrs. Bryner, the International Elementary Superintendent, recently published in the state Sunday School papers the results of her inquiry of state and provincial elementary superintendents concerning the spiritual results that can be reported from the introduction of the Graded Lessons; and the testimony was most encouraging. One school reported that the number of Juniors coming naturally into the church had increased seventy-five percent since the adoption of these lessons in that school.

"In the First Year Senior there is excellent topical study offered on 'The Needs of the World,' 'The Standard of Success,' 'The Challenge to the Individual;' and this year offers also two complete book studies, taking up the Book of Ruth in three lessons and the Epistle of James in nine lessons.

"The opportunity for complete book study is still further extended in the Third Year Senior, just issued by the Lesson Committee, offering opportunity for brief, rapid surveys of more than twenty of the books of the New Testament. The doctrine of salvation is well taught here also, in a lesson devoted to 'Developing the Theology of Salvation,' from Romans.

"In such points as these, and in many other admirable opportunities for thorough-going Bible study, the International Graded Lessons offer the Sunday School a rich field for profitable work.

"Yet in spite of all this there are other factors in this series of Graded Lessons that are fairly characterized as regrettable and harmful. If one asks why these words should be used, here is the answer:

"Because there are elements here that tend to minimize or ignore the unique and supreme character and authority of the Bible as the inspired Word of God; that tend to blur the line between the natural and the supernatural; that tend to place nature study on the same plane as Bible study in gaining a knowledge of God; and that tend to a lack of emphasis on certain vital doctrinal teaching of the Gospel of Christ.

"Extra-Biblical lessons have been inserted throughout this Graded series, that is, lessons the material for which is drawn chiefly from other literature than the Bible. In one instance —in the Second Year Intermediate,—a full six months is devoted to the study of 'Later Christian Leaders,' including such characters as Luther, Calvin, John Wesley, the Earl of Shaftesbury, and Florence Nightingale; and three months of the six are devoted to the study of a single modern missionary, Alexander Mackay. A note from the Lesson Committee points out that the material upon which these three months' lessons are based is found in the well-known book 'Uganda's White Man of Work,' the Committee having previously said: 'It is intended that a more careful analysis of a single character shall prepare the pupil for the nine months' study in the life of Christ which will immediately follow in the lessons for the Third Year Intermediate.' Just what effect will it have upon fourteen-year-olds to bring in a book of this sort, as, in a sense, parallel material to the Bible's record of the life of our Lord Jesus Christ? To be sure, Scripture material is suggested for each of these extra-Biblical lessons, but the Scripture material is subordinate, and the extra-Biblical material is the main theme for study.

"As is well known, in response to a widespread protest the Lesson Committee in 1911 issued Biblical lessons to run parallel to all the extra-Biblical lessons in the Graded Series, and to make such other minor modifications as seemed to it desirable. These Biblical lessons do not *replace* the extra-Biblical lessons; they 'take their place beside the extra-Biblical lessons in the lists already issued.' The International Lesson Committee therefore stands before the Sunday School world committed to offering the Sunday School constituency material from other sources than the Bible as its chief material for study in numerous Sunday School sessions.

"And it has been done with deep-seated conviction on the part of those who favor it. At the conference on the International Lessons held in Philadelphia in 1914, a prominent leader in the work of the Graded Lessons said publicly, and with intense earnestness: 'We deny at every point that our course is a BIBLE course; our course is a CHILD-TEACHING course.'

"As we speak of 'the Sunday School' today, we refer to the very limited opportunity for Bible study offered in the session of an hour or so on Sunday, where the actual Bible studying, Bible teaching period is about thirty minutes. This is the church's chief and only Bible teaching service, at present, in the vast majority of churches. To give any other form of material than the Bible the right of way in this restricted period is a perilous thing. The church *must* have a service of Bible study and Bible teaching. Its very life, and the life of the home and the community, depend upon this. Nothing that is extra-Biblical can be permitted to encroach upon that vital part of the church's work. It will be a sad day indeed when this question is considered even debatable by the majority of the members of the Church of Christ on earth.

"It is important to recognize also that there is no real dilemma between the Bible and child-teaching. We do not have to choose between the two. We must have them both, and we can. The Bible is God's best provision for child-teaching.

"There is a real danger, also, in using nature as the chief material for Sunday School teaching, even with the youngest beginners. Nature study has its valued place as material to illustrate Bible truths. Our Lord used it in that way. But there is no such revelation of God in nature as there is in the Holy Scriptures. Nature is natural; the Bible is supernatural. The two are in no sense equal revelations of the heart of God and of the Gospel of Christ. Indeed, nature is a sin-distorted, sin-cursed thing. God made this very plain when He said in the Garden of Eden, 'Cursed is the ground for thy sake; . . . . . . thorns also and thistles shall it bring forth to thee,' as He told Adam and Eve how they had degraded even the earth beneath their feet through their sin. It may not be

necessary or wise that the little child should be taught this; but it is very necessary that the teacher should have this in mind in using nature material to illustrate the ways and the love and the protection of the Heavenly Father. It puts sharp limitations upon our use of nature materials, and it suggests that such nature material, in and of itself, should not be the leading material in any lessons for Sunday School study.

"Apart from the question of nature studies as such, there is present in the International Graded Lessons the modern steadily encroaching atmosphere of the 'natural' as over against the 'supernatural.' The atmosphere in many colleges today is an atmosphere that denies the supernatural. There are evidences, here and there throughout this scheme of lessons, of such a handling of the Bible as one would give to any other book. Such lesson titles, for example, as 'Gideon, the Man Whom Responsibility Made Great' (First Year Intermediate), 'Abraham—The Challenge of an Ideal' (Second Year Senior), 'The Development of Religious Ideas in Early Israel' (Second Year Senior), are hints of this; as is also the note on Lessons 17 to 22 of the First Year Intermediate, 'David, the Man Who Showed Himself Friendly': 'the aim is to show that David's power to make and retain friends explains his career and his character.' This ignoring of God's sovereign grace as the secret of David's career is not sufficiently offset by the close of the note, that David's 'intimate, constant, and childlike fellowship with God was the supreme friendship of his life, exalting and directing his actions.'

"And there is a certain inadequacy in some lesson topics, a failure to reveal the stupendous riches of the Scripture truth that is to be taught. An example of this is to be seen in the Third Year Senior topics for the study of the Epistle to the Galatians: 'Paul's Assertion of Independence,' 'The Bondage of Tradition,' 'The Christian Idea of Freedom.' The wording of these topics does not do justice to the great eternal spiritual truths of bondage to sin under the law versus the life of victory-by-freedom in Christ which this Epistle so gloriously brings out.

"Many would have been glad to see somewhere in these lessons, among the many statements of aim and purpose of the courses for the different years, a declaration of aim that the pupil shall come to recognize man's lost condition as constituting our need of a Saviour. This is nowhere stated. It is stated that the lessons have the aim of bringing the pupil to the personal acceptance of Jesus as Saviour and Lord; and that is good. But a clear declaration of the universal need of the new birth would have given increased doctrinal strength to the series. This lack is accentuated by such expressions as the following: 'The average age of thirteen calls for a new type of lessons which shall make their appeal to the new sense of selfhood and the new hunger for a satisfying personal ideal.' The emphasis seems to be chiefly 'to deepen the impulse to do right,' rather than to show (not necessarily to the youngest children, but certainly somewhere during the series) the hopelessness of any one's doing right except through the regenerating presence of the Holy Spirit made possible by the acceptance of Christ as Saviour."*

Against all such encroachments upon the Word of God, upon the Gospel of Jesus Christ, and upon a clear vision of men's eternal need of that Gospel, the Sunday School of true evangelism must stand with the firmness of the Rock of Ages. Only the power of Christ can enable us to stand thus firmly in the strength of Christ. He is doing just this, with blessed results, for Sunday Schools that ask Him to do so upon His own terms.

---

*Representatives of two denominational Sunday School Publishing Boards have stated that the helps published by them are free from the objections noted.

I. J. Van Ness, Editorial Secretary of the Southern Baptist Sunday School Board (Nashville, Tennessee), writes: "Many denominations have made radical modifications for themselves. The Southern Baptists have issued a complete series of periodicals for these lessons, using only Biblical material, and making material

The Social Service program, which includes so many things Christian in spirit, but which in many cases so disastrously puts fruit ahead of root, is a danger against which the Sunday School needs to guard, especially in its adult classes. The salvation of society regardless of the salvation of the individual is a hopeless task; and the Sunday School of true evangelism will not enter upon it. But the Sunday School that brings the good news of Jesus Christ to the individuals of any community lifts society as the usual Social Service program can never do. A striking illustration of this principle has been noted in the work of Evangelist "Billy" Sunday. Sunday preaches the individual Gospel of the apostolic church. He says little about social service. But the community-results where Sunday's evangelism has had an opportunity are revolu-

changes in the lessons for the Beginners, Primary and Junior Departments. The Lesson Committee of the Southern Baptist Convention entirely reconstructed the Intermediate courses, using in the main the material put out by the International Committee, but making changes in the arrangement and in the titles. The series of lessons which we are putting out is essentially different from that which you condemn, and has few, if any, of the points which you point out."

Marion Stevenson, of the Christian Board of Publication (St. Louis, Mo.), writes: "It should be noticed that we are following the Biblical lessons so strongly approved by the International Sunday School Association at San Francisco and also at Chicago. As your editorial stands, it is a blanket indictment of the Graded Lessons, to which we would respond that we are not guilty. The characteristics complained of are true of hardly any graded literature except that published by the Syndicate. But the Syndicate is a diminishing association. Since its organization the Presbyterian bodies have withdrawn and are preparing their own literature, thus leaving the Syndicate to the Methodist Church, North and South, and to the Congregationalists. Some smaller denominations are selling agents for the Syndicate material. But from the first the Baptists, North and South, and the Churches of Christ, have chosen their own writers. The indictments against the Syndicate material may not therefore be drawn against all graded lesson literature. They are certainly not true in regard to the graded literature prepared by the Christian Board of Publication."

Every movement away from the perils that would injure the Sunday School is to be heartily welcomed; and the writer gladly gives prominence to these letters of denominational leaders.

tionizing. There is no social service worker in America today whose work can compare, in the very results for which the social service program aims, with that of Sunday's. And so the Sunday School of true evangelism will do an effective work in social service; but it will do it in the Lord's way.

One last word. If the Sunday School is really to do its work as an evangelizing agent, the Sunday School must consist of workers whose personal lives are radiant with victory. The Sunday School of true evangelism declares with convincing power the message of the victorious life.

Here is an evangel, a Good News, which is all too new to many a follower of the Lord Jesus Christ who rejoices in the Sunday School as his field of service. But our Lord wants it to be the experienced possession of His every follower.

Evangelism that is limited to the Good News that there is freedom from the penalty of our sins is only a half-way evangelism. It is a crippled, halting evangelism. If we would tell "that sweet story of old," let us tell the whole story.

And the whole story is that our Lord Jesus Christ came, not only to pay the penalty of our sins, but to break the power of our sin. He laid aside His glory and came from heaven to earth, not only that men might be saved from dying the second death, but also that they might live without sinning in this present life. Here is Good News indeed; so good that to many it sounds too good to be true. But, praise God, it is true! When the Holy Spirit says to us, "Sin shall not have dominion over you: for ye are not under law, but under grace," He *means* it. When Paul declared in the exultant joy of the Spirit, "The law of the Spirit of life in Christ Jesus made me free from the law of sin," he *meant* it. It was *true*. And the same Spirit of life in Christ Jesus is making men free today from the law of sin, when they are ready to take Him at His word. When the beloved Apostle wrote, under the direction of the Holy Spirit, "My little children, these things write I unto you *that ye may not sin,*" he *meant just that.* When our Lord Jesus Himself said, first, "Every one that committeth sin is the bondservant of sin"; and then, instead of leaving us hopelessly there, went on to say: "If therefore the Son shall make you free, ye shall be free indeed," He was trying to tell us what His whole salvation is.

The victorious life is not a life made sinless, but it is a life kept from sinning. It is not, as has well been said, that the sinner is made perfect here in this life, but that the sinner even in this life has a perfect Saviour. And that Saviour is more than equal, while we are still in this life, to overcoming all the power of our sin.

The Keswick Convention in England has for forty years been blessedly used of God in spreading abroad the Good News of the Gospel of victory over sin. The life that is surrendered unconditionally to the mastery of Jesus Christ and that then believes unconditionally in the faithfulness of that Saviour Lord to make His promises true, begins to realize the meaning of the unspeakable riches of God's grace.

There are Sunday School teachers who are rejoicing today in the privilege of telling their classes the whole message of true evangelism. May God mightily increase the numbers of those who shall bear witness, by their victorious lives and by their eager glad message, to the whole evangelism of the Word: the saving and the keeping power of our wonderful Lord and Saviour Jesus Christ. Then, "If He shall be manifested, we may have boldness, and not be ashamed before Him at His coming."

CHAPTER IV

FOREIGN MISSIONS OR WORLD-WIDE EVANGELISM

BY ROBERT E. SPEER,

SECRETARY BOARD OF FOREIGN MISSIONS OF THE
PRESBYTERIAN CHURCH, U. S. A.,
NEW YORK CITY

Argument in behalf of foreign missions is generally either needless or useless. It is needless with believers; with unbelievers it is useless. And yet not wholly so; for often believers and unbelievers alike have taken their opinions at second hand, and an honest first hand study of the facts and principles of the missionary enterprise leads the one group to believe with deeper conviction and a firmer hope, and shakes the scepticism and opposition of the others who have known neither the aims nor the motives which inspire the movement.

Because foreign missions is a religious movement, however, the fundamental argument for it is of necessity a religious argument, and will be conclusive only in proportion as the religious convictions on which it rests are accepted. It rests first of all upon God. If men believe in God they must believe in foreign missions. It is in the very being and character of God that the deepest ground of the missionary enterprise is to be found. We cannot think of God except in terms which necessitate the missionary idea.

He is one. There cannot, therefore, be such different tribal or racial gods as are avowed in the ethnic religions of the East, and assumed in the ethnic politics of the West. Whatever God exists for America exists for all the world, and none other exists. And that cannot be true of God in America which is not true of Him also in India. Men are not free to

hold contradictory conceptions of the same God. If there be
any God at all for me, He must be every other man's God,
too. And God is true. To say that He is one is merely to say
that He is. To say that He is true is to begin to describe Him,
and to describe Him as alone He can be. And if He is true
He cannot have taught men falsehood. He will have strug-
gled with their ignorance in His education of mankind, but it
cannot have been His will (or be His will now) that some men
should have false ideas of Him or false attitudes toward Him.
A true God must will to be truly known by all men. And
God is holy and pure. Nothing unholy or impure can be of
Him. Anything unholy or impure must be abhorrent to Him,
if in religion the more abhorrent because the more misrepre-
sentative of Him, the more revolting to His nature. If anywhere in the world religion covers what is unclean or unworthy, there the character of God is being assailed. And
God is just and good. No race and no man can have slipped
through the fatherly affection of a loving God. Any inequality
or unfairness or indifference in an offered god would send
us seeking for the real one whom we should know was not
yet found. A god who was idols in China, fate in Arabia,
fetiches in Africa, and man himself with all his sin in India,
would be no god anywhere. If God is one man's father, He
is or would be every man's father. We cannot think of God,
I say it reverently, without thinking of Him as a missionary
God. Unless we are prepared to accept a God whose character carries with it the missionary obligation and idea, we
must do without any real God at all.

When men believe in God in Christ the argument for missions becomes still more clear. It is by Christ that the character of God is revealed to us. One of His most bold and
penetrating words was His declaration, "The day will come
when they shall slay you, thinking that they do service unto
God, and these things will they do unto you because they have
not known the Father or Me." The best people of His day,

He declared, were ignorant of the true character of God. Only those truly knew it who discovered or recognized it in Him. "He that hath seen Me hath seen the Father. No man cometh unto the Father but by Me. No man knoweth the Son save the Father, and no man knoweth the Father save the Son and he to whomsoever the Son willeth to reveal Him." These are not arbitrary statutes. They are simple statements of fact. The world's knowledge of the character of God has depended and depends now on its knowledge of God in Christ. A good and worthy, an adequate and satisfying God, i. e., God in truth, is known only where men have been in contact with the message of the historic Christ.

This simple fact involves a sufficient missionary responsibility. Men will only know a good and loving Father as their God, i. e., they will know God, only as they are brought into the knowledge of Christ, who is the only perfect revelation of God. For those who have this knowledge to withhold it from the whole world is to do two things: It is to condemn the world to godlessness, and it is to raise the suspicion that those who think they have the knowledge of God are in reality ignorant of what Christ was and what He came to do. "It is the sincere and deep conviction of my soul," said Phillips Brooks, "when I declare that if the Christian faith does not culminate and complete itself in the effort to make Christ known to all the world, that faith appears to me a thoroughly unreal and insignificant thing, destitute of power for the single life and incapable of being convincingly proved to be true." And I recall a remark of Principal Rainy's to the effect that the measure of our sense of missionary duty was simply the measure of our personal valuation of Christ. If He is God to us, all in all to our minds and souls, we shall realize that He alone can be this to every man, and that He must be offered thus to every other man. The Unitarian view has never produced a mission, save under an inherited momentum or the communicated stimulus of evangelicalism, and it has been incapable of sustaining such missions as it has produced. But when men really believe in God in Christ, and know Christ as God, they must, if they are loyal to themselves or to Him, share Him with all mankind.

For, child of one race and one time though He was, and that race the most centripetal of all races, Christ thought and wrought in universals. He looked forward over all ages and outward over all nations. The bread which He would give was His flesh, which He would give for the life of the world. He was the light of the whole world. If He should be lifted up He would draw all men unto Himself. His disciples were to go into all the world and make disciples of all nations. His sheep were not of a Jewish fold alone. It was not of a race but of a world that the Father had sent Him to be the Saviour. He did not regard Himself as one of many saviours and His revelation as one of many revealings. He was the only Saviour of men, and His was the only revelation of the Father God. "I have long ago ceased to regard the history of the Hebrew race as unique," writes a well-known Christian leader of our day. "It was well for us in our early days that our studies were directed towards it, and we saw how the Hebrew people found God in every event in their history, but we believe that Assyria and Babylon, Nineveh and Rome, could have similar stories written of God's dealings with them." Now, whether the history of the Hebrew race is unique or not is not a matter of theory. It is a simple question of fact. If it was not unique, then where is its like? What other history produced a vocabulary for a revelation? What other history yielded God to humanity? What other ended in a Saviour? As a simple matter of fact, Christianity, which sprang out of this race and this history, is unlike all other religions in its kind. As such, it never contemplated anything else than a universal claim. If it shrinks into a mere racial cult, it separates itself from its Founder and life, and utterly abandons its essential character.

Not only is the missionary duty inherent in the nature of Christianity and in the Christian conception of God, i. e., in the real character of God, but it is imbedded in the very purpose of the Christian Church. There were no missionary organizations in the early Church. No effort was made to promote a missionary propaganda, but the religion spread at once and everywhere. The genius of universal extension was in the Church. "We may take it as an assured fact," says Harnack, "that the mere existence and persistent activity of the individual Christian communities did more than anything else to bring about the extension of the Christian religion."

Bishop Montgomery in his little book on "Foreign Missions" recalls Archbishop Benson's definition of four ages of missions, "First, when the whole Church acted as one; next, when missions were due to great saints; thirdly, to the action of governments; lastly, the age of missionary societies." The Church at the outset was a missionary society. The new Christians were drawn together spontaneously by the uniting power of a common life, and they felt as spontaneously the outward pressure of a world mission. The triumphant prosecution of that mission and the moral fruits of this new and uniting life were their apologetics. They did not sit down within the walls of a formalised and stiffened institution to compose reasoned arguments for Christianity. The new religion would have rotted out from heresy and anaemia in two generations if they had done so.

As an old writer of the Church of England has put it: "The way in which the Gospel would seem to be intended to be alike preserved and perpetuated on earth is not by its being jealously guarded by a chosen order and cautiously communicated to a precious few, but by being so widely scattered and so thickly sown that it shall be impossible, from the very extent of its spreading, merely to be rooted up. It was designed to be not as a perpetual fire in the temple, to be tended with jealous assiduity and to be fed only with special oil; but rather as a shining and burning light, to be set up on every hill, which should blaze the broader and the brighter in the breeze, and go on so spreading over the surrounding territory as that nothing of this world should ever be able to extinguish or to conceal it." The sound doctrine of the Church was safeguarded by the wholesome hygienic reflex action of service and work and conquest. And its light and life convinced men, because men saw them conquering souls. The Church was established to spread Christianity, and to conserve it in the only way in which living things can ever be conserved, by living action. When in any age or in any land the Church has forgotten this, she has paid for her disobedience. So long as there are any unreached men in the world or any unreached life, the business of the Church is her missionary duty.

The fourth deep ground of missionary duty is the need of humanity. The world needs Christ today as much and as truly as it needed Him nineteen centuries ago. If Judaism and the Roman Empire needed what Christ brought then, Hinduism and Asia need it now. If they do not need Him now, no more was He needed then. If they can get along without Him just as well, the whole world can dispense with Him. If there is no missionary duty, the ground falls from under the necessity, and therefore from under the reality of the incarnation. But that world into which He came did need Christ. Men were dead without Him. It was He who gave them life, who cleansed their defilement, who taught them purity and service and equality and faith and gave them hope and fellowship. He alone can do this now. The non-Christian world needs now what Christ and Christ alone can do for it.

It needs the physical wholeness, the fitting of life to its conditions, which, as a matter of fact, men get just in proportion as they get Christ. We do not need to go for proof of such needs to any overcolored, distorted accounts of those who see only the good of Christendom and only the evil of heathenism—heathenism is a good word, and it describes facts. Sir John Hewett's account, as Lieutenant-Governor, of the conditions of sanitation in the United Provinces of India, will suffice: "Speaking generally, the death rates recorded in the Provinces in recent years, both in urban and rural tracts, are nearly three times as high as in England and Wales. It is estimated that in India nearly one out of every ten of the population is constantly sick, and a person who has escaped the diseases and dangers of childhood and youth, and entered into manhood or womanhood, has an expectation that his or her life will extend to only 68 per cent of the time that a person similarly situated may be expected to live in England. . . . . . . Infantile mortality is nearly twice as great as it is in England. . . . . . It is lamentable that one out of every four children born should die before he or she has completed a year of life. . . . . . The average number of persons per house (which frequently consists of two rooms, or even of only one) is 5.3 in important cities, and 5.5 in the rest of the country. It is estimated that the average superficial area per head of the population is something like 10 square feet, and the breathing space 150 cubic feet—just half what is required in common lodging-houses in England." Conditions in Christian lands are not what they should be, but they are infinitely superior to the conditions in other lands, and in proportion as they are Christian, famine and disease and want are overcome. Are these blessings to be ours alone?

The world needs the social message and redemption of Christianity. Paul tells us that it met and conquered the inequalities of his time, the chasm between citizen and foreigner, master and slave, man and woman. These are the chasms of the non-Christian world still. It has no ideal of human brotherhood save as it has heard of it through Christianity. Not one of the non-Christian religions or civilizations has given either women or children, especially girl children, their rights. There is human affection. The statement of a recent writer regarding China, that "children are spawned and not born," is surely most untrue save on the basest levels of life. But the proverb of the Arab women of Kesrawan too truly suggests the Asiatic point of view: "The threshold weeps forty days when a girl is born." And between man and man the world knows no deep basis of common humanity, or if it knows, it has no adequate sanction and resources for its realization. Its brotherhood is within the faith or within the caste, not as inclusive as humanity. It wants what all the world wanted until it found it through Christ. "In his little churches, where each person bore his neighbor's burden, Paul's spirit," says Harnack, "already saw the dawning of a new humanity, and in the Epistle to the Ephesians he has voiced this feeling with a thrill of exaltation. Far in the background of these churches, like some unsubstantial semblance, lay the division between Jew and Gentile, Greek and Barbarian, great and small, rich and poor. For a new humanity had now appeared, and the Apostle viewed it as Christ's body, in which every member served the rest, and each was indispensable in his own place." The great social idea of Christianity is still only partially realized by us. But we do not have it at all unless we have it for humanity, and it can be made to prevail anywhere only by being made to prevail everywhere.

The world needs, moreover, the moral ideal and the moral power of Christianity. The Christian conceptions of truth and purity and love and holiness and service are original. Every ideal except the Christian ideal is defective. Three other sets of ideals are offered to men. The only other theistic ideals are the Mohammedan and the Jewish. The Mohammedan ideal expressly sanctions polygamy, and the authority of its founder is cited in justification of falsehood. The Jewish ideal is wholly enclosed in and transcended by the Christian. Buddhism and Shintoism and Confucianism offer men atheistic ideals, i. e., ideals which abandon the conception of the absolute and cannot rise above their source in man who made them. Hinduism, with its pantheism, is incapable of the moral distinctions which alone can produce moral ideals, and as a matter of fact owes its worthy moral conceptions today exclusively to the influence of Christianity. But it is not ideals alone—it is power for their realization that the world requires. That power can be found only in life, in the life of God communicated to men. Who offers this or pretends to offer it but Christ? How can it be offered by religions which have no God, or whose God has no character?

For this is the great need of the world. It needs the knowledge and the life of the good and fatherly God. Its own religions have given it neither of these, and its own religions are disintegrating. Christianity has detached small companies of people from them, but the influence of Christianity has penetrated them to the marrow. Let alone, it would war against their vicious elements and preserve all in man that is capable of redemption. But it will not be let alone. Other influences are at work upon the religious conceptions of the non-Christian world, and under those influences the conceptions and the institutions of the non-Christian religions are doomed. Never did men face a more solemn responsibility than confronts us now. "The ancient beliefs and customs of the non-Christian peoples," said Lord Bryce while in America, "are destined soon to pass away, and it becomes a matter of supreme importance to see that new and better moral and religious principles are given to them promptly to replace what is disappearing; and to endeavor to find methods for preventing the faults or vices of adventurers and others who are trying to exploit the uncivilized races from becoming a fatal hindrance to the spread of Christianity." Christian peoples are standing face to face with judgment here.

Throughout the non-Christian world there are multitudes who are conscious of their need. They may not regard Christianity as the answer to their need. It is not surprising if they do not. In what way has Christendom not misrepresented Christianity to them? But they know their need. "You speak as if our country is already a dead thing," says one of the characters in Uchimura's dialogue on "The Future of Japan." "Yes," is the reply, "immoral nation is already dead. With all its shows of stability, a nation without a high ideal is a dead corpse. Japan under the Satsuma Choshu Government is a dead nation." "You speak very determinedly." "Yes," replies Uchimura, "I have to; I cannot bear to see my nation die." And there are many who do not wish to see their nations die in Asia, who turn to Christ. "All over India," wrote Dr. Cuthbert Hall to the missionaries there when he left India, with India's need upon his heart and its poison in his blood, "all over India are men unprepared to identify themselves with any Christian denomination, to whom the popular forms of the ancient faith have become inadequate, if not distasteful, and for whom the name of Jesus Christ and the distinctive truths connected with that name for the redemption of individuals and the reconstruction of the social order, are taking on new attractiveness and value." The fact that the world is awaking to its need, whether it understands Christ or not, adds a pathos to its mute appeal to those who have in custody the Gospel of God in His Son.

For it is only that Gospel that can meet the world's need. Commerce and government, philanthropy and education, deal with it superficially, and in the hands of shallow or evil men only accentuate it. A force is needed which will cut down to the roots, which deals with life in the name and by the power of God, which marches straight upon the soul and reconstructs character, which saves men one by one. Here we are flat upon the issue, and not to evade or confuse it, I will put it unmistakably. It is our duty to carry Christianity to the world because the world needs to be saved, and Christ alone can save it. The world needs to be saved from want and disease and injustice and inequality and impurity and lust and hopelessness and fear, because individual men need to be saved from sin and death, and only Christ can save them. His is the only power which will forgive and regenerate, which will reach down deep enough to transform, and will hold till transformation is fixed.

And Christianity does this by striking down to the individual and saving him. It saves him by the power of God in Christ, working in and upon him. The missionary duty is this duty. "I hold education," says Uchimura, "as essentially personal and individualistic." And he uses the term education in its broad sense. There is more to education than this. Society is something more than the sum-total of individuals, but it begins and ends with individuals, and the need of the world is primarily the need of its individuals, and the salvation of the world in Christ's way can only be the salvation of its soul through the salvation of its souls.

A few years ago we heard a great deal about the need of educating and civilizing the world before we try to change its religion. Dr. George Hamilton advanced this argument in the General Assembly of the Church of Scotland in 1796: "To spread abroad the knowledge of the Gospel among barbarous and heathen nations seems to me to be highly preposterous in as far as it anticipates, nay, as it even reverses the order of nature. Men must be polished and refined in their manners before they can be properly enlightened in religious truths. Philosophy and learning must, in the nature of things, take the precedence. Indeed, it should seem hardly less absurd to make revelation precede civilization in the order of time, than to pretend to unfold to a child the 'Principia' of Newton, ere he is made at all acquainted with the letters of the alphabet. These ideas seem to me alike founded in error; and, therefore, I must consider them both as equally romantic and visionary." We do not hear so much of this view now. Civilization has shown what a vain and empty thing it is, and we know that the sin and passion in human hearts, which it cannot destroy, are as real and dreadful in America and in all the neutral nations as they are in the nations at war. God is man's one need. Man cannot save himself or make anything out of himself. He needs what God and God alone can do for him. If that is true of Europe and America it is true of all the rest of the world. Jesus Christ is the one Saviour of men and each man in the world needing that Saviour has a right to look to those who know of Him to tell of Him to all mankind.

Even as a purely religious movement, however, there are some who object to foreign missions on the ground that there are other religions in the world which are true for their followers and which meet their needs as truly as Christianity meets ours. They say that a fair comparison of Christianity with other religions destroys the claim of Christianity and makes foreign missions unnecessary. Is this true? What are the conclusions which such a comparison presents?

1. In the first place it is a significant fact that Christianity is the only religion which is trying to make good its claim to universalism. None of the non-Christian religions is making any real effort to do so. Mohammedanism is spreading in Africa and India, but it makes no effort of any significance to convert America or Europe or Japan. The bounds of Confucianism are contracting. Shintoism has withdrawn from the lists as a religion, and claims now only the place of a court ceremonial and a burial rite. Zoroastrianism, one of the worthiest of the ancient religions, has almost vanished in the land of its origin, and numbers comparatively few adherents in India. Hinduism is geographically limited, save as a philosophy, by its principle of caste, and Buddhism is rejected in Japan by the very men who might succeed in propagating it elsewhere. But Christianity is moving out over all the earth with steadily increasing power, with ever multiplying agencies, with ever enlarged devotion, and with open and undiscourageable purpose to prepare for Christ's kingship over the world. And not less significant than the fact of Christianity's missionary purpose, is the method of it. With no trust in secular support, in spite of all slanders which charge otherwise, with purely moral agencies

and with fair comparison of its treasures with anything that the world can offer, Christianity goes fearlessly forth to deal with all the life and thought of man and to solve his problems and meet his needs in the name and strength of God.

2. At the root of all things is the idea of God. Here all religions meet to be judged. "The truth and the good inherent in all forms of religion is that, in all, man seeks after God. The finality of Christianity lies in the fact that it reveals the God for whom man seeks." (Jevons, "Introduction to the Study of Comparative Religion," p. 258.) The best that can be said of any non-Christian religion is that it is seeking for that which Christianity possesses—the true and perfect God. "The conception of God with which Christianity addresses the world, is the best that man can form or entertain."

If it is asked, "What is that excellence in Christianity by virtue of which it is entitled to be a missionary religion and deserves to be received by all men?"—the answer is:

"Christianity is entitled to be a missionary religion and to displace all other religions, because of its God.

"There are many glories in the religion of Jesus Christ, and it can do many services for men; but its crowning glory, or rather the sum of all its glory, is its God. Christianity has such a conception of God as no other religion has attained; and, what is more, it proclaims and brings to pass such an experience of God as humanity has never elsewhere known. It is in this that we find that superiority which entitles Christianity to offer itself to all mankind.

"It is necessary to tell in few words what this God is who is the glory of Christianity and the ground of its boldness in missionary advances—this God so infinitely excellent that all men may well afford to forget all their own religions, if they may but know Him. The God of Christianity is one, the sole source, Lord and end of all. He is holy, having in Himself the character that is the worthy standard for all beings. He is love, reaching out to save the world from sin and fill it with

His own goodness. He is wise, knowing how to accomplish His heart's desire. He is Father in heart, looking upon His creatures as His own, and seeking their welfare. All this truth concerning Himself, He has made known in Jesus Christ the Saviour of the world, in whom His redemptive will has found expression, and His saving love has come forth to mankind."

Set over against this conception of God the views which we have seen that the non-Christian religions take of Him, and it does not need to be shown that the religion of the Christian God has supreme rights among men.

"A religion that can proclaim such a God, and proclaim Him on the ground of experience, is adapted to all men, and is worthy of all acceptance. Since Christianity is the religion of such a God, Christianity deserves possession of the world. It has the right to offer itself boldly to all men, and to displace all other religions, for no other religion offers what it brings. It is the best that the world contains. Because of its doctrine and experience of the perfect God, it is the best that the world can contain. Its contents can be unfolded and better known, but they cannot be essentially improved upon. At heart, Christianity is simply the revelation of the perfect God, doing the work of perfect love and holiness for His creatures, and transforming them into His own likeness so that they will do the works of love and holiness towards their fellows. Than this nothing can be better. Therefore, Christianity has full right to be a missionary religion, and Christians are called to be a missionary people."

3. From its unique and adequate conception of God, it follows that Christianity has a message to the world which is full of notes which the non-Christian religions do not and cannot possess. Even ideas which some of these religions share with Christianity, such as "belief in an after life, in the difference between right and wrong, and that the latter deserves punishment; in the need of an atonement for sin; in the efficacy of

prayer; in the universal presence of spiritual powers of some kind;" belief in the sovereignty of God, in the immanence of God, in the transitoriness and vanity of this earthly life on one hand, and in the infinite significance of this life and the sacredness of the human order on the other,—have a relationship and a significance in Christianity, with its perfect God, which makes them totally different from the conceptions of other religions. And beside these, Christianity has a whole world of conceptions of its own—the fatherhood of God, the brotherhood of man, redemption, the incarnation of a personal God, atonement, character, service, fellowship.

4. In its conception of sin, in its provision for sin's forgiveness and defeat, and in its ideals of salvation and the free offer of its salvation to every man, Christianity is unique and satisfying. Christianity sees sin as the supreme evil in the world, it regards it as a want of conformity to the perfect will of God, or as transgression of His perfect law; it teaches that sin is not a matter of act only, but also of thought and desire and will—a taint in the nature; it insists that God is not responsible for it or for any evil; it emphasizes the guilt and horror of it, and the deadly consequences both for time and for eternity, and it opens to man a way of full forgiveness and clean victory. In contrast with this view, Mohammedanism teaches that sin is only the wilful violation of God's law; sins of ignorance it does not recognize; its doctrine of God's sovereignty fixes the responsibility for sin on God and dissolves the sense of guilt, and it denies the evil taint of sin in human nature. In Hinduism sin as opposition to the will of a personal God is inconceivable; it is the inevitable result of the acts of a previous state of being; it is evil, because all existence and all action, good as well as bad, are evil, and it is illusion, as all things are illusion. In pure Buddhism there can be no sin in our sense of the word, because there is no God; sin there means "thirst," "desire," and what Buddhism seeks to escape is not the evil of life only, but life itself; and

its conception of the sins that impede, while including much that is immoral, does not include all, and does not include much on the other hand that has no immoral character at all. Confucianism makes no mention of man's relation to God, and totally lacks all conception of sin. In one word, Christianity is the only religon in the world which clearly diagnoses the disease of humanity and discovers what it is that needs to be healed and that attempts permanently and radically to deal with it.

And so, also, Christianity alone knows what the salvation is which men require, and makes provision for it. In Christianity salvation is salvation from the power and the presence of sin, as well as from its guilt and shame. Its end is holy character and loving service. It is available for men here and now. In the Mohammedan conception salvation consists in deliverance from punishment, and deliverance not by redemption and the sacrifice of love, but by God's absolute sovereignty. The Hindu idea of salvation is to escape from the sufferings incident to life, to be liberated from personal, conscious existence, and this liberation is to be won by the way of knowledge, knowledge being the recognition of the soul's essential identity with Brahma, the impersonal God, or by the way of devotion, devotion being not faith in a God who works for the soul, but the maintenance by the soul of a saving attitude of mind toward the deity chosen to be worshiped. This is actual Hinduism, not the nobler doctrine of the Vedas. In Buddhism salvation is the extinction of existence. Indeed, there is no soul recognized by pure Buddhism. There is only the Karma, or character, which survives, and every man must work out his own Karma unaided. "By one's self," it is written in the Dhammapada, "the evil is done; by one's self one suffers; by one's self evil is left undone; by one's self one is purified. Lo, no man can purify another." The best Northern Buddhism draws nearest to Christianity in its conception of a salvation by faith in Amitaba Buddha, but even here the salvation is release from the necessity of continued rebirths, not a creation of new character for human service in Divine loyalty. Confucianism has no doctrine of salvation. The Chinese soul has had to turn, in the attempt to satisfy its needs, to other teachers. In its ideal and offer of salvation Christianity stands alone. (Kellogg, "Comparative Religion," chapters IV, V.)

5. Christianity is the only religion which is at once historical, progressive and spiritually free. Therefore, it is the only religion which can claim universal dominion. Each religion of the world has filled a place in history, but Mohammedanism is the only one whose historical facts are essential to it, and, as Bishop Westcott says:

"Christianity is historical not simply in the sense in which, for example, Mohammedanism is historical, because the facts connected with the origin and growth of this religion, with the personality and life of the Founder, with the experience and growth of His doctrine, can be traced in documents which are adequate to assure belief; but in a far different sense also. It is historical in its antecedents, in its realization, in itself; it is historical as crowning a long period of religious training which was accomplished under the influence of Divine facts; it is historical as brought out in all its fulness from age to age in an outward society by the action of the Spirit of God; but above all, and most characteristically, it is historical because the revelation which it brings is of life and in life. The history of Christ is the Gospel in its light and in its power. His teaching is Himself, and nothing apart from Himself; what He is and what He does. The earliest creed—the creed of baptism—is the affirmation of facts which include all doctrine.

"Dogmatic systems may change, and have changed so far as they reflect transitory phases of speculative thought, but the primitive Gospel is unchangeable as it is inexhaustible. There can be no addition to it. It contains in itself all that will be slowly wrought out in thought and deed until the consummation.

"In this sense, Christianity is the only historical religion. The message which it proclaims is wholly unique. Christ said, I am—not I declare, or I lay open, or I point to, but I am—the way, the truth and the life."

6. The ethical uniqueness of Christianity entitles it to absorb and displace all other religions. It alone makes the moral character of God the central and transcendent thing. Judged by its God, no other gods are really good. It alone presents a perfect ethical ideal for the individual and it alone possesses a social ethic adequate for a true national life and for a world society. It is pre-eminently the ethical religion. All its values are moral values. All the best life of Christian lands is an effort to embody the Christian ethics in life, and those ethics shelter absolutely none of the evil of Christian lands. "There is hardly a more trustworthy sign and a safer criterion of the civilization of a people," says the anthropologist Waitz, "than the degree in which the demands of a pure morality are supported by their religion and are interwoven with their religious life." And this is the true test of religions also. Do they supply men with perfect moral ideals? Do they condemn evil and refuse to allow evil to shelter itself under religious sanction? On one or both of these issues every non-Christian religion breaks down. There is much worthy moral teaching in each of the non-Christian religions, but the Koran enjoined the enslavement of the women and children of unbelievers conquered in battle, and authorized unlimited concubinage, and its sanction of polygamy cannot be defended as in the interest of morality. "Polygamy," said Dr. Henry H. Jessup, "has not diminished licentiousness among Mohammedans." Even in the Vedas there are passages which are morally debarred from publication. "I dare not give and you dare not print," wrote the Rev. S. Williams, "the ipsissima verba of an English version of the original Yajar Veda Man-

tras." ("Indian Evangelical Review," January, 1891.)   In
the Bhagavata Purana the character of the god Krishna is distinguished by licentiousness.   And worst of all in the Hindu
ethics, even in the Bhagavadgita, it is taught that actions in
themselves do not defile one, if only they are performed in
the state of mind enjoined in the poem.   While Buddha and
Confucianist ethics are deficient in active benevolence and
human service.   "Be ye perfect, as your Heavenly Father is
perfect," is a conception peculiar to Christianity.

7.   Christianity is the final and absolute religion, because
it contains all the good and truth that can be found in any
other religion, and presents it to men in its Divine fulness,
while other religions have none but partial good; because it is
free from the evils which are found in all other religions, and
because it alone can satisfy all the needs of the human heart
and of the human race.   It is the one true religion.   We are
glad to find any outreach after truth in other religions which
shows that the hearts of those who hold them are made for
that truth and capable of receiving it in its perfect form in
Christianity.   Christianity is final, because there is no good
beyond it and no evil in it, and because it cleanses and crowns
all the life and thought of man.   It is the end of all men's
quest.   "I maintain," says Tiele, "that the appearance of
Christianity inaugurated an entirely new epoch in the development of religion; that all the streams of the religious life of
man, once separate, unite in it; and that religious development
will henceforth consist in an ever higher realization of the
principles of that religion."   And Christianity is absolute as
well as final; that is, it fills the field.   There can be nothing
higher or better.   There can be nothing else in the same class.
As Bishop Westcott said:

"A perfect religion—a religion which offers a complete satisfaction to the religious wants of man—must be able to meet
the religious wants of the individual, the society, the race, in

complete course of their development and in the manifold intensity of each separate human faculty.

"This being so, I contend that the faith in Christ, born, crucified, risen, ascended forms the basis of this perfect religion; that it is able, in virtue of its essential character, to bring peace in view of the problems of life under every variety of circumstance and character—to illuminate, to develop, and to inspire every human faculty. My contention rests upon the recognition of two marks by which Christianity is distinguished from every other religion. It is absolute and it is historical.

"On the one side, Christianity is not confined by any limits of place, or time, or faculty, or object. It reaches to the whole sum of being and to the whole of each separate existence. On the other side, it offers its revelation in facts which are an actual part of human experience, so that the peculiar teaching which it brings as to the nature and relations of God and man and the world is simply the interpretation of events in the life of men and in the life of One who was truly Man. It is not a theory, a splendid guess, but a proclamation of facts.

"These, I repeat, are its original, its unalterable claims. Christianity is absolute. It claims, as it was set forth by the apostles, though the grandeur of the claim was soon obscured, to reach all men, all time, all creation; it claims to effect the perfection no less than the redemption of finite being; it claims to bring a perfect unity of humanity without destroying the personality of any one man; it claims to deal with all that is external as well as with all that is internal, with matter as well as with spirit, with the physical universe as well as with the moral universe; it claims to realize a re-creation coextensive with creation; it claims to present Him who was the Maker of the world, as the Heir of all things; it claims to complete the cycle of existence, and show how all things come from God and go to God."

As absolute, it must displace all that is partial or false. It must conquer the world. The people who have it must be a missionary people.

This is the solemn duty with which we are charged by our personal experience of the treasure that is in Christ, and this is the solemn duty with which any true comparison of Christianity with the world religions confronts us. Alike from the look within and from the look without we arise with a clear understanding of the missionary character of the religion that bears the name of Christ. The attitude of that religion is "not one of compromise, but one of conflict and of conquest. It proposes to displace the other religions. The claim of Jeremiah is the claim of Christianity: 'The gods that have not made the heavens and the earth, they shall perish from the earth and from under the heavens.' The survival of the Creator, joyfully foreseen, is the ground of its confidence and its endeavor. Christianity thus undertakes a long and laborious campaign, in which it must experience various fortunes and learn patience from trials and delays; but the true state of the case must not be forgotten, namely, that Christianity sets out for victory. The intention to conquer is characteristic of the Gospel. This was the aim of its youth when it went forth among the religions that then surrounded it, and with this aim it must enter any field in which old religions are encumbering the religious nature of man. It cannot conquer except in love, but in love it intends to conquer. It means to fill the world." It must do so in order that the nations may have their Desire and the world its Light.

CHAPTER V

WHAT MISSIONARY MOTIVES SHOULD PREVAIL?
"The love of Christ constraineth us" (1 Corinthians 5:14)

BY REV. HENRY W. FROST,

DIRECTOR FOR NORTH AMERICA OF THE CHINA INLAND MISSION,

GERMANTOWN, PHILADELPHIA, PENNSYLVANIA

VARIOUS KINDS OF MOTIVES

When we contemplate the motives which largely prevail in these days in respect to missionary service, we meet with a surprise. Instead of discovering, as we should anticipate in such a relationship, that these are always upon the high plane of the divine and heavenly, we find often that they are upon the low plane of the human and earthly. And it is to be noted that this condition, as compared with the past, marks a change in the kind of motive which is being presented to men in order to induce them to give themselves to missionary service. There was a time—within the memory of many—when the motives proclaimed were markedly scriptural and spiritual. But more recently there has been in many quarters a positive decline in this respect, the scriptural and spiritual giving place either to the selfish or to the simply humanitarian. And this has resulted in a development of weakness, both in the appeal and in its results. It is certainly true, as men say, that non-Christian nations are in a pitiable state, governmentally, educationally, commercially, socially and physically; and it is equally true that nothing but Christianity will alter the conditions which are existing. But such conditions do not constitute the appeal which God makes to His people when He urges them to Christianize the nations. The conditions above named are all "under the sun," and they have to do with the present temporal life. Besides, though a total transformation might be secured in these respects, the peoples so affected—as the present condition of Japan demonstrates— would have been brought no nearer to God than they were before. For, while it is always true that Christianity civilizes, it is never true that civilization Christianizes.

It would appear from the above, if souls are to be reached, if men are to be made inwardly right, if the things which make for eternal security and blessedness are to be obtained, that divine motives, leading to divine methods and results, must prevail. This is the reason why God sets such high motives before the Church. He would have Christians look high in order that they may live high; and He would have them live high in order that they may lift others equally high. It is supremely important, therefore, to discover from the Scriptures what the divinely given motives are. Our starting text indicates that Paul felt that these could be expressed in one phrase: "The love of Christ"—that is, Christ's love for us— "constraineth us." But other portions of the Word indicate that the Spirit expands the thought so expressed, the one motive including several others. May we anticipate sufficiently to say that these motives appear to be three in number. It is our purpose to consider these, one by one.

A FIRST MOTIVE

During the earlier portion of the ministry of Jesus on earth, that is, between His baptism and crucifixion, He spoke very little about missions; but during the later portion, that is, between His resurrection and ascension, He spoke of nothing else. This last is a striking and impressive fact, especially as there were many other matters, in those last days, about which His disciples might have wished to have Him speak and with which He might have desired to occupy Himself. It is evident then, during the forty days of His ascension, that one theme was uppermost in His mind and that one burden lay most heavily upon His heart. His redemptive work having been accomplished, He longed to have His disciples proclaim the glad tidings everywhere; and hence He spoke of this, and of this alone.

Moreover, on the several occasions when He discoursed upon the theme of missions, He always spoke as a master would address his disciples, as a captain would address his soldiers, as a king would address his subjects. At other times and in other relationships, He suggested, He exhorted, He urged. But here, without exception and without equivocation, He commanded. Not once did He explain how He could demand what He was requiring; not once did He ask if there were any arguments to be expressed in answer to His proposals; in full knowledge of the terrible cost, without allowing any escape from the obligation imposed, He simply said, "Go!"

In face of such a burning passion and heavily imposed obligation, there is but one conclusion to reach; the Church of Jesus Christ has no choice as to whether she will or will not do the thing ordered. One who has purchased His people with His own blood, One who owns them in spirit, soul and body, One who is indeed Master, Captain and King has positively commanded that His Gospel shall be preached throughout the world. Of course, the Church, if she chooses, may disobey, as—speaking generally—she is disobeying. But under the conditions prevailing, this on her part is high treason, and it is at her present loss and future peril. The thing which Christ has commanded, in all rightful consideration, is the thing which ought to be fully and immediately undertaken. This then, is the prime motive which God sets before Christians, individually and collectively, namely, that He who has had a right to command has done so, and that the command, because of the Person, calls for unhesitating, uncompromising and continuous obedience, until the task ordered is fully and finally accomplished.

A SECOND MOTIVE

There are five several passages in the Gospels which speak of Christ as having, or as being moved with, compassion. One is when Jesus saw two blind men and where He gave them sight; another is where He saw a leper and where He touched and healed him; another is where He saw a widow mourning the loss of her dead son and where He raised that son to life; another is where He saw the hungry multitudes and where He fed them; and the last is where He saw multitudes uncared for and where He asked His disciples to offer prayer in their behalf.

Now, all of these passages are interesting, as revealing the heart of Christ, He being the "God of compassion" whose "compassions fail not." But the last passage is particularly interesting, as it gives to us a view of present world-conditions and of the thought of God concerning them. For what was true that day in Galilee is still true the world over; and what Christ was He still is. Let us, for a moment, consider the passage.

Jesus had come to His own city of Nazareth, and later He had gone forth from thence throughout the neighboring districts. Both in the city and out of it, He had dispensed His largess of healing, from, apparently, early morning until late evening. As a result of His ministrations, He had gathered at last great crowds about Him, made up of men, women and children, and now these had no place to turn to for the night and had many physical and spiritual needs still unsupplied. That Jesus had had compassion upon the people all through the day, His words and acts attest. But now, seeing the multitudes in such a pitiable condition, it is recorded—for this is the implication—that He had peculiar compassion upon them. He saw that they were hungry and weary, just as sheep are at the close of the day when they are unfed and exhausted; and He saw also that they were like a great harvest field, whose past-ripe grain, for lack of hands to gather it into the garner, was rotting on the stalk. Then it was—these physical conditions suggesting the spiritual—that the great heart revealed its longing, and that there came forth the appealing, pathetic cry: "Pray ye therefore the Lord of the harvest, that He will send forth laborers into His harvest."

We would not imply, for a moment, that there was not sufficient cause in the sight of the multitudes that day to thus mightily move the heart of the Son of God. At the same time, we can but think that not a little part of the emotion which Jesus experienced was occasioned by the fact that the multitudes before Him were a picture of those other, greater multitudes which went to make up a lost world, and also of those other and still greater multitudes which were yet unborn and which would go to make up the lost world which was yet to be. For Christ ever looked on things with a divinely prophetic eye; and there was everything in that present view to suggest the wider vision. And so the heart bled out its grief; and so the voice plaintively asked the help of man. And thus this same Christ is ever looking down from heaven's throne, the same heart is ever feeling its weight of compassionate woe, and the same voice is ever pleading with His disciples to see as He sees and to feel as He feels. This then is the second motive which God sets before Christians, namely, to enter into Christ's compassion for the lost souls and lives of men, and thus to be moved as He was moved, and to be constrained to do as He did.

A THIRD MOTIVE

The Gospels, recording the earthly life of Jesus, are full of promises—mostly from the lips of the Master—concerning a coming which would be for the purpose of establishing a kingdom. The Epistles, representing the testimony of the risen and glorified Christ, continue this theme, and always give the same order, first the coming and then the kingdom.

And at the end of the New Testament, a whole book—Revelation—is taken up with the expansion of the now familiar thought and tells in detail how Christ will come, and what the kingdom will be.

In addition to the above, Gospels, Epistles and Revelation speak of a work to be accomplished, which is preliminary to the coming and kingdom, and which, in the divine economy, makes the one and the other possible. As these passages are more than interesting, as they are vital to our subject, we make a selection from them, quoting them without comment: "The Son of Man is come to seek and to save that which was lost." "Other sheep I have, which are not of this fold; them also I must bring; and they shall hear My voice; and there shall be one fold [flock] and one Shepherd." "Go ye therefore, and teach [disciple] all nations." "Go ye into all the world, and preach the Gospel to every creature." "Ye are witnesses of these things." "Ye shall be witnesses unto Me both in Jerusalem, and in all Judéa, and in Samaria, and unto the uttermost part of the earth." "Delivering thee from the people [the Jews], and from the Gentiles, unto whom now I send thee; to open their eyes, and to turn them from darkness to light, and from the power of Satan unto God, that they may receive forgiveness of sins." "That by me the preaching might be fully known and that all the Gentiles might hear." "Blindness in part is happened to Israel, until the fulness of the Gentiles be come in." "And this Gospel of the kingdom shall be preached in all the world for a witness unto all nations; and then shall the end come." "A great multitude which no man could number, of all nations, and kindreds, and peoples, and tongues."

Impressive as these passages of Scripture are, and clear as their teaching is to the effect that missionary service is related to all the world and is for the purpose of gathering to God an innumerable number of people in preparation for the King and the kingdom, there is yet another passage which is even more impressive and clear as related to the same particulars. As if to remove any possible misunderstanding in regard to the divine plan, the Spirit led to the declaration and preservation of words which tell us what God purposes to do in this present age in preparation for the age to come, and what part the Church is to play in the fulfilment of the purpose so announced. We refer to Acts 15:13–18. There James, quoting Peter, is the spokesman, and the great Apostle confirms his utterance by stating it as a foundation truth that "known unto God are all His works from the beginning of the world." He thus says: "Simeon hath declared how God at the first did visit the Gentiles to take out of them a people for His name; and to this agree the words of the prophets; as it is written, After this I will return and will build again the tabernacle of David, which is fallen down; and I will build again the ruins thereof, and I will set it up; that the residue of men might seek after the Lord, and all the Gentiles upon whom My name is called, saith the Lord, who doeth all these things."

Here then, is a divine utterance and program. And simply speaking, it sets forth the following facts in the following order: first, a present work of grace in which God visits and gathers out, preeminently from the Gentiles, a people for His name; second, the return of Christ; third, the restoration and establishment of the Jewish theocratic kingdom with its attendant worship; and fourth, the salvation in the kingdom-age of the "residue" of the Jews, and of "all" the Gentiles upon whom God's name shall be called. And this program, in its first article, makes it clear what share the Church has in its fulfilment. To put it in a single sentence, it is this: God is visiting the nations, and Christians have the high privilege of visiting them with Him. He goes forth, in the persons of the missionaries, not to convert all the world—since not all men will accept of Him—but to gather out from it a willing people, heavenly in quality and innumerable in quantity, which shall be to the glory of His name throughout time and eternity.

And, manifestly, this preparatory work will bring to pass the event which is described as following it, that is, the coming of Christ. This then is the final and consummating motive which God sets before Christians, namely, to go forth everywhere, preaching the good tidings to every creature, in order that the Church may be made complete and that the King and the kingdom may come.

THE EFFECT OF SCRIPTURAL MOTIVES

It will need only passing consideration to discover that the three motives which have been mentioned, namely, the command, the compassion and the coming of Christ, are like the God who gave them, and are thus worthy of being accepted by the noblest and most devoted of men. And there are two reasons why they are this. First, because they represent spiritual and eternal truths; and second, because they make for the highest glory of God and the greatest good of mankind. As to the last effect, no other motives are so uplifting and purifying to the person who is moved by them, and no other motives are so sure of divine favor and blessing in their exercise. There is enough power in these motives, singly and collectively, to raise the missionary propaganda above everything earthly, selfish and narrow, and to place it, where it ever belongs, upon the plane of the heavenly, the spiritual and the infinite. Moreover there is enough potency here to turn the "forlorn hope" of present-day foreign missions, in which a Gideon's band of men and women are bravely fighting on against overwhelming odds, into an ever victorious army of the Church, where the battle will not only be fought but also be won, and where the end of saving the elect, and thus of bringing back the King and bringing in the kingdom, will be surely and speedily brought to pass. For what foes on earth, or what demons in hell, could stay the onward progress of a people which had determined, in the power of the Holy Spirit, to obey Christ's command, to show forth His compassion, and to press forward with uplifted faces to the rapturous and victorious meeting with Him who one day will descend with a shout, with the voice of the archangel, and with the trump of God? Such motives as these are not simply constraining; they are invincible and triumphant.

AN ILLUSTRATION

Some years ago, while living in Toronto, I received a call from a Miss Kathleen Stayner, of that city. Miss Stayner had come to confer with me about the possibility of her serving in China. I saw at once that she had been born and bred a gentlewoman; and I learned afterwards that she had had an exceptionally good education both in Canada and in Europe; that she was an heiress; and, being an orphan, that she was free to come and go as she might choose. Also, I perceived, as our conversation advanced, that she was a young woman of great devotion, having turned her back upon all social allurements and having committed herself to an earnest and self-sacrificing service for Christ, including work for the Chinese in Toronto. The situation in respect to her going to China, therefore, was a most promising one, for there was nothing to hinder her proceeding to that land. But my growing confidence as we talked was suddenly arrested by Miss Stayner, for she unexpectedly declared that there was one difficulty in her way which was insurmountable. Asking what this was, I received this reply:

"I have to confess that I do not love the Chinese." And then she explained: "They are so ignorant and dirty!"

This was a real obstacle, especially as she had been working among the Chinese. But in spite of it I replied:

"Do you know, Miss Stayner, I do not think the question whether or not you love the Chinese is the one to be considered; it seems to me that the real question is whether or not you love the Lord."

At this, her eyes kindled and she exclaimed: "Oh, yes, I do love Him!"

"Then," I said, "if you love Him, how can you do anything else but obey His command and go?"

At this, she looked at me earnestly and said: "Do you think then that I may dare to go?"

"Under the circumstances," I replied, "I do not see how you may dare to stay."

A few days later Miss Stayner applied to the Mission; a few months later she was accepted for service; and shortly after her acceptance she went on her way to China.

Miss Stayner, however, was not to have the easy time in China which many missionaries experience there. For a period all went well and happily. She was located at the inviting station of Wenchow; she entered into the old, well developed and very promising work at that place; she made remarkable progress with the language; and she gained the confidence and love of the people. But one night, when she was staying with her Bible-woman at an out-station, she was suddenly aroused from her sleep by lights and voices, and thereupon discovered that robbers had forced their way into her room and were stealing what they could lay their hands upon. Miss Stayner protested, whereupon one of the robbers struck her with a bamboo pole. Later, she and the Bible-woman got out of a door at the back of the house, and, clad as they were and in the cold of the winter night, they fled over the hills to a clump of trees and bushes and hid themselves from view. There they remained for a long time, chilled and horror-stricken, until the robbers had sacked their house and departed. After this they were found by some of the villagers and brought back to their almost ruined home. Miss Stayner was seriously affected, physically, by this trying experience, and it became necessary that she should visit Shanghai for quiet and rest. Just at that time I visited that place, and I was thus able, one evening, to ask her about her work and to hear from her lips the account of her recent experiences. After the tale had been told, I said:

"Miss Stayner, may I ask you a question?"

"Yes," she replied, "what is it?"

"It is this," I answered; "do you love the Chinese?"

I shall never forget the look of astonishment which she gave me. "Why," she said, "what do you mean? Of course, I love the Chinese!"

"I was just wondering," I replied, "if, having gone through such an experience at their hands, you were sorry you had come to China, and if possibly you now almost hated the Chinese."

This remark perplexed her more than my first had done. But I then reminded her of our conversation in Toronto, which had quite passed from her mind.

"Oh," she finally answered, "I had forgotten that I ever said that; but that was before I knew the Chinese; I love them all now!"

But Miss Stayner was not at an end of her appointed trials. For only a few years had passed when she became afflicted with a climatic disease, which is terrible in its process and effects. It soon became evident that she must leave the country. This she did, coming home to Canada, and later going to a certain "Spa" in Germany. Happily she got better, and at last she was able to go back to her much loved work. But still later, her old trouble returned. She fought against it, and for a considerable time would not give up. But at last it was a question of life and death, and she reluctantly took her way back, first to Germany and then to England. Here, her strength gradually failed, and, finally, she finished her earthly course by falling asleep in Christ. It was my privilege to see our friend during this last visit. She was, in spite of her youth, a physical wreck, her hair being gray, her face being thin, and her strength and vigor having departed. But she had not one word of regret to express at having gone to China and was full of grateful praise to God that such a privilege had been hers. And she confessed that the one thing which had led her on and which gave her ever ample compensation for all that she had suffered was the knowledge that she was doing what she could to take the Gospel to the heathen and thus to hasten the return to earth of her beloved Lord.

Miss Stayner's life is more than an illustration; it is an interpretation. For it shows beyond misunderstanding what is the effect upon an open mind and heart of true scriptural motives. Here was a woman who had everything, naturally speaking, to keep her at home, but who deliberately chose to go abroad. Here was one who had faced the question of her responsibility toward the heathen, not emotionally, but calmly, and who finally had gone forth for no other reason than that her Master had commanded her to do so. Here was one who at first had little love for the heathen, but whose heart, in the path of obedience, became filled with compassion for them. And here, finally, was one who had remained steadfast and even praiseful through all her suffering and sorrow because she had learned to serve with her eyes fixed upon Him who is the Coming One. And thus the interpretation becomes an inspiration. For Miss Stayner's life and service are a constraining call, to all who know and love the Lord, to do as she did, in being wholly obedient to God and in committing all to Him. And it is not too much to say that if Christians should follow her as she followed Christ it would not be long before there would be produced a veritable revolution in missionary methods and results. Then indeed we might hope to see foreign missions turned into an apostolic triumph, where the old figure of speech, "terrible as an army with banners," would but feebly express what God would make His Church on earth to be. For it is manifest that our Father in heaven has large thoughts toward the heathen, and that He is ready to use His saints in their fulfilment whenever they will allow Him to do so. But it is to be remembered, that this last can only come to pass in the measure in which the followers of Christ are possessed and controlled by those motives which are truly and wholly divine.

CHAPTER VI

THE PLACE OF PRAYER IN EVANGELISM

BY REV. R. A. TORREY, D. D.,
DEAN OF THE BIBLE INSTITUTE OF LOS ANGELES,
LOS ANGELES, CALIFORNIA

The most important human factor in effective evangelism is PRAYER. Every great awakening in the history of the Church from the time of the Apostles until today has been the result of prayer. There have been great awakenings without much preaching, and there have been great awakenings with absolutely no organization, but there has never been a true awakening without much prayer.

The first great ingathering in human history had its origin, on the human side, in a ten days' prayer meeting. We read of the small company of early disciples: "These all with one accord continued stedfastly in prayer" (Acts 1:14). The result of that ten days' prayer meeting is recorded in the 2nd chapter of the Acts of the Apostles: "They were all filled with the Holy Ghost, and began to speak with other tongues, as the Spirit gave them utterance" (2:4), and "there were added unto them in that day about 3,000 souls" (2:41). That awakening proved real and permanent; those who were gathered in on that greatest day in all Christian history, "continued stedfastly in the apostles' teaching and fellowship, in the breaking of bread, and in prayers" (2:42). "And the Lord added to them day by day those that were being saved" (2:47).

Every great awakening from that day to this has had its earthly origin in prayer. "The Great Awakening" in the 18th century, in which Jonathan Edwards was one of the central figures, began with his famous "Call to Prayer." The work of David Brainerd among the North American Indians, one of the most marvelous works in all history, had its origin in the days and nights that Brainerd spent before God in prayer for an enduement of power from on high for this work. In 1830 there was a revival in Rochester, New York, in which Charles G. Finney was the outstanding human agent. This revival spread throughout that region of the state and 100,000 persons were reported as having connected themselves with the churches as the result of this work. Mr. Finney himself attributed his success to the spirit of prayer which prevailed. He says in his autobiography:

"When I was on my way to Rochester, as we passed through a village some thirty miles east of Rochester, a brother minister whom I knew, seeing me on the canal boat, jumped aboard to have a little conversation with me, intending to ride but a little way and return. He, however, became interested in conversation, and upon finding where I was going, he made up his mind to keep on and go with me to Rochester. We had been there but a few days when this minister became so convicted that he could not help weeping aloud at one time as he passed along the street. The Lord gave him a powerful spirit of prayer, and his heart was broken. As he and I prayed together, I was struck with his faith in regard to what the Lord was going to do there. I recollect he would say, 'Lord, I do not know how it is; but I seem to know that Thou art going to do a great work in this city.' The spirit of prayer was poured out powerfully, so much so, that some persons stayed away from the public services to pray, being unable to restrain their feelings under preaching.

"And here I must introduce the name of a man, whom I shall have occasion to mention frequently, Mr. Abel Clary. He was the son of a very excellent man and an elder of the church where I was converted. He was converted in the same revival in which I was. He had been licensed to preach; but his spirit of prayer was such—he was so burdened with the souls of men—that he was not able to preach much, his whole time and strength being given to prayer. The burden of his soul would frequently be so great that he was unable to stand, and he would writhe and groan in agony. I was well acquainted with him, and knew something of the wonderful spirit of prayer that was upon him. He was a very silent man, as almost all are who have that powerful spirit of prayer.

"The first I knew of his being in Rochester, a gentleman who lived about a mile west of the city called on me one day, and asked me if I knew a Mr. Abel Clary, a minister, and I told him that I knew him well. 'Well,' said he, 'he is at my house, and has been there for some time, and I don't know what to think of him.' I said, 'I have not seen him at any of our meetings.' 'No,' he replied, 'he cannot go to meetings, he says. He prays nearly all the time day and night, and in such an agony of mind that I do not know what to make of it. Sometimes he cannot even stand on his knees, but will lie prostrate on the floor, and groan and pray in a manner that quite astonishes me.' I said to the brother, 'I understand it; please keep still. It will come out all right; he will surely prevail.'

"I knew at the time a considerable number of men who were exercised in the same way. A Deacon P—— of Camden, Oneida County; a Deacon T—— of Adams, in the same county; this Mr. Clary, and many others among the men, and a large number of women partook of the same spirit, and spent a great part of their time in prayer. Father Nash, as we called him, who in several of my fields of labor came to me and aided me, was another of those men that had such a powerful spirit of prevailing prayer. This Mr. Clary continued in Rochester as long as I did, and did not leave it until after I had left. He never, that I could learn, appeared in public, but gave himself wholly to prayer."

Perhaps the most remarkable awakening ever known in the United States was the great revival of 1857. As far as its human origin can be traced it began in the prayers of a humble city missionary in New York named Landfear. He not only prayed himself but organized a noon meeting for prayer. At first the attendance was very small; at one meeting there were only three present, at another two, and at one meeting he alone was present. But he and his associates persisted in prayer until a fire was kindled that spread throughout the whole city, until prayer meetings were being held at every hour of the day and night, not only in churches but in theaters. When this had gone on for some time, Dr. Gardner Spring, one of the most eminent Presbyterian ministers in America, said to a company of ministers, "It is evident that a revival has broken out among us, and we must preach." One of the ministers replied, "Well, if there is to be preaching, you must preach the first sermon," and Dr. Gardner Spring consented to preach. But no more people came out to hear him preach than had come out for prayer. So the dependence was put upon prayer and not preaching; the fire spread to Philadelphia, and then all over the land until it is said that there was no part of the country where prayer meetings were not going on, and the whole nation was moved and there were conversions and accessions to the Church everywhere by the hundreds and thousands. This awakening in America was followed by a similar awakening, though in some respects even more remarkable, in Ireland, Scotland and England, in 1859 and 1860. The most important human factors in the origin of the wonderful work seem to have been four young men who began to meet together in the old schoolhouse in the neighborhood of Kells in the north of Ireland. Here night after night they wrestled with God in prayer. About the spring of 1858 a work of power began to manifest itself. It spread from town to town and from county to county; congregations became too large for any building, meetings were held in the open air, oftentimes attended by many thousands of people. Hundreds of persons were frequently convicted of sin in a single meeting; men were smitten down with conviction of sin while working in the field. In some places the criminal courts and jails were closed because there were no cases to try and no criminals to be incarcerated. The fruits of that wonderful work abide to this day. Many of the leading persons even in the churches of America were converted at that time in the north of Ireland. While men like Dr. Grattan Guinness and Brownlow North were greatly used at that time, the revival spread not so much through preachers as through prayer. The wonderful work of Mr. Moody in England, Scotland and Ireland in 1873, and the years that followed, beyond a question had its origin on the manward side in prayer. His going to England at all was in answer to the importunate prayers of a bedridden saint. The first demonstration of God's power through his preaching was in a church in the north of London a year before he went to England for this work. In this meeting 500 people definitely accepted Christ in a single night. This was the direct and immediate outcome of the prayers of this same bedridden saint. While the spirit of prayer continued, Mr. Moody went on with power, but as is always the case, in the course of time less and less was made of prayer and his work fell off perceptibly in power.

The great Welsh revival in 1904 and 1905 was unquestionably the outcome of prayer. A year before the writer began his work in Cardiff, it was announced that he was going to Cardiff, and for a year prayer went up from thousands of devoted Christians that there would be not only a revival in Cardiff but throughout Wales. When we reached Cardiff we found that early morning prayer meetings had been held in Penarth, one of the suburbs of Cardiff, for months. Yet at first the work went very slowly. There were great crowds, most enthusiastic singing, but little manifestation of real convicting and regenerating power. A day of fasting and prayer was appointed. This was observed not only in Cardiff but in different parts of Wales. There came an immediate turn of the tide; the power of God fell. On that day, at a meeting held in another part of Wales by a few devoted men of God, the power of God was manifested in a most remarkable way. For a whole year after our meetings closed in Cardiff, the work went on in that city, meetings every night with a very large number of conversions. The week following the meetings in Cardiff a minister associated with the work went up into one of the valleys of Wales, and there was a mighty manifestation of the power of God with large numbers of conversions, and all over Wales the work of God continued, largely without human instruments except in the way of prayer. 100,000 conversions were reported in a year. Of course, not all of these proved steadfast, and doubtless there were extravagances in some places, but after making all allowance, it was one of the most remarkable works of God in modern times, and from Wales there went forth a fire from God to the uttermost parts of the earth and only eternity will reveal the glorious results of that work.

And not only has it been demonstrated over and over again in a large way that widespread revivals are the certain outcome of intelligent and prevailing prayer, but in smaller circles the power of prayer has been demonstrated over and over again. In a very obscure village in the state of Maine, where apparently nothing was being accomplished by the churches, a few earnest Christian men got together and organized a prayer band. They selected apparently the most hopeless case in all the village and centered their prayers upon him, importuning God for his conversion. The man was a drunkard and a wreck. In a short time the man was thoroughly converted. Then the praying band centered its prayers upon another man, the second hardest case in the village, and he was converted; and so the work went on until about 200 were converted in a single year.

In a little village in the state of Michigan, way off from the railroad, a Presbyterian and a Methodist minister united in an effort to win the unsaved to Christ. They were backed by a faithful praying band. While the Presbyterian preached and the Methodist exhorted, this praying band were in the back room crying to God for His blessing on the work. They would select individuals in the community to pray for. In some instances these men would come into the meeting the very night they were being prayed for and be converted. The work grew to be so remarkable that ministers and multitudes of the people would drive for miles to witness the wonderful work.

The history of foreign missions abounds in illustrations of the importance and power of prayer in world-wide evangelism. All will recall "the haystack" prayer meeting and its results, and the sending out of the 100 by the China Inland Mission in 1887.

Illustrations of this character could easily be multiplied. The history of the Church demonstrates beyond a question that the most important human factor in the evangelism of the world is prayer. The great need of the present hour is prayer. In our work at home and abroad we are placing more and more dependence upon men, machinery, and methods, and less and less upon God. Evangelism at home is becoming more and more mechanical, and methods are being resorted to that are more and more revolting to all spiritually minded people; while evangelism abroad is becoming more and more merely educational and sociological. What is needed above everything else today is prayer, true prayer, prayer in the power of the Holy Ghost, and prayer that meets the conditions of prevailing prayer so plainly laid down in the Word of God.

All that is said thus far is more or less general, but if anything practical is to be accomplished we must be specific. In what directions should we put forth prayer, if we would see that effective evangelism for which so many are longing?

First of all, we should pray for individuals. Under God's guidance we should select individuals upon whom we should center our prayers. Every minister and every Christian should have a prayer list, i. e., he should write at the top of a sheet of paper the following words (or words to the same effect): "God helping me, I will pray earnestly and work persistently for the conversion of the following persons:" Then he should kneel before God and ask God definitely and in the most thoughtful earnestness and sincerity, to show him whom to put on that prayer list, and as God leads him to put different persons on that prayer list, he should write their names down. Then each day he should go to God in very definite prayer with that prayer list and cry to God in the earnestness of the Holy Spirit for the conversion of these individuals and never cease to pray for them until they are definitely converted. If there were space we could record most marvelous instances of conversion in many lands as the outcome of such prayer lists.

Second, we should pray for the individual church and community. Pray definitely for a spiritual awakening, pray that the members of the church be brought onto a higher plane of Christian living, that the church be purged from its present compromise with the world, that the members of the church be clothed upon with power from on high and filled with a passion for the salvation of the lost. We should pray that through the church and its membership, many may be converted and that there be a genuine awakening in the church and community. Any church or community that is willing to pay the price can have a true revival. That price is not building a tabernacle and calling some widely-known evangelist and putting large sums of money into advertising and following other modern methods. These things may all be right in their place, but they are not the price of a revival. The price of a revival is honest, earnest prayer in the Holy Spirit, prayer that will not take no for an answer. Let a few people in any church or community get thoroughly right with God themselves, then let them band themselves together and cry to God for a revival until the revival comes, with a determination to pray through no matter how long it takes; then let them put themselves at God's disposal for Him to use them in any way He will, in personal work or testimony or anything else, then let them go out as God leads them, dealing in love and wisdom and persistence with the unsaved, and a genuine revival of God's work in the power of the Holy Ghost is bound to result. The writer has said substantially this around the world; time and again, the advice has been followed, and the result has always been the same, a real, effective, thorough-going work of God. In the church in Chicago of which he himself was pastor, during the eight years of his active pastorate there was a constant revival, and in all those eight years there was never a week without conversions. The great majority of those converted united with other churches, but the smallest number ever received into that church in any one year was 250. In the thirteen years that have elapsed since he left the active pastorate of that church, the work has continued to go on, at first under another pastor, and now for several years with no pastor at all. Many illustrations of the same thing could be given. A most notable instance is that of the Charlotte Chapel in Edinburgh under the leadership of Rev. Joseph W. Kemp.

Third, we should pray for the work in foreign lands. The history of foreign missions proves that the most important factor in effective missionary work is prayer. Men and women are needed for foreign missions, money is needed, but what is needed most of all is prayer. We should pray very definitely for God's guidance upon the secretaries and other officers of our foreign missionary boards. The problems that confront them are beyond the wisdom of any man to solve; the secretaries need wisdom from above and that wisdom is given in answer to prayer. We should pray very definitely that laborers be thrust forth into the harvest which is so plenteous and so ripe at the present time. (Matt. 9: 37, 38.) Not only should we pray that men and women be called into the foreign field, but we should pray for definite fields and for the definite thrusting forth of laborers into those fields. We should pray very specifically for the men and women who have gone into the field. Only one who has visited the foreign field can have any realization of how much the missionaries need our prayers. One feels when he gets to the foreign field as if the very atmosphere was taken possession of by "the prince of the power of the air." The burdens that the foreign missionary has to bear and the conflicts that he has to endure would be appalling if we did not believe in a God who answers prayer. But we have no right to leave the devoted men and women who have gone out to the foreign field to fight the battle alone. Realizing that their "wrestling is not against flesh and blood, but against the principalities, against the powers, against the world-rulers of this darkness, against the spiritual host of wickedness in the heavenlies," we should with all prayer and supplication pray at all seasons in the Spirit, and watch thereunto in all perseverance, that God would give to these men and women victory in their personal conflict, and power in their efforts to win men from the delusions of the false religions that eternally destroy to the truth of the Gospel that eternally saves. We should pray too very definitely for the converts on the foreign fields, for their deliverance from error and delusion and sin, and that they may become intelligent, well-balanced, strong and useful members of the body of Christ. We should pray for the churches as organizations that are formed as the outcome of missionary effort in foreign lands.

Finally, we should pray for the evangelization of the world in the present generation. The awful war now in progress emphasizes the need of prayer, especially in connection with our foreign work. The past few years have been years of marvelous opportunity in foreign missionary work. God has been calling the church as never before to the evangelization of the world, but the church as a whole has slept on and not responded to the call, and it almost seems as if the door was at last being closed and that our Lord was saying to us as He said to the disciples who slept in the Garden of Gethsemane, "Sleep on now, the opportunity I gave you and that you despised is now gone." We cannot have it so. Let us pray that God will give us one more opportunity. I believe He will, as dark as the present day seems. Let us pray just as earnestly that God will lead His church to improve the one more opportunity as it is given. Let us be very earnest, very persistent in our prayers. Let us determine that we will not take no for an answer, and we shall see world-wide evangelization, and that glad day for which we are longing above all other days will speedily come when "the Lord Himself shall descend from heaven with a shout, with the voice of the archangel and the trump of God," and when His completed body, the church, will be caught up to meet Him in the air. "Even so, come, Lord Jesus."

CHAPTER VII

THE CHURCH AND SOCIALISM

BY PROFESSOR CHARLES R. ERDMAN, D. D.,
PRINCETON THEOLOGICAL SEMINARY,
PRINCETON, NEW JERSEY

The *sudden rise of Socialism* is the most surprising and significant movement of the age. A few years ago the term suggested a dream of fanatics; today it embodies the creed and the hope of intelligent millions. For example, in America the Socialistic vote increased from 20,000, in 1892, to 900,000 in 1912. In France this vote numbers 1,104,000, and in Germany more than 3,000,000; and in these and other lands multitudes who are not openly allied with political Socialism are imbued with Socialistic principles and are advocates of Socialistic theories.

With this great movement *the Christian Church* is deeply concerned; first, because of the endeavor which many are making to identify Socialism with Christianity; and, secondly, because, on the other extreme, popular Socialism is suggested as a substitute for religion and is antagonistic to Christianity; and, thirdly, because the strength of Socialism consists largely in its protest against existing social wrongs to which the Church is likewise opposed but which can be finally righted only by the universal rule of Christ.

I. *Socialism,* strictly defined, is *an economic theory* which proposes the abolition of private capital and the substitution of collective ownership in carrying on the industrial work of the world. This collective ownership is to extend to all the material instruments of production; these are to be publicly operated, and the products to be equitably distributed. The government is to be wholly in the hands of the people, and it is to assign to each individual his task and to determine his wage. Every citizen is to be actually a government employee.

It is evident that Socialism is to be distinguished from *Communism* with which it is often confused. The latter advocates a collective ownership of all wealth. Socialism does not deny the right of private property, but of private capital. In a Socialistic state one might own a house, but he could not rent it to increase his income. He might own a yacht, but he could not use it to carry passengers for pay. Under Communism there would be no private ownership, but it would be literally true that "no man could call aught that he possessed his own."

Socialism is still more easily distinguished from *Anarchism*. The latter seeks the abolition of all government; but Socialism advocates the extension of the functions of government to regulate the life and labor of every individual and even in the most minute details. Anarchy means no government; Socialism proposes more government than any nation has ever known.

Quite as obviously Socialism should never be confused with that extreme form of Anarchy known as *Nihilism*. The latter advocates the violent abolition of all existing institutions, social and political. It is true that Socialists often propose revolution and violence; but an ever increasing number believe their ends will be attained by a gradual process of social evolution moving toward the goal of a collective ownership of capital. It is not right therefore to identify Socialism with assassination, lawlessness and outrage.

Most important of all is the distinction between Socialism and *Christianity*. This might seem to be self-evident. Christianity is a religion; Socialism an economic theory, or a political proposal, and with such theories and proposals Christianity and the Church have nothing to do. At the present time, however, there is a strong endeavor and an evident tendency to identify Socialism and the Christian Church.

Some are insisting that Jesus Christ was a Socialist and that the early Church was established on Socialistic principles. Others declare that Socialism is merely the application of Christianity to industrial problems, and that it is the duty of a Christian minister to preach Socialism, and the supreme function of the Christian Church to introduce and support Socialism as the one cure for all existing social evils.

As to Jesus Christ, it is impossible to identify Him with any social theory or political party. His teachings are of universal application and eternal validity; but they do not deal with the questions of political economy any more than with those of physical science. That He insisted upon justice, and brotherhood, and love, and self-sacrifice is evident; but to suggest that these virtues are the monopoly of any one political or economic party is presumptuous, and to prove that Christ advocated "collective ownership of property" is impossible. The fundamental economic problem relates to the division of wealth; and as to that Christ refused to speak. He rebuked social sins and injustice and selfishness, but when requested to divide a possession on a certain occasion He asked, "Who made Me a judge or a divider over you?" and that question has wide implications for the present day.

When we read the story of *the early Church* there are statements which suggest Socialism or even Communism, as for instance when we read that "they had all things common," but a fuller investigation shows their Communism was *local, voluntary, occasional, temporary*. It was practiced only in Jerusalem, no one was compelled to divide or sell his property; not all adopted the practice, but many like Mary the mother of Mark kept their homes in the city. Furthermore, this Communism was only practiced for a time. It was prompted by love and designed to meet a special crisis, but never admitted or established as an abiding principle of Church life.

As to *the Church of today*, it would be gross injustice to its members should it be identified with Socialism. While

Socialists may adopt many of the Christian principles and feel impelled by Christian motives, they must remember that Christianity is something other than a social propaganda and far more than an economic theory. On the other hand, the Church recognizes that it has no right to ally itself with any political party, or to commit itself to any one form of social or industrial organization. The Church leaves its members free to adopt or reject Socialism as they may deem wise. A man may be an ardent Socialist and a sincere Christian, or he may be a true Christian and a determined opponent of Socialism.

Most Christians admit the wisdom of many Socialistic proposals, but feel that they are at liberty to act without the interference of the Church. In America, for example, the public school system and post office department of the government are instances of the application of Socialistic principles. Government ownership might be extended to the railroads, mines, public utilities, factories; this would not involve questions of religion, but of expediency and political wisdom, with which problems the Church has nothing to do.

On the other hand many Christians are persuaded that there are fallacies and weaknesses in the Socialistic scheme. They believe, for instance, that Socialists are mistaken in assuming that labor is the sole factor in producing wealth, and that capital is the result or embodiment of robbery; they do not believe the formation and government of a completely organized Socialistic state would be practical or possible; they are convinced that Socialism, if realized, would involve a tyranny and slavery which would be incredible and intolerable. These are their sincere convictions and men who hold them should not be denied a place in the Church nor rebuked by the Church as though they were lacking in intelligence or in Christian sympathy and love. It should be recognized that the Church is not to invade the field of political economy, nor is it allied with any political or social order or propaganda.

It is in this connection that the movement called *"Christian Socialism"* should be criticised. To say the least, the name it has adopted is unfortunate, for it implies, whether intentionally or not, that other Socialists are not Christians, and that other Christians should be Socialists. One might as well speak of Christian Democrats, or Christian Republicans, or Christian Suffragists. The implications would be much the same.

"Christian Socialism," however, is not only an imperfect name; it is in most of its forms an unfortunate thing. In some cases, it is true, it is merely the expression of a benevolent desire that a spirit of justice and brotherhood should be shown by men in their social and industrial relations. This is innocent enough; but as presented by the great mass of its advocates, "Christian Socialism" is neither Christian nor Socialism. It is disappointing to Christians and irritating to Socialists. It minimizes or denies such Christian truths as the incarnation, the virgin birth, the atonement, the resurrection, justification by faith, the work of the Holy Spirit, the second coming of Christ, and insofar it ceases to be true Christianity. On the other hand, it is not real Socialism. Few of its adherents deny the right of private capital, or insist upon the "collective ownership of the instruments of production." In the effort to unite Christianity and Socialism justice is done to neither. Such a union should never be attempted. From Socialism as a strict economic theory, Christianity is absolutely distinct, and as a political proposal Socialism has no relation to the Church.

II. *Popular Socialism,* however, is something quite different from a scientific economic theory. It is a social creed, offered as a substitute for religion, promising material benefits to all mankind, and bitterly opposed to Christianity and the Church. Much of this hatred is due to ignorance and prejudice. Great multitudes who call themselves Socialists have vague conceptions of the problems of political science or of the serious difficulties involved in the establishment of a Socialistic state, but they are vividly conscious of their hatred against existing institutions which they hold responsible for the present social inequalities and wrongs. Christian teachers, therefore, do well to meet fairly and generously the attacks which Socialists are making upon the Church, and they should explain to Socialists their misconceptions and the obvious defects of their creed.

1. Popular Socialism is mistaken in *identifying the Christian Church with "capital,"* and in regarding the Church as responsible for the present social order. It is commonly asserted that the Church is the "rich man's club"; that Christian ministers are controlled by men of wealth and afraid to rebuke social evils, that the Gospel is preached with the purpose of making poor men content with their present conditions and of preventing them from rising to assert their rights. As a matter of fact the Church is committed to no one social order. It has flourished under imperial rule as it has in great republics, but it is opposed to the wrongs and injustice of every system. Instead of being "the rich man's club" the great proportion of its members are wage earners, and a very small proportion are rich. For instance, of the 36,000,000 Church members in the United States only a few could be classed as capitalists. On the other hand, very many capitalists, unfortunately, are not professed Christians nor actively interested in the Church.

As to the ministry, it is rarely recruited from the ranks of the wealthy, and its representatives are usually fearless in their rebuke of social sins. It is the glory of the Church that it welcomes to its services and blesses by its offices both rich and poor alike, and does more to obliterate class distinctions than any other agency in the world.

2. Popular Socialism unjustly *places all capitalists under suspicion* of dishonesty and selfishness. It is true that the more intelligent advocates of Socialism, as an economic proposal, discriminate between the responsibilities of individuals

and the defects of a system. They even sympathize with capitalists who are compelled to act under conditions and laws which are beyond their control, and they attack no one class in a community, but seek for new institutions which, without violence or injustice, will secure a truer equality of opportunity and condition. But "popular Socialism" regards all men of wealth with enmity. Its outcries against the rich are engendering the bitterest class hatred and arousing passions which, unless controlled, will result in violence and anarchy and universal disaster. There can be no doubt that capital is often cruel, that at times it depends upon injustice and tyranny, and frequently exploits the helpless, and produces misery and distress; but these abuses are not universal. Where they exist they can be corrected by law; and it is merely begging the question to assert that they can be removed only by abolishing capital and substituting collective ownership. On the other hand, it must be remembered that large numbers of capitalists are scrupulously honest in their dealings and are devoted to the welfare of their employees. So far, however, has "popular Socialism" poisoned the public mind that these last statements would be received in many quarters with ridicule and incredulity. Yet it is undoubtedly true that many employers are conducting large business enterprises with a deep sense of their personal responsibility and in a spirit of sympathy and helpfulness. It should be noticed further that the very principles of industry, fidelity and honesty, taught by Christianity, enable men to increase their power and wealth, and this should be true under any form of social organization. The mere fact that one is possessed of wealth should not be regarded as evidence that he has been guilty of robbery and greed.

3. Popular Socialism *fails to recognize* that the principles of justice, fraternity and charity, by which its leaders claim to be animated, are *Christian principles,* and have been expressed by the Church as by no other society of men. It is

hardly rational for Socialists to contend, as they do, that all the hospitals and orphanages and benevolent institutions in Christian and pagan lands, established and conducted by the Church, are mere weak endeavors to bolster up a false and decadent social system. They are rather the expression of the spirit of Christ, without which no social system can ever attain perfection or can long endure.

4. Popular Socialism is vitally defective in that it *places the physical above the spiritual* needs of mankind. It is, as a philosophy, definitely materialistic. It insists that better social conditions will produce better men; Christianity teaches that better men are needed to produce better conditions. Socialism endeavors to elevate individuals by elevating society; Christianity contends that society can be elevated only by the regeneration of individuals. To secure such regeneration is the supreme effort and function of the Church, and its chief message to Socialism is that the "life is more than meat and the body than raiment." To those who are crying for equality and opportunity and improved material conditions and fondly dreaming of a new age of universal plenty and comfort and happiness, the Church repeats the divine message, "Ye must be born again." If Socialism is ever to succeed as an economic theory, it can only be by the aid of the Church; for of all conceivable social systems, none would be more dependent upon high character and exalted principles than a socialistic state; and the production of such character and enforcement of such principles are the proved function of the Christian Church.

III. *Socialism* is, however, something else than a scientific economic theory, or a popular materialistic philosophy; it is *a serious protest against the social wrongs* and cruelties of the age, against the defects of the present economic system, against special privilege and entrenched injustice, against prevalent poverty, and hunger, and despair. It is not always an intelligent protest. Its cry is sometimes inarticulate and wild; but it voices the social unrest, the sullen discontent, the bitter envy and sorrow of thousands who are attracted to Socialism merely by its protest against the present social order and its prophecies of a better age to come.

1. This protest of Socialism is a call to the Church *to proclaim* more insistently *the social principles of Christ*. This does not mean the adoption of a so-called "social gospel" which discards the fundamental doctrines of Christianity and substitutes a religion of good works; but a true Gospel of grace is inseparable from a Gospel of good works. Christian doctrines and Christian duties cannot be divorced. The New Testament no more clearly defines the relation of the believer to Christ than to the members of one's family, to his neighbors in society, and to his fellow-citizens in the state. These social teachings of the Gospel need a new emphasis today by those who accept the whole Gospel, and should not be left to be interpreted and applied by those alone who deny essential Christianity or substitute for religion some modern social creed.

The Church must emphasize anew the teachings of Christ and His apostles relative to *marriage* and the family. Upon this sacred institution many professed Socialists are making a deadly assault. Socialism is not necessarily related to any one theory of marriage, but unfortunately it is too frequently allied with lax theories of divorce and proposals of free love which are destructive to the family and subversive of society.

The Church must proclaim anew the teaching of her Lord relative to *the stewardship of wealth*. Many a man who believes himself to be an orthodox Christian becomes restless and declares he wishes to hear only "the simple Gospel" when his pastor begins to expound the Scriptural principles relative to Christian stewardship. It must be insisted that one is as responsible for the methods by which his power and position and property are acquired as for the way in which these are used; and that every man must render an account to the Lord not only for his use of one-tenth of his income, but for every fraction he selfishly retains or spends. Christians must be reminded that an infallible test of being a child of God is the treatment shown to one's neighbor who is in need.

There must be a similar emphasis on the Scriptural principles relating to *masters and servants,* to employers and employees. If, on the one hand, there is an insistence upon justice and sympathy, so there must be on the other, upon absolute loyalty and fidelity. The conflict between capital and labor could be avoided without a reorganization of society should both parties be controlled by the plain teachings of the Gospel of Christ.

There must be a new insistence upon the sacredness of *the state* and the truth that government is a divine institution. This means a new emphasis upon the duties of Christian citizenship. Every expression of anarchy and lawlessness should be severely reproved and speedily repressed; and every Christian citizen should seek by patient endeavor to solve the complex problems of modern social and industrial life, and to aid in the establishment of better customs and of juster laws. Social-ism would lose much of its power if the Church were more careful to proclaim the explicit social doctrines which form an integral part of the Gospel of Christ.

2. This protest of Socialism demands of the Church a *more consistent practice,* on the part of her members, of the social teachings of Christ. It is easy to bring false charges against Christians; it is even customary today to hold the Church up to ridicule and scorn as a society of hypocrites untrue to their professions and their Lord. It is not necessary to even consider these accusations which spring from ignorance or prejudice or spite. The great masses of Christians are striving to be faithful and seeking to live well-pleasing to their Master. However, it is true that there are some in the Church who are consciously guilty of sins against society, and others who, because of the difficulty of the questions involved, excuse themselves on the ground that their wrong practices

are necessitated by the industrial system of the age. Some are quite comfortable under what they regard as orthodox preaching, even though they know their wealth has come from the watering of stocks and from wrecking railroads, and from grinding the faces of the poor. The supposed orthodoxy of such preaching is probably defective in its statements of the social teachings of the Gospels. One might be a social bandit and buccaneer and yet believe in the virgin birth and in the resurrection of Christ; but one cannot be a Christian unless he believes "that if One died for all, then were all dead: and that He died for all, that they which live should not henceforth live unto themselves, but unto Him which died for them, and rose again;" and to live for Christ means to live for Him in every sphere and relationship of life, whether employer or employee, capitalist or laborer, stock-holder or wage-earner.

We must all admit the grave complexity of modern life, and the delicacy and difficulty of the problems involved, yet we must not be content to countenance practices which are unjust or unchristian. To be absolutely true to conscience and to Christ will mean sacrifice and loss of money and social prestige. It is never easy to take up the cross daily and to follow Christ; but there is a new call for heroism, for martyrdom. Absolute loyalty to Christ in the business and social world today often means crucifixion, pain, death, but "it is the way the Master went; must not the servant tread it still?"

3. The protest of Socialism is a distinct call to the Church to define anew to herself her function, and to interpret anew *the prophecies of her Lord*. There are many who, in the name of Christianity, have been promising a new social order, a kingdom of God, which they declare the Church will introduce. The long continued failure to realize these promises has led to criticisms of the Church, and has done not a little to increase the bitterness of socialistic attacks upon her. The Church is now being held responsible for social sins and injustice, for the wrongs and grievances of the age; and for this unfor-

tunate position she must largely blame herself. She has arrogated functions which are not her own; she has made promises for which there is no written word of Scripture. It should be remembered, for instance, that the state is quite as purely a divine institution as is the Church. It is for the state to secure social reconstruction when necessary; it is for the state to punish offenders, and to secure by legal enactments and legislative processes the abolition of abuses, and the establishment of justice. When the Church assumes functions belonging to the state, she involves herself in needless difficulties and places herself in a false position before the world. More important still it is to ask what predictions of Scripture support the assertion that the Church is herself to introduce the kingdom of God. She is certainly to promise the coming of that kingdom; she is even now to insist that her members shall obey its laws, but it is impossible for her to compel Christless men to accept the principles of her Lord. Her supreme function is to secure, on the part of individuals, whole-hearted devotion and allegiance to Christ. It is for her to increase as rapidly as possible her membership and to extend in every legitimate sphere her benevolent influence; but the real blessedness of the Church and of the world awaits the personal return of Christ. The hope of the world is not in a new social order instituted by unregenerate men; not a millennium made by man; not a commonwealth of humanity organized as a Socialistic state; but a kingdom established by Christ which will fill the earth with glory at the coming of the King.

THE FIFTEEN BOOKS MOST INDISPEN-
SABLE FOR THE MINISTER OR
CHRISTIAN WORKER

For several years the Committee having in charge the publication of "THE FUNDAMENTALS" has been endeavoring to get a list of the five most indispensable books for the minister and the Christian worker, and the ten and the fifteen and the twenty-five. They have been in correspondence with various leaders in Christian thought on both sides of the water. It was hoped that a comparison and combination of all the answers could be made, but the replies have been so divergent that this has been impossible. We are, therefore, giving here nine different lists sent, classifying the books in the order of their importance according to the various persons furnishing the lists. The other lists submitted were not classified or specific.

List of Rev. W. J. Erdman, D. D.:

Best Five:

> "The Divine Unity of the Scripture." Adolph Saphir. (This book is published in cloth covers at $1.50; paper cover, 15c.)
> "Divinity of Christ," Liddon.
> "The Progress of Doctrine in the New Testament," Bernard.
> "History of Doctrine," Shedd.
> "Confessions of St. Augustine."

Second Five:

> "History of the Reformation," D'Aubigne.
> "Old Testimony Theology," Oehler.
> "Life and Epistles of St. Paul," Conybeare and Howson.
> Rutherford's Letters.
> Bacon's Essays.

Third Five:

> "Many-Infallible Proofs," A. T. Pierson.
> "New Acts of Apostles," A. T. Pierson.
> "Law of Love and Love as Law," Mark Hopkins.
> "How to Study the Bible for Greatest Profit," R. A. Torrey.
> "Facts of the Future State," Frederick Grant.

List of Rev. Charles R. Erdman, D. D., Professor in Princeton Theological Seminary, Princeton, N. J.:

First Five:

> "The Bible," American Standard Edition.
> "Bible Dictionary," J. B. Davis (new edition).
> "Bible Handbook," Angus-Green (new edition).
> "The Progress of Doctrine in the New Testament," Bernard.
> "The Divine Unity of Scripture," Adolph Saphir.

Second Five:

A Reference Bible (either Scofield's or the Cross Reference Bible).
"Strong's Concordance."
"The Historical Geography of the Holy Land," G. A. Smith.
"How We Got Our Bible," Smyth.
"Introduction to the New Testament," Kerr.

Third Five:

"Old Testament Introduction," Raven.
"Outline Studies of the Books of the Old Testament," Moorehead.
"The Mosaic Institutions," Moorehead.
"Outline Studies of the Four Gospels," Moorehead.
"Outline Studies of the Acts and Epistles," Moorehead.

List of Rev. Cleland B. McAfee, D. D., Professor in McCormick Theological Seminary, Chicago, Ill.:

First Five:

A good concordance. (I have found nothing better than Young's Analytical.)
A good commentary. (The best I know in one volume is Dummelow, which includes a good introduction to each book.)
A good Bible dictionary. (The best two are that by Jacobus and Zenus and that by Davis.)
A good church history. (Fisher's is the best I know.)
A good history of the world, either Meyer's or Ridpath's.

Dr. McAfee does not give a second and third list, but says: "The next five books should be on special phases of Christian truth, probably such as (1) The Person of Christ; (2) The Atonement; (3) Sin; (4) The Holy Spirit; (5) The Inspiration of the Bible.

List of Rev. James M. Gray, D. D., Dean of the Moody Bible Institute, Chicago: (He gives his list as the Ten Indispensable Books for the Pastor's Library, or, "to put it in another way, what ten books have most helped me.")

1. Oxford Two Version Bible.
2. "The Cyclopædic Hand Book of the Bible," Rev. Samuel G. Green, D. D.; Introduction by the late Joseph Angus, M. A.
3. "Analytical Concordance of the Bible," Robert Young, LL. D.
4. "Theopneustia" ("The Plenary Inspiration of the Bible"), Dr. L. Gaussen.
5. "Outlines of Theology," Rev. A. A. Hodge, D. D.
6. "Pre-Millennial Essays" of the Prophetic Conference held in the Church of the Holy Trinity, New York City, with an appendix of critical testimony, by Nathaniel West.
7. "Aids to Prophetic Enquiry," B. W. Newton.
8. "Christianity and Anti-Christianity in Their Final Conflict," Rev. S. J. Andrews.
9. "The Life of Our Lord Upon the Earth," Rev. S. J. Andrews.
10. "The Two-Fold Life," Rev. A. J. Gordon, D. D.

List of Rev. C. I. Scofield, D. D., Editor "Scofield Reference Bible":

First Five:

Young's Concordance.
"Bible Dictionary," Angus-Green.
"Darby's Synopsis."
"What the Bible Teaches," Torrey.
"Personal Work," Torrey.

Second List:

Andrews' "Life of Christ."
"Synthetic Bible Studies," Rev. James M. Gray, D. D.
"Jukes on the Four Gospels."
"Harmony of the Prophetic Word," Gaebelein.

List of Rev. Professor W. H. Griffith-Thomas, D. D., of Wycliffe College, Toronto, Canada: (Dr. Thomas has not divided his list into the first five, etc.)

"The Christian View of God and the World," Orr.
"Galatians, Philippians and Colossians," Lightfoot.
"Psalms and Colossians in the Expositor's Bible," McLaren.
"The Cross in Christian Experience," Clow.
"Christ in the Social Order," Clow.
"Romans in the Expositor's Bible," Moule.

List of Rev. John H. Hunter, of the Bible Institute of Los Angeles:

Strong's or Young's Concordance.
"Bible Dictionary," Davis.
"The Bible Text Cyclopædia," Inglis.
Matthew Henry's or Jamieson, Faucett and Brown's Commentary.
"Synthetic Bible Studies," Rev. James M. Gray, D. D.
"The Life and Times of Jesus, The Messiah," Edersheim.
"The Life and Epistles of St. Paul," Conybeare and Howson.
"What the Bible Teaches," Torrey.
"How to Work for Christ," Torrey.
"Tongue of Fire," William Arthur.
"Many Infallible Proofs," A. T. Pierson.
"New Acts of Apostles," A. T. Pierson.
"Memoirs of Robert Murray McCheyne."
"Christian Leaders in England in the Eighteenth Century," Bishop Ryle.
"Handbook of the Bible," Angus-Green (new edition).

List of Rev. R. A. Torrey, D. D., Dean of the Bible Institute of Los Angeles:

First Five:

Scofield Reference Bible.
American Standard Version Bible. (The best edition is the Cross Reference Bible, but quite expensive.)

"Treasury of Scripture Knowledge."
"Cyclopædia of Bible Texts," Inglis.
Strong's Concordance (by far the best concordance).

Second Five:

Finney's Autobiography.
"Revivals of Religion," by Chas. G. Finney.
"The Divine Unity of the Scripture," Adolph Saphir.
"Harmony of the Prophetic Word," A. C. Gaebelein.
"Wonders of Prophecy," Urquhart.

Third Five:

"With Christ in the School of Prayer," Andrew Murray.
"Demon Possession and Allied Themes," Dr. Nevius.
C. H. M.'s Notes on Genesis, Exodus, Leviticus, Numbers and
   Deuteronomy.
"The Spirit of Christ," Andrew Murray.
"The Epistle to the Ephesians," Rev. H. C. G. Moule, M. A., Bishop
   of Durham. (The Cambridge Bible for Schools and Colleges.)

List of Rev. John M. MacInnis:

Best Five:

Strong's Exhaustive Concordance.
A good, reliable Bible dictionary.
"Book by Book, Popular Studies on the Canon of Scripture."
Salmon's "Introduction of the New Testament."
"The Life of Our Lord," Andrews.

Second Five:

"How to Bring Men to Christ," R. A. Torrey.
"The Personal Life of the Clergy," A. W. Robinson.
"The Preacher, His Life and Work," Jowett.
"The Holy Life," MacGregor.
"The Ministry of Intercession," Murray.

Third Five:

"The Living Messages of the Bible," G. Campbell Morgan.
"The Progress of Doctrine in the New Testament," Bernard.
The best single commentary on each book in the Bible as taken up;
   e.g., Plummer on the Gospel of Luke; Sanday on Romans,
   McLaren on Psalms, Godet on John. (I do not favor sets of
   commentaries very much, because in all of these sets there is
   a great deal of useless matter.)
"Pilgrims' Progress," Bunyan.
"What the Bible Teaches," R. A. Torrey.

INDEX OF ARTICLES APPEARING IN THE TWELVE VOLUMES OF "THE FUNDAMENTALS"

———

TITLES IN THIS SERIES

The Evangelical Matrix
1875-1900

The Formation of
A Fundamentalist Agenda
1900-1920

Fundamentalism Versus Modernism
1920-1935

■ 24. Joel A. Carpentar, ed.
Modernism and Foreign Missions:
Two Fundamentalist Protests
New York, 1988

■ 25. John Horsch
Modern Religious Liberalism: The Destructiveness
and Irrationality of Modernist Theology
Scottsdale, Pa., 1921

■ 26. Joel A. Carpenter,ed.
Fundamentalist vesus Modernist
The Debates Between
John Roach Stratton and Charles Francis Potter
New York, 1988

■ 27. Joel A. Carpenter, ed.
William Jennings Bryan on
Orthodoxy, Modernism, and Evolution
New York, 1988

■ 28. Edwin H. Rian
The Presbyterian Conflict
Grand Rapids, 1940

Sectarian Fundamentalism
1930-1950

■ 29. Arno C. Gaebelein
Half a Century: The Autobiography of a Servant
New York, 1930

■ 30. Charles G. Trumball
Prophecy's Light on Today
New York, 1937

■ 31. Joel A. Carpenter, ed.
Biblical Prophecy in an Apocalyptic Age:
Selected Writings of Louis S. Bauman
New York, 1988

■ 32. Joel A. Carpenter, ed.
Fighting Fundamentalism:
Polemical Thrusts of the 1930s and 1940s
New York, 1988

■ 33. *Inside History of First Baptist Church, Fort*
Worth, and Temple Baptist Church, Detroit:
Life Story of Dr. J. Frank Norris
Fort Worth, 1938

■ 34. John R. Rice
The Home — Courtship, Marriage, and Children: A
Biblical Manual of Twenty -Two Chapters
on the Christian Home.

Wheaton, 1945

■ 35. Joel A. Carpenter, ed.
Good Books and the Good Book: Reading Lists by
Wilbur M. Smith, Fundamentalist Bibliophile
New York, 1988

■ 36. H. A. Ironside
Random Reminiscences from Fifty Years of Ministry
New York, 1939

Rebuilding, Regrouping, & Revival
1930-1950

■ 43. Joel A. Carpenter, ed.
The Youth for Christ Movement and Its Pioneers
New York, 1988

■ 44. Joel A. Carpenter, ed.
The Early Billy Graham:
Sermons and Revival Accounts
New York, 1988

■ 45. Joel A. Carpenter, ed.
Two Reformers of Fundamentalism:
Harold John Ockenga and Carl F. H. Henry
New York, 1988